Sydney-based Debbie Malone, the 2013 Australian Psychic of the Year, is an acclaimed and highly respected psychic, clairvoyant, psychometry expert and spirit medium.

Debbie assists police Australia-wide to solve murder investigations and missing persons' cases. She conducts private readings and workshops on how to tune into the spirit world, and is regularly interviewed in national print and on television and radio. Television appearances include *Today Tonight, Sensing Murder, Sunrise, Today, The Project* and most recently *The One.*

Her extraordinary gift has enabled her to receive visions from both the living and the dead, from the past, present and future, and to convey messages to bereaved families from their departed loved ones. Debbie also specialises in paranormal spirit photography.

Debbie's book *Awaken Your Psychic Ability* was published in 2016, followed by *Clues from Beyond: Insights from the living and from the dead* in 2017.

Debbie has also created a series of bestselling Angel cards – *Angels Whisper* & *Angel Wishes Cards, Angels to Watch Over You, Angel Reading Cards* and *Guardian Angel Reading Cards.*

Debbie Malone's gift has enabled her to see beyond the here and now and she draws strength from using the world of spirit to help herself and others, and from knowing that we are never alone.

www.betweentwoworlds.net

Never Alone

True crime stories from a
real-life psychic detective

DEBBIE MALONE

Gelding Street Press
An imprint of Rockpool Publishing
PO Box 252
Summer Hill
NSW 2130
Australia
www.geldingstreetpress.com

Originally published by William Heinemann Australia in 2009
First published by Rockpool Publishing in 2017 under
ISBN 978-1-925429-54-1
This edition published in 2020

ISBN 978-1-925924-63-3

Cover design by Tracy Loughlin, Rockpool Publishing
Cover photographs by Shutterstock
Internal design by Midland Typesetters, Australia
Typeset in Minion Pro 12.5/17 pt by Midland Typesetters, Australia
Printed and bound in China

10 9 8 7 6 5 4 3 2 1

A catalogue record for this
book is available from the
National Library of Australia

To my very patient and understanding husband, Warwick, and my inspirational children, Ryan, Blake and Shannon. Your encouragement has given me the motivation and strength to see this journey to fruition. Without your love and support, this book would not have been possible.

Oasis in the Sand
The gentle shimmer in the breeze,
It looks like an oasis in the sand.
It is a glimpse that life lives on,
And is closer than you think.
They are only a thought away,
An image in your mind,
A feeling in your heart,
A feeling so close you can almost touch it.

But are you kidding yourself?
Is it wishful thinking, or contact from beyond?

I leave that up to you –
I know what I see and feel,
I know what is real.
They are here amongst us;
Their love lives on forever.
We are never alone;
Love and spirit endures.
All it takes is for you to believe,
And they will do the rest.

Debbie Malone

Contents

Chapter 1

Childhood Encounters with Spirit

My life has been unusual and often very challenging, but I wouldn't change a thing. I feel that I am a truly blessed and privileged human being to have been allowed to see and feel the experiences I will share with you in this book. Through my gift of mediumship, I have met many wonderful people, both living and in the realm of spirit.

I was born in Sydney, Australia, in September 1963 to my loving parents, Robin and Leonie Gee. My only sibling is my darling brother, Michael, who arrived in 1968. Our parents have always been very hard-working people and have done all they can to provide a positive life for us. Both Michael and I were christened Catholic and had an open and not overly religious upbringing.

When I was three, my family moved into our newly built home in the suburb of Lalor Park, in the west of Sydney. There, my health took a turn for the worse. I suffered bronchial pneumonia and was admitted to hospital. My family had to travel the long distance into the city to visit me in the Royal Alexandra Hospital for Children at Camperdown. It was during my time there that I believe I had my first encounter with the spirit world.

I remember waking up in the ward coughing uncontrollably one night and seeing all of the other sick children lying in their beds. I felt so alone and frightened, and all I wanted was to be back at home with my parents, tucked snugly in my bed. It seemed as if I lay there in the bed coughing for an eternity. I waited for a nurse to come, but none came. Then a beautiful lady dressed in white suddenly appeared before me, comforting me and assuring me that I would be safe. Perhaps this vision was a dream or just wishful thinking, but at the time I felt so calm and surrounded by love that I settled down and went back to sleep. This vision has stuck with me for all of my life and I would like to think that the lady was one of my guardian angels.

After spending three or four weeks in hospital, I was allowed to go home. I can't tell you how happy I was to be back in my parents' arms. From that time on, my mum wanted to wrap me up in cotton wool so I wouldn't get sick again.

At the age of five, I started at the local infants school, and unfortunately this was the beginning of a very harrowing time for me. From almost my first day there, a group of girls bullied me on the way home. I became terrified of going to school and I told my parents how frightened I was of this gang of girls. My parents simply said that I should stand up for myself and hit them back. This was an even more frightening option, as there was one of me and five of them. And anyway, I have never agreed with using violence against violence. (Back in those days, parents didn't intervene in school bullying like they thankfully do now.)

The bullying followed me right through to primary school and affected my health and confidence greatly. I became a very timid and nervous child, a loner. I preferred to be by myself as I felt that I would never fit in with any of the groups of kids at school.

I have always been very artistic, so I spent a lot of my spare time painting and drawing at home. On weekends, our family would often go to my paternal grandparents' place in Bankstown and I would spend hours with my gorgeous grandfather, a great man in my eyes who was in the navy during the Second World War. My memories of my grandfather are always of joy. My poppa was a very artistic man and he was able to paint or draw on anything he could get his hands on. When we would go to visit, he would surprise me with a new work of art painted on a leaf, piece of bark or canvas.

It was Poppa who gave me my appreciation of art. He would spend many hours sitting with me, telling me stories about his life and teaching me how to draw and paint; he was also very gifted with calligraphy and taught me how to do hand lettering. My memories are of him always being surrounded by big, blue clouds of smoke but at the time I never thought much about the damage his heavy smoking was doing to him.

My nanna was also a very gifted woman. She would sit patiently, teaching me how to embroider, knit and crochet. Each visit to their house was an adventure, as I never knew what I would learn next. Now, as an adult, I realise what a blessing these two loving people were in my life and I miss them dearly.

It was at their house that I was introduced to the idea that fairies exist. On the wall above her bed, Nanna had a special Chinese hat that her brother had given her after the Second World War, and she said that behind the hat was where the fairies lived. I felt in awe of the fact that the fairies were always at her house when we went to visit and not at my own home. This was another very enticing reason to go to visit Nanna and Poppa as often as possible, to see what the fairies had been up to between each visit.

My father's side of the family were tested with a lot of illness and during my childhood I seemed to suffer the same fate. I constantly had bronchitis and never-ending stomach problems. The poor doctor didn't know what to do with me; he diagnosed me with nervous dyspepsia but couldn't offer anything to help improve my condition. I look back now on this period of my life only to realise that the gang of bullies who caused my anxiety had actually hurt me in more ways than one.

Due to my nervousness, I suffered many fears, the biggest one being of the dark. I wouldn't be able to go to sleep at night unless my mum left the light on in the bathroom, which was next to my bedroom. Mum humoured me enough to keep the light on until I fell asleep each night.

Another fear was of all of the strange things I could see and hear in my bedroom. Each night, I would complain

4

to my mum that there was something or someone in my room. I could hear footsteps and creaking; I could hear snippets of conversation and at times it sounded like some unknown person was talking to me. A blue-white glow would materialise, sometimes taking the form of a person walking around the room. Other times, the glow took the form of a ball of light flying around above my head.

When it all became too much for me, I would call in my mum and make her check whether there was anyone else in the room besides me. As soon as she got to the door, everything would suddenly stop.

My constant complaining about what was going on when I went to bed began to drive my poor parents crazy. Mum told me that I had an overactive imagination and asked me to stop going on about nothing. I knew better: I knew that there definitely was someone or something making nightly visits.

Thankfully, Mum gave me her old radio and suggested that I listen to it to help me get to sleep at night. I discovered that if I focused on what the radio was playing, whoever or whatever was coming to visit me wasn't able to get through any more. I was so relieved to be able to finally get some sleep and leave the family in peace.

There were still times when I would see the blue-white glow moving around but I would quickly slide down under the covers and pretend it wasn't there. Even to this day, the glow still comes to visit me. It doesn't communicate with me. I feel that it is a spirit who wants to make his or her presence known to me. It doesn't frighten me any more; I accept it as part of my life.

When I was finishing year five, our family received the devastating news that Poppa, my very special mentor when it came to the artistic side of my life, had been diagnosed with throat-and-lung cancer from smoking. At the age of eleven, I didn't realise the consequences of cancer; it would be some time before I understood what an impact it would have on my family. After the initial shock of Poppa's diagnosis, I just accepted that he had to make frequent trips to hospital. Over the next three years, he would be in and out of hospital more often than I care to remember for tests, many operations and chemotherapy. This was a traumatic time for all of the family; we were very close to my grandparents and it was a shock to everyone that Poppa had cancer.

*

By the time I reached year six at school, I finally felt stronger and more confident than I had in the previous years. I still had the bullies in my class but I didn't let them get to me like I had done before. I had decided that if I learnt to focus my energy into studying and doing well at school, then at least I could feel happy that I had been successful in one area of my life. In addition to this, I put my efforts into doing things that others could benefit from. I established an anti-litter campaign at the school and introduced an aluminium-recycling program, which was an excellent fund-raiser. The extra activities I undertook at school were very uplifting, and in my last year I was finally enjoying primary school.

My life was going really well until I was struck down

by illness once again, after a weekend outing with my family to Oktoberfest. Multiculturalism didn't really exist in Australia then like it does now, so it was exciting to try different types of German food. Unfortunately for me, somebody serving the food was suffering from hepatitis A. The rest of my family all ate at Oktoberfest but I was the only one who got sick. As hepatitis A is so highly contagious, I wasn't allowed to finish my final months of year six. I finished the rest of the school year by doing my schoolwork and exams at home when I was well enough. Luckily, my grades were good enough to allow me into high school even though I had missed the last three months of school.

Beginning at a new school presented me with the exciting prospect of meeting new friends and doing new things. My endeavours to do well at primary school had paid off, as I was placed in higher-graded classes than the bullies, so I didn't cross paths with them very often any more. They no longer played a part in my life and I no longer had to listen to their taunts. I felt relieved that I could finally feel at peace and enjoy going to school. I met a new group of friends, who were all great fun to be with. Jayne, Chantal and Alison were all very adventurous girls, and I was a bit of a tomboy.

The western suburbs of Sydney can be a very hot place in the summer months. My entire life, I have been drawn to the water and, though my parents couldn't understand the attraction of the beach, they were understanding enough to let me spend most summer weekends there with my girlfriends.

We would all meet at the local train station at about 6 am, after a half-hour walk to get there with either surfboards or boogie boards under our arms. Then it was a two-and-a-half to three-hour trek, changing trains at Redfern station to continue on to Cronulla Beach. We would arrive hot and sweaty and just dying to swim in the cool, blue ocean. The summer days were very memorable and we had a great deal of fun.

As the end of year seven approached, I began to get sick again. After my bout of hepatitis A, I constantly suffered stomach cramps and needed to be careful with what I ate. My mother was always taking me to doctors, but they just couldn't put their finger on the problem. It wasn't until one particularly bad attack of stomach cramps that it was discovered that I had a grumbling appendix.

The doctor arranged for me to go to hospital the following day to have my appendix out, because he feared that it might burst. I was quite excited to be going into hospital, as it felt like a kind of adventure. Little did I know how the upcoming events would begin to alter my future.

On the morning of the operation, the nurse came in to give me a needle to calm me down before the surgery, and this is the last thing I remember until after the operation. It was late afternoon when a nurse woke me up. I didn't know how I could possibly have been excited beforehand because all I could feel now was the pain in my side. After taking my blood pressure, the nurse then told me that I needed to go back to sleep – I couldn't understand why she hadn't just left me asleep in the first place.

As I slowly dozed off, I began experiencing the strangest dream-like vision. I felt my body lifting off the bed and flying very quickly towards the ceiling. It felt like I was floating on the surface of a swimming pool.

Looking down, I could see my body still lying in the hospital bed. I desperately tried to get myself back into my body, but it was as if I was a cork floating in water, and I constantly kept popping back up to the ceiling of my hospital room.

The nurse came back into the room to recheck my blood pressure. A worried look came across her face and she quickly rang the buzzer. Another nurse entered and, after speaking with the first nurse, left the room and returned with a trolley containing an oxygen bottle.

I suddenly woke up safely back in my bed when an oxygen mask was placed over my face. The first nurse was looking straight at me with a panicked expression. I couldn't work out what all of the commotion was about – I thought I was just having a vivid dream.

The following morning, the doctor told me that even though the operation had gone well, something had gone wrong during the night and my heart had stopped. The doctor ran tests, which all came back normal; he couldn't explain what had happened.

After this experience, I felt very peaceful, although a nagging voice in the back of my head started telling me to read about near-death experiences (NDEs). At this point, I barely knew what an NDE was, let alone had the courage to admit that I may very well have had one of my own.

I decided to visit the library as soon as I recovered from my operation. Much to my surprise, the school library contained exactly the book I needed: *Life After Life*, by Raymond A. Moody. It described what an NDE was and detailed other people's experiences. From the moment I opened the book, I couldn't read it quickly enough.

When I finished, I was positive that I had actually had my own NDE. Friends at school asked me why I had been away from school and I told them about the operation – but when I told them I thought I'd had a near-death experience they thought I was strange. I didn't feel that I could tell my parents, either, as I'd already felt quite stupid trying to discuss it with my friends. I began to withdraw into my own little world, like I had done in primary school. I had experienced one of the most amazing things in my life and yet I didn't have anyone I could verbalise it to.

Chapter 2

My Very Own
Guardian Angel

My first NDE was a life-changing event. I felt that it was a good time to question why I was here. I began to wonder more and more about the Bible and whether there really was life after death. I certainly believed that something else was out there.

When I was younger, I attended the local Catholic church every Sunday, and I also made my First Holy Communion and then my Confirmation. None of these experiences made me feel any closer to God. In fact, they made me feel more alienated from Him, because of the way the people at church seemed to look down upon each other. For instance, there were certain areas where certain families of the congregation would sit, depending on whether their children went to the local Catholic school that was attached to the church. Those of us who were not part of the school were relegated to the back few pews, if we were lucky enough to find a seat. Goodness forbid if you thought that you should sit closer to the priest and the altar than the other members of the church, as the looks and stares that came from those at the front were enough to make you drop dead on the spot. I wondered: if God loved us all so much, then why didn't he let everyone be treated in the same way? So, after a number of years of not feeling any more enlightened by going to church, I decided to stay at home and talk to Him in private.

I also joined a local youth fellowship run by the Uniting Church. We would meet every Friday night for Bible study and then an outing. It would vary from going to the movies, roller skating or putt-putt golf, to meeting up for a barbecue.

I made many new friends and had a great time each week. I couldn't wait for Friday night to come, as my new group of friends were very welcoming and they helped me to feel that I belonged.

All was going well, until one night when the minister who ran the fellowship gave me a lift home. When he stopped the car and I was about to get out, he suddenly made an advance towards me. I quickly pushed him away and jumped out of the car.

I ran inside and spoke to my parents about the incident; they were upset about his behaviour and suggested that the best thing was for me not to go to fellowship any more.

This experience was very upsetting and it was a disappointment for me that a religious person – a minister –

would behave in such an improper and unreligious way. To make matters worse, he lived in the next street to me with his lovely wife and five young children. His wife was quite oblivious to the type of man he was and I didn't want to cause any problems by telling her about what had happened. I knew the minister's children well, as I had gone to school with them through infants and primary.

I stopped going to youth fellowship, but I did tell one of the youth leaders about my experience. He admitted that another young girl had unfortunately had a similar unpleasant experience with this minister. I heard no more about him until his house was put up for sale and he left the parish. After that, I didn't hear of him again.

I returned to the youth fellowship and became close friends with one of the boys, Luis, who would pick me up each week. Luis – or Lou, as he preferred to be called – was a gentle and caring boy. On the weekend of our local fair, Lou and I decided to go and watch the fireworks display with my family.

Lou had two siblings, Mary and Jimmy. Their father was quite controlling of the children, and Mary, who was seventeen, wasn't allowed out very often unless she was chaperoned by her father or Lou. On the afternoon of the fair, Mary joined Lou and my family. When we got to the fair, we went on some rides and then got seats in readiness for the fireworks display. Mary told us that she wanted to meet up with some friends and that she would join us later to see the fireworks. Unbeknown to us, she had used the excuse of coming with us just so she'd be able to slip away and meet these friends.

When the fireworks display began and Mary still hadn't returned, Lou became worried and went off to look for her. He came back quite distressed, telling me that his father had followed us to the fair and had caught Mary with her friends, smoking a cigarette. He had forced her to return home with him. Lou said he needed to follow them home urgently, as he was concerned about what his father might do to her.

When Lou got back, their father was holding a gun to his sister's head while he forced her to smoke a whole box of cigars. He said he wanted to teach her a lesson so that she would never smoke again.

Mary was traumatised and seriously feared for her safety; she decided that it was better to leave home and move in with some friends than to stay at home with her father. Within a week, Mary had moved out and was trying to live a normal life.

A few weeks passed, and Mary's father, unhappy that she no longer lived under his roof, rang her and said that he wanted to speak with her. He promised to drive her to work after they finished their meeting.

Mary never made it to work, as a violent argument broke out and her father lost control. He produced a knife and stabbed her many times in an unprovoked, frenzied attack, for which he was later jailed.

On the morning of the attack, I was getting ready for school when a newsflash came across the radio saying that a young woman had been stabbed to death by a man in the Blacktown area. Shortly after, I received a phone call from Lou, who was in a very distraught state. When he told me what his father had done, I was in total shock. I had never had anybody close to me die before, let alone a friend near my age, murdered by her own father.

The weeks that followed are still a blur. I suffered severe headaches and couldn't cope with the shock. I tried to comfort Lou for the loss of his sister but I was only fourteen years old. I had to grow up a lot quicker than I would have liked.

During this period, Lou changed immensely. The gentle boy I once knew had gone and I became quite wary of him. Understandably, the things that Lou had been through would be imprinted on his mind forever. I felt that, with his sister's death, the friend I once had had also died within. I found it more and more difficult to keep up our friendship and felt it was better that we go our separate ways. Lou didn't take this decision very well and he began to contact me constantly.

My severe headaches would last for days. I just wanted this horrible nightmare to end and I wanted to resume the life that I had prior to the murder of Mary.

*

Things settled back down to normal and the new school year had just begun when Poppa's cancer took its final turn. I remember going to visit him in a hospital ward that had nine other men in it, and as the weeks went by the other men in the room would go missing one by one.

I asked Poppa if these gentlemen had gone home and, with sadness, he replied that they had all died. Suddenly, the realisation came to me that, more than likely, Poppa wasn't coming back home and he would die in hospital like the others.

15

Watching someone die is such a hard thing to do; seeing a healthy person so full of life fade away to a mere shell is a traumatic experience. My poppa suffered greatly with the cancer. Towards the end, he was unable to talk, as he had been given a tracheotomy and his voice box was removed to help him breathe; he could only communicate by writing on a slate board. I much prefer to remember him sitting in his chair at home, teaching me how to draw, rather than as the sick man lying in the hospital bed.

Poppa was a very proud man and towards the end of his life he asked for the grandchildren not to visit him any more. At the time, I was heartbroken, because I loved him so dearly and felt that I must have upset him. I later realised that he saw how distraught I became when I visited him and he didn't want to go on upsetting me.

I was fifteen when my poppa died, the first close relative I had ever lost. My parents thought it was better that I didn't go to his funeral, as they thought I would get too upset. I actually was more devastated that I wasn't allowed to go. I felt that I was never given the chance to say goodbye and he would think that I didn't love him enough to go and pay my respects.

After he died, when we went to my grandparents' place I would always feel him in his bedroom. I loved to go in and sit quietly on his bed because I could feel I was close to him. My parents didn't question what I was doing. They always knew where to look for me – I would either be in Poppa's favourite chair or in his room, waiting and hoping that he might talk to me and let me know that he was okay.

I started to feel his presence more and more. At night, I would lie in bed and think about him and cry. One night,

I saw a beautiful blue glow float into my bedroom and come and sit on my bed. I could feel the weight on the bed as though someone was really there; the longer I stared at the presence, the more the blue glow began to take on the form and features of my poppa. I was scared yet excited at the same time. I wanted to scream with fright, yet Poppa's presence made me feel calm and protected. The glow then mysteriously disappeared. I had a number of visits like this from Poppa but whenever he came he didn't really say anything; he just sat there on the bed and smiled at me.

When you are a child, you never think that anyone is ever going to die; it seems that everyone lives forever. What I was now realising was that after we die, we do still exist but in a different form. His presence became more of a regular occurrence in my life and I realised I had myself a real live guardian angel. Boy, did I feel blessed!

This special gift wasn't something I could tell my friends about. The one thing I did know was that I was never alone.

During this period in my life, I suddenly developed a small white streak in my hair beginning right at the top of the head (an area I later came to know as the crown chakra). As the years have gone on, the white streak has widened, though I colour my hair so you can't see it, as people have called it my witch's streak. I prefer to call it my psychic streak. At first, I didn't understand why this was happening to me, but, on looking back on my life, I now realise that the psychic development taking place within me was changing the colour of my hair. When I do any form of psychic or medium work, the top of my head becomes extremely hot.

It was very sad to lose a wonderful, loving mentor like Poppa. I decided that I would try to not dwell on his loss but focus on doing my best at school; I felt that would make him happy.

*

My last two years of school flew by very quickly and soon it was time to start making decisions about what I wanted to do when I left.

I loved art and photography and had a strong interest in becoming a graphic designer. At the end of year ten, I left school and got an apprenticeship as a typesetter at the magazine publisher Australian Consolidated Press, where I was taught many aspects of the printing industry. I also went to trade school at technical college.

I was sixteen and I would catch the train daily to get to work. In my first year, my aim was to save up enough money to buy a car so I could get my driver's licence and my ticket to freedom.

My father and I found a blue 1966 Ford Cortina for sale in the local paper and paid the asking price of $450. The car was old and in need of a lot of work, but I thought it was a bargain and that if my dad and I worked on it, it would soon look a lot better than it did in its current state.

My father has always been good with cars and he took great pride in restoring them. Every night after work, if I didn't have tech homework to do, I would help my father rub back the paintwork on the car and rebuild the motor. It took us about four months and, when we were finished, the car looked like new.

I thought I was invincible in my little old car and, every now and then, I was probably a bit more adventurous than my driving skills would allow. At times like this, I suddenly felt a warm presence in the back seat and I would get the impression that my grandfather was with me. He would always give me the message that I should slow down, and sometimes he warned me that there was a police radar up ahead. (He was always right!) I believe that he would accompany me in the car to protect me from other motorists – and most of all from myself. I began to listen to his messages and I always felt protected. As I grew up, I didn't feel his presence around me as much any more but I always felt blessed for the times he was with me.

I remember that, when I was little, the scripture teacher would come to school and give out holy cards bearing a picture of a little boy or girl and a lovely guardian angel standing behind them protecting them. I now felt like I was one of the children from those cards, as I had the wonderful experience of knowing that I had my very own angel, my poppa.

Chapter 3

The Catalyst to Hearing Spirit

By the age of eighteen, my career had become an important focus and I was very busy at work. I would do as much overtime as possible so I could save up to follow my next dream, which was to learn scuba-diving.

I lived to go to the water. Jacques Cousteau was someone I admired and I was curious to see underwater life with my own two eyes. The shore dives and deep-water boat dives we did in my first week of training at a dive school in Cronulla were enough to get me hooked on diving forever. I was in love and the ocean was my new playmate. I felt like I had finally found a place in which I truly belonged.

If people think heaven only exists above the earth, then they need to experience the sea, as heaven certainly has made her presence known there. The feeling of freedom in the water and the beauty of the sea creatures that so innocently let me share their existence made diving one of the most wonderful experiences of my life. I felt that I had found my heaven.

But, from the very beginning, I experienced problems with my ears. Divers need to equalise their ears before they descend for a dive, so that the pressure of the water doesn't cause damage to their eardrums or inner ears. It wasn't uncommon for me to come to the surface with a mask full of blood from a bleeding nose. I was told by the instructors that this was pretty normal and not to worry about it. I would later find out, though, that nosebleeds can be a sign of ear damage while diving.

Aside from the nosebleeds, I had a fabulous time during my diving course and it made me more ambitious to further my diving experience. Over the next couple of years, I worked my way through a number of courses in the hope of one day becoming an instructor.

After passing my advanced diving course with a group of other diving friends, we all decided to go on a diving weekend down to Jervis Bay, in New South Wales, to celebrate. It was just the perfect weekend – the weather was great and we had multiple boat dives planned.

The first dive was at a place called Point Perpendicular, a headland at the opening to Jervis Bay. I had a new dive buddy, whom I had met during the course; he was a nice-enough guy but I didn't have much prior experience of diving with him. The dive site was about thirty metres deep. Most of the other divers had already gone before us and, as the visibility was great, I could see them on the bottom. Everyone looked to be having a great time.

When my buddy and I went to descend, I was hit by an overwhelming pain in my right ear. I tried numerous times to clear my ear but the more I did this the more my ear and head throbbed. Then my mask filled up with blood and I realised that my nose was bleeding.

My buddy left me and descended. I could see him having a great time down below with the others, so I thought I would try to clear my ear one more time to try to join him. Only thing was, I heard a very large pop in my right ear and then felt a lot of cold water gushing into it. I felt dizzy and disorientated, so I returned to the boat. The pain was now excruciating.

I spoke to my dive captain on board the boat and he told me not to worry as my ear would probably clear on the next dive. The pain did indeed subside, so I went on the next one, a shallow dive on a scallop bed. There were beautiful caves and two of the largest cuttlefish I have ever seen – they were almost as big as me – swimming in one of the caves.

I had descended fine and thought my ear was okay but when I decided to ascend I thought my head was going to explode into many pieces. My poor dive buddy panicked and tried to pull me to the surface very quickly. (Unbeknown to both of us, this quick ascent only increased the damage to my inner ear.)

For the rest of the weekend, I dived being told that my ear problem would probably go away. The rest of the dives went off without much pain. But I did have this new noise in my right ear, which sounded like a group of crickets having a party. I still suffer with this today – a condition known as tinnitus – and it is a permanent reminder of my diving days.

On returning home, I went to a diving doctor, only to be referred on to an ear specialist. The first thing the specialist told me was that I would never dive again. I was pretty unimpressed with this news and became quite upset. The doctor informed me that I had ruptured a membrane and the fluid in my inner ear that helped me to keep my balance had begun to leak out, into my middle ear. After much discussion – of not many options – I was booked in to have a skin graft to repair the membrane.

It was six weeks before I could have the operation and the wait seemed to take forever. It was very embarrassing trying to walk up the ramp to the train station and run for the train, as I would fall all over the place; I had lost quite a bit of fluid from my inner ear and I had trouble keeping my balance. I am sure that during the period before the operation people thought I was constantly drunk. (I most certainly felt like it.)

The doctor told me that after the operation there was a chance that the tinnitus could go away, but unfortunately it didn't. The noise in my head was beginning to drive me mad, not to mention my disappointment that the new career I'd hoped to embark on was lost to me forever.

I was finding it very hard to concentrate at work, as the noise would never end. I was lucky enough to have an understanding boss who let me wear earphones and listen to the radio while I did my work so as not to be overwhelmed by the constant ringing. If only I had known then that, for me, tinnitus was to be a gift more than a curse. As my psychic abilities developed, it would become apparent that spirits could come through on the same frequency as the ringing – to this day, it is only through my right ear that I hear messages from spirit.

But, as a young woman, the ringing was a constant annoyance. I reluctantly sold my dive gear and bought a windsurfer instead and spent most weekends taking it out on the ocean. Windsurfing was enjoyable but it just wasn't the same as scuba-diving. I had lost the freedom I felt under the water and the ability to witness the beauty of all the delicate sea creatures that I had come to know and love.

I felt quite angry and lost and had numerous trips to the doctor, who thought I should go on antidepressants. I wasn't too impressed with this suggestion, as I didn't believe in taking anything like that and felt that I could sort things out myself. To escape my frustration, I decided to work hard and save my money to go on a working holiday.

I went up to Queensland on an under-thirty-fives bus tour, similar to a Contiki Tour, and when it finished I was lucky enough to get a job on Green Island, off the coast of Cairns, in north Queensland. I worked on the island as a waitress at night and during the day I would go snorkelling and windsurfing. Sometimes, I would run the windsurfing and boat hire for one of the guys on the island. My life was settling down and my frustration with the tinnitus began to subside; I was beginning to enjoy my new island lifestyle.

One morning, I received the news that Nanna Gee had died. Devastated, I decided to leave my job immediately and return to Sydney for the funeral. I felt that it was most important I attended. As I wasn't given the opportunity to go to Poppa's funeral, I wanted to be able to say my goodbyes to Nanna.

After her funeral, I travelled to Geelong, where friends I had met on my working holiday lived. I decided to stay there a few months, get a job and see some of Victoria. I rented a flat in Geelong and started work at the local paper, *The Geelong Advertiser*, as a graphic artist. During the evenings, I worked part-time as a waitress.

On weekends, I would travel to Apollo Bay to visit one of the friends I met in Queensland, a guy named Glenn. His house was very old and had a link to the area's maritime history. In 1880, the captain of a three-masted sailing vessel, *Eric the Red*, believing he was at least six miles (about ten kilometres) off Cape Otway, steered towards the lighthouse on the cape. But he had miscalculated his position and the ship struck the Otway Reef, about three kilometres south of the lighthouse. The ship broke in two quickly, leaving her crew and passengers struggling in the water. Twenty-three men, including the captain, were rescued but three crew and one passenger were lost. Only one body was recovered and it is buried in the Cape Otway Lighthouse Cemetery. The following day, ships in the area reported wreckage in the sea, much of which washed ashore at Point Franklin. Large quantities of timber were salvaged by local residents and later used as building material – including as flooring in the house that Glenn rented. Apparently, the sails were also used in the ceiling of the house, as makeshift insulation.

My first experience with the ghost from *Eric the Red* happened one Saturday morning. I had just driven down from Geelong, and Glenn was at work. When I arrived at his house, I felt quite sick in the stomach. I decided that if I lay down, I might feel a bit better. While I was dozing off, I heard the back door open and shut; I heard the shower turn on for some time and then it was turned off. I thought that Glenn's flatmate, who went by the nickname of Dasher, had come home from work to have a shower. It was only later, when I spoke to Glenn about it, that I found out Dasher was actually at work, at the local butcher shop. Nobody but myself was in the house. Glenn thought that I was imagining things.

Another evening, I was alone in the house, as Glenn had to work and Dasher had gone out with some friends. I was sitting in the lounge room watching TV when the kitchen seemed to come alive. I could hear the cupboard doors opening and banging shut; crockery began rattling and, to my amazement, the kettle turned itself on. I went into the kitchen, only to hear everything stop. The strangest thing was that I could see a young man dressed in long, white, baggy pants and a white short-sleeved shirt. He was wearing a sailor's hat and was leaning in the doorway, smiling at me. I thought I was seeing things. I shut my eyes and then opened them again, only to see him grinning back at me. The sailor was very cheeky and the hairs on the back of my neck went up. Then, he suddenly vanished.

I brought Glenn's dog inside to keep me company until Glenn came home. The dog didn't want to be inside with me, so I waited outside with him, as I felt that was a safer place to be.

Later, I spoke with the neighbour next door, who owned the property, and he told me that the previous tenants had moved out because of the goings-on in the house. He told me that it seemed the ghost only showed himself to female occupants, as none of the males ever complained about his presence.

Another time, my parents came down from Sydney and we stayed with Glenn and Dasher for the weekend. The ghost from *Eric the Red* had a field day with us. Mum and Dad were sleeping on a blow-up bed in the lounge room, I was sleeping on the couch and my friends, Glenn and Dasher, were sound asleep in their bedrooms.

The house was situated in an area where there weren't any street lights, so it was very dark at night. I was woken by a huge ball of light glowing on the back of the closed lounge-room door. At first, I thought I was dreaming – until the light began to move around the room and the floorboards began to squeak loudly.

I thought that if I shut my eyes and pretended I didn't see anything, the light would go away, but I began to feel a cold hand stroking the side of my face. I called out to my mum and asked her if she could see the same glow that I could. When she agreed that she could, I became more frightened. Mum then told me that she could feel someone playing with her hair and stroking her face. It was quite funny, really, as my father lay sound asleep snoring quite loudly, oblivious to the whole scene.

Mum shook Dad violently to wake him up, in the hope that he might scare the presence away. Grumpily, he got up and walked to where Mum and I could see the light, but it moved away from him quite quickly. Having decided that there was nothing there, he became quite annoyed and told Mum and me to go back to sleep and forget about it.

As soon as he went back to sleep, though, the fun and games started once more. I could feel the presence playing with my hair and stroking my face. I could then feel someone lying down beside me on the lounge and cuddling me. It felt like a male presence and I presumed that it was the sailor I had seen on the previous occasion. I told Mum the story of what the sailor did the last time I saw him and she became even more frightened. She said that we would talk about it in the morning and that she didn't want to hear another word about him during the night.

For the rest of the night, I lay curled up in my sleeping bag with my eyes tightly shut. I could still feel the ghost and hear the creaking floorboards as he walked around the room.

When first light came, I couldn't believe how quickly my mum packed up her things and announced that we would be going home early because she didn't want to ever have to spend another night in the house at Apollo Bay.

Prior to this, my parents never believed that ghosts existed. After the night in Apollo Bay, their beliefs changed, and to this day Mum doesn't like to talk about the night with the ghost.

Chapter 4

Love, Loss and a Very Special Gift

After living in Geelong for nine months, I became quite homesick and returned to Sydney. As I had spent most of the money I'd earned in Victoria, I decided to get a job back in Sydney and save up to further my travels around Australia. I hadn't planned on meeting a boyfriend at this stage, as I had only seen part of the east coast of Australia and there were still many destinations left on my wish list. Then I met a man named Warwick through my friend Jody, with whom I had gone to technical college. Warwick and I got on very well and we had a lot of things in common, especially our love for the water and the beach.

I told him that I was only back in Sydney long enough to save up and travel again, but since we hit it off so well we decided that we would travel together. While saving for our trip, the cost of living rose very quickly. Interest rates soared to 18 per cent, so we decided it would be wiser to save for a house and put our travel plans on hold.

After two years together, Warwick asked me to marry him. We were engaged in April 1986. We bought our first house in a suburb called Corrimal, on the south coast of New South Wales, near Wollongong, as we couldn't afford to buy a house in Sydney, close to our family and friends.

We moved into our new home in early March 1988, a couple of weeks before getting married, but I went home to my parents' place three days before the wedding, to prepare. When I walked into my old bedroom, there was a familiar smell that I knew meant that my pop was close by. I could see Poppa and Nanna sitting patiently on my bed, waiting for me to arrive.

It blew me away, as when they were both alive they always said that they wanted to live long enough to see all of their grandchildren get married and to watch them walk down the aisle.

On my wedding day, I felt so blessed because I knew they were both present at the church. Even though they were in spirit, they still made the journey to share my special day with me.

Warwick and I settled down to married life, both working hard to save enough to renovate our house and pay our mortgage. Warwick worked as a carpenter for a local builder and I managed to get a job at the local newspaper as a typesetter.

Not long after we were married, I began having

reproductive problems and a specialist told me that I probably would not be able to have any children. This was devastating news. I wasn't planning on becoming a mum right at that time but it was a blow to our future hopes and dreams. After some exploratory surgery, I was advised by the specialist that if I wanted to have a child then I had better start trying right away, just in case I needed to have IVF treatment.

We decided that we would go away with one of our best friends, Steven, for a week of snow skiing, and try to chill out and not worry about my health. During that week, I started feeling quite strange and nauseous. I told Warwick and Steven that I thought I could be pregnant. The pair of them just laughed and told me I must have eaten something that made me feel a bit off.

I discovered that I couldn't stand the smell of any sort of raw meat. Each evening, when it came time for me to cook dinner for Warwick and Steven, who loved eating big, juicy steaks, I would spend more of the time throwing up in the bathroom than cooking in the kitchen.

After our week's holiday, we returned home and I visited the doctor, to find that we were going to be proud parents. I had proved the doctors wrong.

My pregnancy was very draining, as I was constantly sick. Then I caught glandular fever and was rushed to hospital, where they initially told me that I had lost our baby. Thankfully, they were wrong.

I was so happy when I finally went into labour and gave birth to our beautiful healthy son Ryan James, who arrived on 1 April 1990. Ryan and my poppa share this birthday. I remember thinking how blessed I was that my first child would share my grandfather's birthday and that he would now be my son's spirit guide as well as my own. Ryan has proven to be a gifted artist, and I hope that Poppa teaches him as much as he taught me about art.

After two and a half years in Corrimal, Warwick and I moved back to Sydney. We purchased an old, run-down house. It desperately needed to be renovated, but it was in a nice street. We thought it might be nice to make a new addition to the family, by giving Ryan a baby brother or sister for company.

I fell pregnant after some months of trying and unfortunately had a miscarriage. The doctors then discovered I had early cervical cancer. Adding to my distress, as we couldn't afford to be in a health fund at the time, I had to wait nine months before I was able to have an operation to remove the early cancer cells.

After many subsequent trips to multiple doctors and getting second opinions, the doctors told me they had doubts that I would ever have any more children.

Our son, Ryan, was now aged two and a half, and he wondered why Mummy and Daddy couldn't just buy him a new baby brother or sister at the shop. Ryan constantly asked when he would have a baby brother or sister like his friends at daycare did. This was a very trying time, as I felt I was going to let Ryan down. When I walked down the street, I saw pregnant women and babies everywhere; it seemed I was being bombarded with pregnant ladies and new mothers.

*

After the miscarriage, I began to have many strange visions and to hear voices that weren't my own. And, due to all of the stress, I found it harder and harder to have a good night's sleep; I seemed to be getting more tired by the minute.

One evening in late September 1992, I was watching the nightly news and the main story was about two young English backpackers named Joanne Walters and Caroline Clarke who were missing. The two women had last been seen hitch-hiking on the Princes Highway, in the Bulli Tops area of Wollongong. A body had been found in Belanglo State Forest, in the Southern Highlands, south-west of Sydney, and it was believed to be that of Joanne Walters. They were still looking for Caroline Clarke. Task Force Air had been set up to look after the case. On the news, they asked anyone who had any information to call the task force.

I went to bed about 9.30 pm, after watching a few other programs on television. I didn't really give much thought to the English girls, apart from the fact that I thought it would be sad for their families and friends to lose them so young and senselessly.

I began to have yet another restless night. I finally fell asleep, and then the dream began. Suddenly, I was in a forest and I could see two girls in front of me. They were walking away from me, and a strongly built man dressed in green clothing – it could have been camouflage gear – was walking behind them, making the girls walk up a slight hill. It looked like he had something in his hand.

The two girls turned to look behind them and they seemed to look straight at me. They didn't say anything, but somehow I got the feeling that they were pleading with me to help them.

Suddenly, the man turned to see what the girls were looking at and I realised that he was looking straight at me. I wanted to stop the man, but somehow I knew it was already too late. A very strong feeling came over me that the girls were already dead. I couldn't see the man's face clearly, even though I had a full-frontal view. All I could see were his cold, piercing eyes. This is the most scary thing I remember about the dream.

I woke up in a cold sweat and tried to shake the memory of the dream. The frightening thing was that, even though I was awake, I could still clearly see the two girls and the outline of the man, standing in my bedroom. I began to think I was losing it, so I got up and poured myself a glass of water and hoped that when I returned to bed the images would disappear.

Back in bed, I tried to think happy thoughts. Just as I felt that I had finally settled down to a nice, calm sleep, I began to see a thick swirl of purple-and-black clouds floating before me. At first, the feeling I got was very warm and welcoming, then the colours began to melt, with blues and greens mixing in, and it was like I was floating in a void. I got the feeling I was falling and I heard a sudden popping sound, then I was thrust back into the scene of the two girls and the man.

I saw a green kombi van parked in a clearing and what looked like a two-man tent pitched nearby, and then the dream ended.

I didn't know what any of this meant and I got the strong feeling that I really didn't want to find out.

Over the next couple of months, I kept having the same dream. Each time, the girls pleaded with me and I saw them walking further and further into the forest. The man always looked at me as if he knew I was there but I still couldn't see his entire face, just his eyes.

As the months went by, I became increasingly nervous about going to sleep – some might say the word 'paranoid' would describe my feelings better. My husband, Warwick, was getting quite sick and tired of me constantly talking of the visions, and he wanted me to get control of myself. I became obsessed with the media reports about Joanne and Caroline, and Warwick couldn't understand why. As he rightly said, in the scheme of things, what did this case have to do with our life? I wasn't related to any of these people and I didn't know them from a bar of soap, so what did it matter if I dreamt about them or not? He just wanted the whole issue to go away and for me to go back to being the normal wife and mother I was before.

I initially put the visions down to stress and the fact that the media was flooded with information about the case. It seemed that everywhere I looked, whether it was in the newspaper or on television, or when I listened to the radio, I would hear about the girls. I believed that in some way this was making me dream about the case.

Then the visions began to invade my waking hours. I would be at work focusing on a task when the images would pop into my head. It was becoming quite unnerving, as I felt that these two girls were beginning to take over my life. I tried concentrating on positive thoughts in the hope that the images would stop as suddenly as they had started, but unfortunately I continued to be bombarded with them.

Next, I began to see visions in my sleep of the journey that the girls had undertaken before they went missing. In these visions, the girls seemed happy and carefree. They seemed to be having the time of their life. It was only when I saw the girls in the forest that their despair took over.

One of the last reported sightings of the girls was at a hotel called the Blue Boar, in Bowral, a quiet country town in the Southern Highlands that is a popular tourist destination. In July 1993, Warwick and I were invited on a weekend away for a friend's surprise thirtieth birthday party at Bowral. We were to stay for two nights at a lovely motel just on the outskirts of town with six other couples. I was very excited, as this was to be our first weekend away in ages. My one concern was that I was going to be down in the neighbourhood of the girls' disappearance and I hoped that this wouldn't stir up any more visions. Worse still would be if my friends discovered what I was seeing. I was afraid that they might think I was going crazy.

On passing the Blue Boar hotel as we approached our accommodation at the southern end of Bowral township, I told my husband about its link with Joanne and Caroline. He became annoyed and asked whether I could leave all that stuff alone for at least one weekend. He wanted to know why I couldn't just act normal and forget about the whole thing, at least for this weekend – and, if possible, forever.

I tried to just enjoy the weekend and be normal like everyone else, but I felt quite weird; something just wasn't right. My girlfriends made comments that I was acting a little strangely. I couldn't explain to them what I was experiencing, as I didn't quite understand it myself.

In Berrima, we passed an old sandstone pub and I began to pick up more visions. I could see the man with the two girls and I wondered if he had taken the girls to the pub for a drink before he killed them, or if it was a place that the murderer had frequented prior to the killings.

That evening, we all celebrated our friend's birthday with a lovely dinner and a few drinks. I was tired, so I went to bed earlier than the others. Warwick was still with the boys, having a good time, but I felt that I wasn't alone and that the two girls were trying to make contact with me. I could feel their presence and I could see their faces when I shut my eyes. I was seeing visions of the girls and the forest the whole night and woke up numerous times.

The following morning, I asked my husband to come up to the Blue Boar with me. When we arrived, I began to feel very cold and I got the shakes just standing outside the hotel. I felt so bad I thought I was going to be sick. We didn't go in, and I just asked Warwick to take us back to our motel so we could pack and get going on the journey home.

The next weekend, I went to meet a girlfriend at an antiques fair in Camden, south-west of Sydney near Campbelltown. I got lost while I was trying to find it and ended up near some farms down towards the river. I felt a very strong connection with the man I had seen with the girls in the forest, either that he was a local or that he often visited the area. That night, I had a vision of a farmhouse on a property with a verandah overlooking a dam. There was a small row boat on the edge of the dam and the house was a creamy colour. I didn't know what connection the farmhouse had to the man and the missing girls, but somehow I felt that they all were part of a bigger picture.

The following night, the visions abruptly came to a halt and I had my first restful night's sleep in ages. I was quite perplexed and yet thankful to have a sense of peace back in my life.

Chapter 5

Messages from the Backpacker-Murder Victims

I was still suffering from a number of health issues after the miscarriage and, as the doctor was concerned that I might not be able to have any more children naturally, I had an appointment with an IVF clinic. There, I underwent blood tests to check my hormone levels.

The next weekend, I went to stay at my parents' and I decided to go to the nearby Parklea markets to do a bit of shopping. There, I spotted a stall that sold New Age crystals and other products. A lovely charm of a mother and baby dolphin intertwined around a pink crystal caught my eye. I asked the lady if the charm was also sold without the crystal in it and she said no. She then told me that the crystal was a rose quartz and it boosted feminine energy. It was known as a love stone and was good for female energy and reproductive problems. I didn't know whether this was true but, as I have a love for dolphins, I bought it anyway.

Two weeks later, when I went to the IVF clinic for my next appointment, I told the doctor that I thought I was pregnant. He told me that was impossible, because on top of my existing reproductive problems my blood-test results showed that my hormone levels were not right. I told him that I just knew I was pregnant. He told me to come back in two weeks so I could have a new blood test to ascertain whether I was or I wasn't.

The results came in, and I was over the moon at the news that I was becoming a mum again. I felt ecstatic, but I also felt nervous, as I didn't want to experience another miscarriage.

I tried to think positive thoughts and hoped that the powers that be would allow me to carry my baby full-term.

*

My visions returned on 1 October 1993, as suddenly as they had stopped. I was quite alarmed, as I didn't want it to affect my pregnancy or my unborn baby.

Joanne and Caroline were seemingly trying to show me that something was about to happen with the case. Back in September 1992, the body in Belanglo State Forest had been quickly confirmed as that of Joanne Walters, and a body found nearby the day after the first discovery had been confirmed as Caroline Clarke's. I now felt very strongly that more bodies were about to be found.

My feelings were confirmed when more missing backpackers began appearing on the nightly news. Two Australians named Deborah Everist and James Gibson were the first to be linked to what was now being named the backpacker murders. Then missing German backpackers Simone Schmidl, Anja Habschied and Gabor Neugebauer were also feared to be victims of the same killer. The strange thing was that I knew the bodies of Gabor Neugebauer and Anja Habschied were in the forest but for some reason it wasn't their time to be discovered yet.

Four days later, the news broke that two more bodies had been found in the forest: those of Deborah Everist and James Gibson. They had been missing since 1989 after leaving Frankston, in Victoria. I then began getting visions about the German couple, and what I was seeing was very distressing. I hoped that this wasn't doing anything to upset my unborn baby.

A close girlfriend named Peta, who had been with me when I went away to Bowral, was aware of what was happening to me. We would speak frequently, as she was concerned about the visions I was seeing. She had noticed the changes in me since they had begun.

Thank goodness she was a good support at this time, as she was one of the only people I could talk to about the horrors I was witnessing. Peta suggested I pass on the information I was receiving to the police, as my premonitions were beginning to be borne out by reality. She called her friend Julieanne, who was a police officer, and Julieanne suggested that I get in touch with her husband, Scott, who was a police detective.

I initially felt embarrassed telling Scott what I was

43

seeing. I hadn't ever witnessed psychic-type visions like this before, let alone told the police about them. Scott rang Bowral Police and they said they would get in touch with me.

Later the same day, 9 October, I had a very strong vision. It was one of the clearest I have ever witnessed. In it, I was suddenly inside a house; it looked like an older-style house and the walls of one room were painted blue. My attention was drawn to a large number of Polaroid photographs pinned up on the wall.

The photos looked like they were taken at night, as the background was dark and the various faces were all lit up as if by a flash. There were a number of men and women in each photograph, approximately eighteen to twenty in total, all looking straight at me. I could see the faces of Joanne Walters, Caroline Clarke, Simone Schmidl, James Gibson, Deborah Everist, Anja Habschied and Gabor Neugebauer amongst them. All the people were smiling – the photos looked like holiday or party snaps. In one photo, I could see what looked like a campfire in the background. A couple of the males had cans of beer in their hands and they looked relaxed and happy. I felt that some of these people had drunk quite a lot, as they looked like they were intoxicated. I wondered if they had been lulled into a false sense of security, in the belief that they were there to have a good time. I felt that these photos were taken by the perpetrator before he killed his victims, and he kept them as some kind of sick record of how many people he had killed.

While I was looking at the sea of faces on the wall, the murderer realised I was in the house and saw me. He came running along the hallway towards me, with something in his hands.

The moment was broken and the vision abruptly ended. I felt quite shaken and tried to gather my wits and make sense of what had just happened.

The images on the blue wall suddenly reappeared. I was back looking at them, only this time I was seeing the pictures through someone else's eyes: I was one of the victims, a male, and I had just discovered the wall of photographs. I was in one of the images on the wall, and the murderer wasn't very happy that I had seen the pictures. He came running at me, his face red with anger. He was dressed in the camouflage clothes again. This time, I could see his face clearly. His skin was olive and sun-beaten, his hair dark brown and wavy, his eyes hazel to grey, and he had chiselled features. He needed a shave and was close to a hundred and eighty-two centimetres in height. He was in his thirties and had very broad shoulders. He was wearing a singlet and I could see his biceps bulging. I felt that I had met him earlier that day and the friendly person he had seemed to be then had disappeared, exposing a quick-tempered, very dark quality.

As these thoughts rushed through my head, the murderer came towards me. I felt something cold and sharp in my chest, and everything went black. I separated from the male energy and knew that he had just been murdered.

A few days later, I told Scott of my latest visions, and that this was the first time I had been able to see the perpetrator's face clearly. I felt that I could do an identikit picture if I was given the chance. Scott took my information seriously and said he would see what he could do.

A day later, the name 'David' kept popping into my head; I wasn't sure if it was the victim's Christian name or that of the murderer.

I was sick of waiting for Bowral Police to contact me, so I rang them myself. I spent about twenty minutes giving a detective details of the visions I'd had. She said that she would record all of my information on a computer database; I hoped that she was telling me the truth.

The next day, a detective from Bowral rang and asked me to repeat all of the information I'd previously given. He didn't sound at all impressed with what I had to say and told me that people like me rang up all the time. He gave me the impression I was wasting his time and abruptly said that I should ring him back if I had any further information.

While having a shower before going to work, I saw a vivid flash of the Belanglo State Forest sign. Something told me that the police were searching in the wrong area. The message I received was that they needed to search to the right-hand side of the sign.

I phoned the detective to ask him if that area had ever been searched before, and it hadn't. I told him that the two missing German backpackers Anja Habschied and Gabor Neugebauer would definitely be found in that area. He went very quiet on the other end of the phone, then said, 'God, I hope you're wrong!'

I said, 'So do I, but unfortunately I know that I'm not.'

He then told me that the dogs would be searching an eighteen-kilometre radius, so if the bodies were in the place I had described, they should be found.

That night, I got another vision – a clearer view of where the bodies were. It was as if I was flying above the area and suddenly dropped into the forest. I could see a large sandy area with a track nearby; there was a big white gum tree and I could see a couple digging. I couldn't see their faces, as they had their backs to me. The hole they were digging wasn't very deep – only thirty centimetres or so. What looked like leaf mulch littered the area. The girl in my vision was standing closest to me and I could only see the back of her from the waist down: she had brown hiking boots on and was wearing light-coloured jeans and a matching-coloured top. She was bending over digging. The second person, a male, I could sense in close proximity to me. I got a strong feeling that I was seeing the German couple and that the murderer was making them dig their own grave. No one knew that I was there, watching.

I received another vision during the early hours one morning in late October. I could see a vehicle in a clearing, a deep-red four-wheel-drive station wagon; it could have been a Toyota Land Cruiser or a Holden Jackeroo. The vehicle was parked on a sandy track not far from where I had seen the people digging in the vision a week earlier.

I rang Scott when I got home from work the next day and told him what I had seen. Disappointed with the way the Bowral detectives were treating me, he put me in contact with Detective Inspector Lynch, who was part of Task Force Air. We spoke at length and he seemed quite open to listening to what I had to say. He asked me why I was picking up the information that I was getting. When I told him it began at the time of having a miscarriage and suffering with health issues, he said that he had heard of past cases where someone suffered a trauma and their psychic ability came to the fore. I thought to myself, 'At least this man understands what I'm going through.'

He asked me if I was keeping a diary of my visions. I had been keeping it all in my head; I had a few tattered notes but that was all. He advised me to write down everything I could remember and from then on to keep my visions in a diary, as this would be a useful way to help him. He said that when I had gathered enough information, he would send someone out to pick it up.

Inspector Lynch also said that he would assign two detectives to work with me directly, so I wouldn't have to go through various departments to get the information across. He seemed very understanding of how frustrated I must be feeling. He explained that the task force had received over a thousand phone calls from psychics and would-be psychics and that because they were so busy, some officers' tempers had been tested by the crackpots ringing. I told him I was sure that some of the other officers had already put me down as being a crackpot.

On and off during the next day, the visions kept recurring. I found it hard to think of anything else. At 4 pm, there was a newsflash that a fifth body had been found – it was a missing German woman, Simone Schmidl.

I was frustrated with myself for not getting any information about this victim other than seeing her face in the Polaroid. I wondered why I could pick up so clearly on some victims and not others. Beating myself up over it wasn't going to do me any good, though. I needed to remember that the victims chose to come to me and not the other way around.

As the day drew to a close, the German couple Anja Habschied and Gabor Neugebauer still hadn't been found. I was overwhelmed by a sense of frustration, as the vision of the site of their burial wouldn't leave me. I felt this frustration more from the victims' point of view than my own. They were so strongly around me that I was picking up their feelings.

Desperate to help the police find the couple's bodies, I rang Bowral Police to talk with Inspector Lynch, but he had already gone home. I spoke with another detective, who was the rudest officer I had spoken with yet. He was abrupt with me and implied that I was wasting his time. He made me feel like I was some kind of weirdo. Before I hung up, I asked him if the police had searched a sandy area to the right of the Belanglo State Forest sign, and he sharply said that he didn't want to make any comment.

When I went to work at Fairfax Community Newspapers the next morning, my head was bursting with visions. Over the previous months, I had been telling a journalist friend at work, Colin, about what I was seeing. At first, he was quite sceptical, but as time went on he agreed that I had given him a lot of information that had later been verified on the news. Hearing of my frustration with the police, Colin decided to do a story based on the information I had already gathered.

Fairfax Community Newspapers published a large number of papers across the greater Sydney area. We wanted the story to be printed in the paper that could be the most influential in helping to solve the crimes, so Colin asked me which area I thought the perpetrator lived in. He gave me a map showing the areas that all of the papers covered, and I chose the Macarthur district, in Sydney's south-west. I didn't know why, but I had a very strong feeling that the perpetrator lived in that region.

I rang back Bowral Police and told Inspector Lynch of the visions showing me where the German couple's bodies would be found. His reply was that he thought I was being influenced by the media reports. I was very disgruntled by his reaction, because I had thought that at last I'd found someone who was taking me seriously. I had been recording my visions in a diary as he'd suggested, yet he still hadn't sent anyone to pick it up or assigned me the two detectives that he'd promised.

I didn't bother to tell him that Colin and I intended to do a story about my visions. Perhaps when there was something in print pertaining to them, the police might finally start to take me seriously.

The next night, I had very strange dreams; numbers and letters were constantly floating through my head. I saw quick flashes of a red four-wheel drive and then a New South Wales number plate: LLZ–316. I wrote the number down in my diary for future reference. I never found out if it had been linked in any way to the case.

The next day, 4 November, there was a newsflash at 11.30 am: a sixth victim had been found. I knew in my heart that finally Anja Habschied and Gabor Neugebauer's bodies were in the process of being uncovered. At around 3 pm, the seventh victim was found. These bodies were later confirmed to be the German couple's.

I was most interested in what the nightly news would show. I hoped it would reveal that the bodies were found in a sandy area with a white gum tree close by. To my relief, it did – I finally had confirmation that I truly was receiving messages from the victims.

With a new sense of urgency, I rang Inspector Lynch to tell him the number plate I had dreamt about and that I felt it belonged to a red four-wheel drive associated with the murders. Inspector Lynch said he would send someone to see me as soon as things quietened down with the case. The police just seemed to keep fobbing me off; nobody took me all that seriously, except for Scott and Julieanne, who had gone out of their way to help me.

Chapter 6

Face to Face with the Backpacker Murderer

In November 1993, my visions took an even darker turn. I dreamt of animals lying on the ground, tied down with blackened rope that looked as if it had been burnt. All of the animals had been bleeding and they were laid out in a big circle. The first one was still alive and it looked like it could be a golden retriever – the poor animal had both of its paws bandaged and it was lying on its back, bleeding. The next animal was black and I thought that it too was a dog. It was lying in the same pose. I felt that it was dead and that the other animals in the circle – I wasn't sure if the rest were dogs or goats – were also dead.

All of the animals had their throats cut and some had their stomachs slashed open. There was blood everywhere and it looked like someone had tried to set the animals on fire, as there were black burn marks around the circle. I saw a close-up of a scabbard. The murderer drew a long, sharp knife out of the scabbard and I saw the blade glisten in the light. It looked like some type of a hunting or diving knife. Then the vision abruptly ended.

I woke up feeling like I was going to vomit. I had never seen such horrific things before in my life. I hoped that it was only a dream but my feeling was that it was real. It looked to be the site of some kind of sacrifice or black-magic ritual. Whatever it was, this ritual was connected to something very dark and sinister.

I tried to settle down and get back to sleep but, as soon as I shut my eyes, I immediately had a floating feeling, blackness surrounded me, I saw a purple-green swirl and had the familiar feeling of falling. I seemed to drop back into the house with the blue wall again. The perpetrator had moved an antique kitchen dresser with leadlight doors in front of the Polaroid shots I had seen earlier on the wall.

This time, I saw different photos on another part of the wall. Two females and three males appeared in them. One of the faces was very clear: a pretty girl in her late teens to early twenties. Her eyes were big and blue and she had long blonde hair pulled back in a ponytail. She was not smiling; she was just looking back at me from the photograph.

I recognised the girl from reports I'd seen long ago on the news. It was Trudie Adams, who went missing one night in 1978 after leaving a surf club on Sydney's Northern Beaches. I suddenly saw the murderer's face again. He reminded me of Clint Eastwood, as he seemed to squint and he had wrinkles at the side of his eyes; his lips were thin and he held them tightly together.

The vision changed and I saw two men in bushland, one watching the other bend down and stab something or someone uncontrollably. This vision was extremely brutal and I felt that I was witnessing the death of Anja Habschied.

I saw that Anja was murdered first and Gabor Neugebauer was bound and gagged and made to watch. Gabor was struggling, trying to break free to stop the brutal death of his girlfriend. Anja, also bound and gagged, had been made to kneel over what looked like a type of altar – a large, flat rock or wooden slab that she was forced to place her head on. The perpetrator stabbed her. I could see blood splattered all over his face, but it didn't seem to stop him. Then, suddenly, everything turned to red and the vision ended.

In the next vision, I was again seeing the man who had been murdered in the house with the blue wall, only this time I was looking at him, rather than through his eyes. I felt that he had willingly gone to the murderer's house. The two men were initially quite social, as I saw them sharing a few drinks together in the backyard, around a fire of some sort, like a bonfire. The victim then went inside to the kitchen; on seeing the wall of Polaroid photographs, he asked the perpetrator what they were there for. The murderer became violently angry and grabbed the man, shaking and punching him. I again got the feeling that this man was killed here.

I saw that the victim was dressed in a pale blue-white T-shirt, jeans and white Adidas leather runners with two stripes down the side. He was around a hundred and eighty centimetres tall and between twenty-five and thirty years of age. His eyes were hazel to brown. He had quite short, dark-brown or black wavy hair. He was a slight build but very fit looking. From his accent, he was from the United Kingdom. The victim told me that his name was Will – William Shorter or William Souther; I'm not sure. Then the vision abruptly ended. I don't know whether the man's name was correct or whether he even existed.

I didn't get any more visions for the rest of the week. I got the feeling that all of the bodies in the forest had been found, at least for the moment. And indeed, no more bodies have ever been recovered. However, I was – and still am – absolutely sure that the perpetrator had killed more people, possibly including Trudie and Will. I felt very strongly that he might have killed some of the victims on his property or a property that he had access to and that the remains of these victims were on the property or close by. I would, however, like to add that I don't feel he acted alone on all occasions.

*

On 10 November 1993, Colin's story was published in the *Macarthur Advertiser*. He showed me the story before it went to print and I was happy with it, but unfortunately another of the editors at the paper decided to spice it up a bit. I must say that I wasn't completely happy with the end result, although I did have to admit that it got the message across. I was very thankful that my name was changed in the story to protect my identity because I felt quite stressed after it was published. Colin told me he thought that I didn't have anything to worry about, but I still couldn't get rid of the sickening feeling I had in my stomach.

I just didn't know whether going ahead with it had been the right decision. I was angry with myself for trying to prove a point to the police, as now I feared that I might have jeopardised the safety of myself and my family through being so pig-headed.

The concern deepened when my visions began to change. I started to feel as if I was being watched. I felt that someone was now tuning in to me and knew that I was watching him. I got the impression that this person was also psychic. I began to panic that the person was trying to find me.

Trudie Adams began to appear to me too. She was at a bus stop and was wearing a white Hawaiian-print dress with orange hibiscus flowers on it. A man enticed her into his car, a white or light-coloured vehicle, and the next thing I saw was that he had taken her to a house. In this vision, the house was different to the one with the blue room that I had seen in past visions. I was suddenly standing in what seemed to be a kitchen and saw the man stabbing her uncontrollably.

The visions of the perpetrator were quite confusing, as they didn't come in any particular order. One moment, I was in the present, then suddenly I was going back five or ten years. He seemed to have had numerous vehicles throughout all of the visions, so I wondered if he borrowed them from family and friends or changed his own frequently.

In another dream, I saw a woman whom I felt to be

Trudie Adams being carried in the kind of basket that search-and-rescue crews use to rescue hikers in the bush. The perpetrator seemed to be carrying the basket down a steep slope into some very dense bush. I couldn't work out how one man could be strong enough to carry the basket on his own, but this is what I was being shown. From what I could see, the area dropped down into a deep ravine. I could hear water running swiftly nearby and could see that the rocks were worn by it. Above the waterline, the rocks were black and dark grey in colour and they looked very sharp and rigid.

My next vision was of the perpetrator, much younger than in previous flashes, with a group of men who looked like they were members of a soccer team. They were all gathered at an oval as if waiting to play a game, but most of the team had pitchforks in their hands. They all had the pitchforks facing skyward. The perpetrator seemed to be the captain of the team: the other men were all dressed in identical black-and-white horizontal-striped football jerseys, while on his jersey the stripes were vertical. In the vision, I felt that the men were aware that I was watching them. I saw the perpetrator turn and look directly at me and smile, as if in acknowledgement of my presence. The impression I received was that the pitchforks had some connection to black magic or devil worship. There was some type of cult connection and the perpetrator seemed to be the one in charge.

These visions were quite odd and I am not sure what they were meant to show me.

While I was experiencing all of this, my poor husband, Warwick, was becoming increasingly angry with me, as the backpacker-murder case was taking over my every waking moment. I look back now on this period of my life and feel blessed that he was able to endure the frustration I was putting him through.

I woke up on the morning of 16 November and turned the television on, to be greeted with a newsflash: Task Force Air was searching a section of Galston Gorge, in the northern suburbs of Sydney. The report showed scenes of the gorge and it looked very familiar, from what I had seen in my visions. There was a river with fast-moving water and dark-coloured rocks. The surrounding area was very dense bush, like the type in the area where I felt Trudie Adams' body could be.

I immediately rang Julieanne and arranged a time the following day to give her a copy of my diary so she could pass it on to the task force.

At lunchtime about a week later, I began receiving constant flashes involving Trudie Adams. In the back of my mind, there was a nagging feeling that I should try to contact the police. The most important thing I needed to find out was what Trudie was wearing at the time of her disappearance, to see if it matched up with the dress she wore in my vision. I contacted Missing Persons, who advised me to ring the police station at Mona Vale, on Sydney's Northern Beaches. Mona Vale Police told me that Trudie's file was tied up with Task Force Air and I should ring them. For weeks, I had been waiting for a promised phone call from them. I felt like I was going around and around in circles trying to work on this case; it was at this point that I wondered whether I should just forget about it.

I decided to ring Julieanne one more time and ask her whether she thought that I should bother trying to help the police with the backpacker case any more. Julieanne suggested that I be patient and see what happened.

At five o'clock that afternoon, I received the phone call I had been waiting for. It was Inspector Lynch of Task Force Air and he said that he had two officers he wanted me to meet. We arranged for them to meet me while I was on my lunchbreak at work the following day.

After our phone conversation, I didn't know whether to be happy or nervous about our arranged meeting. I had failed to tell the police that I was five months pregnant, so I was concerned that they would think I was some crazy pregnant woman suffering with some sort of hormonal disturbance. I told Warwick about the meeting we had arranged and he didn't look too impressed with me. He just said that now was my chance to really make an idiot of myself and that I should never have got this involved. I tried to explain to him that I couldn't help what was happening and that I hoped if I passed on the information to the police, all of the visions would disappear. I could see by his face that he still wasn't convinced.

The detectives, Brett Coman and Gae Crea, were both quite approachable, although I couldn't help feeling that I was being evaluated. They were very open to what I had to say and I finally felt that I was being listened to. I gave them a copy of my diary and they told me to ring them if I had any more information to pass on as they were now my direct link to the task force.

*

Another night of visions: I was shown more scenes of the murderer in the forest. He was shooting, doing some target practice. I also saw him watching something or someone through a pair of binoculars. Then I saw him driving through the bush; the road was lined with trees on both sides. It could have been the Galston Gorge area, as it looked like the scenes I had seen on the news reports. I hadn't been there before, though, so I couldn't be a hundred per cent sure.

The next vision I saw was of him and a bushfire. I wondered if the visions were trying to show me a connection to the bushfire brigade, because I saw back-burning going on. Perhaps he was trying to get rid of evidence. If he was in the bushfire brigade and back-burning, then he wouldn't attract any suspicion for lighting fires. I got a strong feeling that he had something to hide and that a fire could destroy whatever it was.

The vision changed and I saw a road – it began as gravel and then turned into a dirt track – leading up to a clearing, like the car park at a lookout area. There was a big post on the right-hand side of the clearing and just in front were a number of boulders on either side of the road. I could see a view of a valley in the distance and felt that I was being drawn up to the top of the track. I felt that I needed to get there, because whatever I was supposed to see was obscured from where I was standing. But I wasn't able to reach the top. The vision ended and I felt frustrated that I couldn't see whatever it was I was meant to be shown.

The name David kept popping into my head, as it had some weeks earlier. I thought to myself that I still needed to know what David's surname was supposed to be, and the name Frazer or Fraser flashed in front of me, then the name Mark appeared. I didn't know if this was correct, but as I was still learning to understand my psychic abilities, I decided to just record the information in my diary and let the police decipher what it may or may not mean.

In late November 1993, the television program *Real Life* on the Seven network had a story about a suspect for the backpacker murders, a man named Graham Lachlan Harris. When I saw this story, alarm bells went off, because this was not the man that I had seen in my visions. He had a strong likeness to the killer but I definitely didn't think it was him. I hoped that the story wouldn't confuse the public into believing that he was the backpacker murderer.

Very good friends of mine, Wendy and Michael, had been sympathetic in listening to my visions and they suggested that we go for a drive through the Galston Gorge to see if I recognised any of the scenes from my visions.

When we arrived at the gorge, I could feel a very strong resonance with the area. The road through it is very winding; it meanders through a lot of bushland and at the bottom there is a bridge and then a sharp bend and a car park that leads off to a walking track. When we drove to the bottom of the gorge and neared the bend, I felt drawn to walk along the track; there was something I needed to see that was near it. We parked the car and were about to go for a walk along it when a huge electrical storm hit.

The rain was pelting down, so we went back to the car and continued driving through the gorge. Next, we drove around Arcadia Road and passed a monastery. The road I had seen previously, with the car park and the valley in the distance, was now making sense: this area looked exactly like my vision. There was a signpost with the name Vision Valley on it and I wanted to go there, but the weather was still terrible. We passed the bushfire-brigade station and I wondered if this was the connection that I'd felt to the bushfires.

I took the electrical storm as a warning that I shouldn't be investigating any further, so we decided to leave.

At home, I looked in the street directory of the area we had driven through and it was only then that I saw there was a rifle range in Galston Gorge. Perhaps the flash I had of the perpetrator target shooting was connected to this area. The map also had a place on it called Rocky Rapids and I wondered if this was the place that I had seen in my visions with the rapidly moving water and the dark-coloured rocks. I felt that things were falling into place.

That evening, my visions stopped. I felt like I had a blockage of some sort. I questioned whether or not the killer was also psychic, as I felt that he knew I was watching him. Whenever I started to get a vision, I saw him staring at me and next I saw a closed door.

Chapter 7

I Embrace My Psychic Journey

I started to do yoga for pregnancy. The only problem was that at the end of the yoga class, when we would do a meditation, I started having visions again. What I saw was the killer walking in the bush. He seemed to be going down a hill, into what appeared to be a cave, as everything would then go dark. Sometimes at yoga I was the last one in the class to come back from the meditation. Everybody else felt very calm and relaxed but all I was seeing was more information concerning the murderer.

I told my teacher that I was having visions and also asked her what the symbols on the yoga chart on the wall meant; she informed me that the chart was of chakras, which are areas in the body. She questioned why I was asking and I told her that I was also seeing the two symbols at the top of the chart during my dreams and meditations. The symbols were of the third eye and the crown chakra.

In our body, we have seven main chakra points: the first is in our reproductive area, called the base or root chakra (colour red); the second is close to our navel, called our sacral chakra (orange); the third is our solar plexus, located in our stomach, also known as our gut feeling (yellow); the fourth is in the heart area (green); the fifth is located on the throat (blue); the sixth is between our eyes, known as the third eye and also as the brow chakra (indigo); and the seventh is our crown chakra, located on the top of the head (violet).

My teacher asked me how I was seeing the sixth and seventh chakras and I told her that when I tried to meditate and relax, the symbols would come into view, followed closely by the colours. The teacher told me that it was impossible to see these symbols, as only highly spiritual teachers and gurus are able to see such things during meditation. I told her that I wasn't that type of person but was definitely seeing the symbols on the wall and that I wondered what it all meant.

She recommended that I speak with a woman she had met who was a psychic, to ask her for some guidance. I finally worked up the courage to ring the woman, Elizabeth, nervous that she would think I was a fruitcake.

I introduced myself, explained to her what was going on and asked if she could help me, to which she abruptly said no. She said that it was too frightening and she didn't like to deal with such evil things. However, she did pass on the name of another medium, Patricia, whom she thought could help me. I was hesitant to ring Patricia because, after having such a negative response from Elizabeth, I didn't want to feel rejected again.

I went to a New Age shop and asked the assistant if there were any books I could read that would help me to find out about the spirit world. The assistant suggested a book called *The Eagle and the Rose*, by Rosemary Altea. She also suggested I buy a meditation tape to help balance my chakras and an amethyst crystal, which was supposed to give me psychic protection from the evil spirits. After purchasing these items, I was about to leave the shop when she said, 'I also have the name of a medium for you to ring.' The woman's name was Patricia.

I got home and decided to ring her, as it seemed too much of a coincidence that the same name would pop up twice. When I spoke to her, she was lovely; she was very understanding and made an appointment with me to meet her in a week's time. I couldn't wait for the day to come. I was nervous and hoped that finally I had found someone who could help me.

The day finally came, and I was very excited. Meeting Patricia was wonderful. I felt like I had known this woman all of my life. Not to mention that she didn't make me feel weird or strange. She explained many things to me about the spirit world and quickly taught me exercises that could help me to protect myself from the negative spirits. Patricia also asked me to join her learning circle, a psychic-development group that met each Tuesday night. She thought that it would be good for me to meet others with similar abilities and it would help me learn how to use my gift.

One of the first things I learnt was that everybody makes contact with spirit in different ways. One week in the learning circle, it was my turn to relay visions I had seen after we all did a guided meditation. I told the others that I saw a large, craggy mountain with an old tree on the top that had died. The tree was huge and all of the branches were bare; it looked almost like a skeleton.

I was standing under the tree and looking down at the vast view below me. The strange thing was that there were thousands of people coming up the mountain towards me. They were lined up for miles and looked as small as ants in the distance. The path they followed up the mountain was well worn. I wondered why all of these people were ascending when there was nothing very interesting when you reached the summit. The tree and I were the only two things there. I relayed to the group the scents and sounds I could smell and hear, and I wondered why some of them were looking at me strangely.

Then Alan, the only man in the group, asked me how I could see, hear and smell all of these things just from doing a meditation. I replied, 'I don't know!' and asked everybody, 'Isn't that how you get your messages?' Most of the group said they only received messages through a feeling, some through hearing voices and a few in the same way that I did. One of the group was quite annoyed. I didn't go to the Spiritualist Church like the others and I didn't study like some of them, so she wanted to know why *I* could do all of this.

Beautiful Patricia stepped in and explained that it is spirit that gives us the ability to communicate and it is their choice how and when we receive our messages. In

fighting them. Frequent images of firefighters were being shown on the TV and I watched them in the belief that there was some sort of link to be found.

Around this time, I woke in the middle of the night with the vision of two men finding a piece of the murderer's gun in bushland. The area looked as though it had been burnt out by the fires.

Another night, I saw the gravesite of the most recent victim, which was very similar to one of the earlier gravesites that had already been found. The backpacker was buried in front of a fallen log or tree stump, one side of which was rotten, making it concave. The body was hidden there, with leaves and branches over the top to conceal it. I felt this new grave was down in the Belanglo Forest, as the terrain was very similar to what I had seen on TV of where the other victims' bodies had been located, and the area in my vision hadn't been affected by the fires. It would make sense for the murderer to go back there as he felt comfortable there. I passed the information on to Detective Crea.

In late January, there was a story on the news about a memorial plaque to be laid in Belanglo State Forest in memory of all the victims of the backpacker murders. I felt very strongly that the murderer would be watching the memorial service closely and I wondered if he would actually be there, as he loved to watch when the police were in the area and he also loved all of the media attention.

I felt that he was going to be caught very soon. He was getting too sure of himself. I kept getting the strong feeling that something good was going to happen soon. Patricia agreed that the perpetrator was close to being caught; she said that he would be undone by his own actions. She agreed that he was psychic and that he knew I could see him. I had a very strong psychic message that warned me that no matter how compelled I felt to go to the forest, I shouldn't, as he was waiting there for me and was trying to draw me to the spot.

In February, I saw a vision of the murderer walking into a forest – it looked like Belanglo again – and he seemed to be burying something . . . it was a baseball bat and his gun.

A few days later, I was woken at about two in the morning by another hideous nightmare. I was tied onto a brown-and-white pinto horse; it walked up a street and the backpacker murderer was there waiting for me. He was with some other men and they had archery equipment. They had been sacrificing animals again and there was blood and guts everywhere. The perpetrator then aimed his bow and arrow at the horse, shot two arrows into it and the horse bolted out of control.

I wondered what on earth it was supposed to mean – until I watched the news the following evening. There was a report of a brown-and-white pinto horse being found alive in a paddock in the Newcastle area with two arrows shot into it. An RSPCA officer made an appeal for any witnesses to come forward.

*

My son Blake was born at Hurstville Community Hospital on the evening of 31 March 1994. After everything I had experienced during the pregnancy, I was lucky to have had a very calm and easy birth. I was so pleased when I saw that I had given birth to a beautiful, serene and healthy baby boy.

After Blake's birth, Warwick had gone home and I had just had a shower and was trying to get some rest when I was woken up by a loud banging sound. I sat bolt upright in bed and couldn't believe my eyes: every door in the delivery suite had been flung open. Prior to me going to sleep, all of the doors were closed tightly shut.

I immediately rang the buzzer for the nurse and waited for her to come while lying in the bed, terrified. When she arrived, she asked me what the matter was. I showed her how every door in the room had been opened when I was asleep, and she just smiled and said, 'So, you've met the ghost.'

Before giving birth to my son, I wasn't aware of the ghostly visitor, but in the delivery wards at Hurstville Community Hospital it has been reported by a number of nurses that a man frequents the ward and is often heard walking up and down the corridors, followed by the strong smell of smoke. This gentleman seems to be more active at night. I'd had my first meeting with the spirit of Dr William Fenton.

The nurse informed me that I was staying in the most haunted room in the labour ward. I thought to myself that it was just my luck to be given the haunted room – I couldn't even give birth without having ghosts come to visit. I was comforted, though, when she told me that many of the nurses had met the presence and said that he was quite friendly and that he liked to stay with the babies and look after them.

*

Blake was a little over seven weeks old when, on 22 May, I awoke to a newsflash on the radio: a man, later identified as Ivan Milat, had been arrested in a dawn raid at a residence in Eagle Vale, near Campbelltown, in connection with the backpacker murders. Eagle Vale was in the Macarthur district of Sydney, which I had been drawn to when Colin had shown me his map.

I turned on the TV and on the news they showed Ivan Milat's house and his vehicle: a deep-red four-wheel drive just like I had seen in my visions. The only problem was, I didn't think that Ivan Milat was the man I kept seeing. He certainly looked similar to the man in my visions, but Milat was somewhat older and not tall enough. I felt that there was a strong connection between Milat and the crimes, but I didn't feel that he was the main or only perpetrator. I also had a feeling that there was some type of cult connection to these murders and that the man in my visions was involved in it. I felt very strongly that he was helping to cover things up for Milat.

The next night, I had a very frightening dream of a man coming to my front door. It was night-time and the sensor light at the front of my house suddenly went on. As the door is made of leadlight, I could see the light shining through the glass. Then there was a knock at the door. My four-year-old, Ryan, ran to open it but for some reason I felt that he shouldn't. I tried to stop him but it was too late. He opened it and the man standing in the doorway said, 'You know what I'm here for, Debbie.'

I also kept being shown a property that I had seen in a past vision, where the animals were sacrificed, but these new images were more focused on the house. It was old, with a chimney and a red roof and walls that were discoloured white fibro or cladding. A couple of steps led up to an aluminium screen door. I could see a big dirt track, a trail bike leaning up against the house and a pile of firewood close to the back door. There was bush adjoining the property and I kept getting the feeling that I had to go to the property's edge on the right-hand side as there were more bodies to be found in this bush area.

Chapter 8

In Too Deep: The Ivan Milat Trial

In the six months after the publication of Colin's article about my visions regarding the backpacker murders, the *Macarthur Advertiser* had received many phone calls from people wanting to speak with 'Julia' – the alias I went under in the article to protect my privacy.

Two days after Ivan Milat's arrest, Colin rang to tell me that a woman, whom I'll call Claire, had rung the paper in a very distraught state wanting to speak urgently with 'Julia'. Being naive (or stupid), I rang the woman and answered her questions about my visions. It was only some time into our conversation that she revealed she was, in fact, Ivan Milat's girlfriend. She said that Ivan was not guilty. She knew he could get very angry and that he had done things in the past, but his past didn't matter as far as the two of them were concerned. He was always very nice to her, she said, and she hoped to spend the rest of her life with him. Claire said that I must help her get Ivan off the charges and set him free. I told her I couldn't help her.

Her tone was sincere and friendly, and she seemed quite upset, so when she then asked me what the man I was seeing in my visions looked like, I told her that Ivan didn't fit his description exactly, because he was shorter and older, but that one of the cars I had seen in my visions matched the one that Ivan owned. Claire said that the police had been able to link Ivan to the case by a white car he had driven. She then added that a silver ute with a stripe was also connected.

I gave her a description of the man who I thought could be the perpetrator: a hundred and eighty-something centimetres tall, with dark, collar-length, wavy-to-curly hair, hazel-to-grey eyes, well built and thirty to thirty-five years of age. Her tone of voice immediately changed, as though I had described a person she knew.

Claire asked if she could have my phone number and address, which I declined to give her, as I thought it could be far too dangerous for my family. She said she understood and warned me that I should be concerned for my safety, as I was in grave danger. Her warning, and the way she was speaking, gave me the impression that I should take her seriously.

When I got off the phone, I immediately rang Task Force Air to tell detectives Crea and Coman what had happened, but they weren't available. I suddenly realised how deep I had got myself in when the officer I spoke with told me that I could be charged for speaking with Claire, as I might influence the investigation. I later received a phone call from a female detective who asked me for details about the conversation and told me to call her if I had any other contact with Claire.

Claire rang Colin a couple of times to tell him she wanted to speak with me again. I finally rang her on her work number and when we began talking she said that I sounded strange. I told her that I was feeling quite nervous, as this case was now getting personal. It had been bad enough dreaming about the case for months on end but to be personally involved, with my safety under threat, was a completely different matter.

We talked more about my visions and Claire told me that these images were like pieces of a jigsaw puzzle, and in the future the pieces would all start to fit and I would know exactly what it all meant. She said she thought it would take a long time for everything to come out in the open.

Claire wanted to know everything that I had seen in my visions, and I realised that I might have been giving too much away. My gut feeling was that I shouldn't get any more involved than I already was, and I shouldn't contact her again.

*

My next vision was of a woman with dark hair around shoulder-length or maybe a little longer. She was dressed in a long gown, riding a horse and holding a wooden cross above her head. I got the feeling that she was a high priestess in a cult. It looked like she was performing a holy ritual.

A friend of mine who is psychic rang at eight o'clock one morning during this period and told me to make sure that I was not alone in the house. I took my son Ryan to daycare and returned home briefly with my baby, Blake, who was close to two months of age. At about 10 am, as I was getting ready to go out, I noticed a man out the front of my house. He seemed to be hiding behind the telegraph pole on the footpath.

I watched through the front window as he started walking onto my property. There was a knock at the door and my gut feeling was not to open it under any circumstances. I called out 'Who's there?' and nobody answered. I quickly ran to the kitchen window and looked out. My car was parked in the driveway and I could see the man's reflection in the car window. He had his back flat against the wall of my house and a coil of electrical wire in his hands.

I ran to the front window again and could see that the car the man had arrived in was a Sydney Electricity car, but I thought it was strange that he was there because our electricity meter had only been read two weeks ago.

The man again knocked on the door, went around to the side of my house and opened and banged shut the meter box, then went back to his car. He stood on the road in front of my house for about twenty minutes, opening and closing the boot of his car or staring at the house. Finally, he got into his vehicle and drove off.

I immediately rang Sydney Electricity and asked if anybody was supposed to come to my place that day.

They said that to their knowledge no electricity man was supposed to have been at my property. They thought it was very suspicious.

I reported this to Task Force Air, and they asked me to go to Sutherland Police to make a statement, just in case anything happened. After taking their advice and making my statement, I rang Patricia and asked her if it was all right if I stayed at her place for the day. When I told her what had happened, she said to come over right away.

Patricia's son Brad, whom I had never met before, came to visit his mother while I was there. He suddenly looked at me and said he could see a vision of a man dressed in black standing on a ridge. The ridge was surrounded by thick bush. Brad said the man had a message for Julia: 'How many?' or 'How much?' This greatly disturbed me, as Brad wasn't aware of the fact that I was getting visions about the backpacker murders and he had absolutely no idea that my alias was Julia.

It further confirmed my fears that the murderer was tuning into me and that he wanted to know how much I knew about the crimes. I felt sure that the perpetrator of these murders had some dealings with the occult. The most recent visions I had been receiving involved more people than just the perpetrator. I strongly felt he wasn't working alone. After the visit from the fake electricity man to my home, I was concerned that the people involved were very much aware that I was in contact with the police and I could be their next victim.

That night, when I went to bed, I had another vision. I could see the perpetrator standing on a black, rocky outcrop in thick bushland. The rocks looked hard and craggy, like black granite. I got the feeling that this was private property – it felt like a home – where he felt safe and knew that he wouldn't be seen by intruders. But I could see that he could see me. I sensed he was annoyed that I was watching him and he wanted to let me know that he was aware of me.

I woke up in a cold sweat. I just wanted these frightening visions to end. Why on earth did I have to be the one to be given such visions? I didn't ask for any of this; I just wanted to have a normal life again.

*

When Anja Habschied's body was located in Belanglo State Forest back in November 1993, her head was missing. To this day, Anja's head hasn't been found. One morning in late May 1994, I woke up feeling that I knew the significance of the fact that she had been decapitated and her head was still missing: it was because of her red hair. The fur of the golden retriever I had seen sacrificed in an earlier vision had a reddish tinge to it. I felt that the cult had some ritual they performed requiring this colour of fur or human hair.

Six weeks later, I had another, more disturbing vision about Anja Habschied. Her head had been put in a very ornate silver and gold metal box with symbols on the front of it. The box had been placed on an altar in the bush and a girl dressed a bit like a gypsy came to offer flowers to it. The box was then opened – it had a hinged door at the front – and the head looked mummified, all dried out. The main feature that stood out was Anja's long, red-orange hair. This vision was one of the most unpleasant I had seen to do with this case, and the memory still haunts me.

Suddenly, I saw Anja standing before me, pleading with me to help find her missing remains so that she could be laid to rest.

*

During this period, I also had a vision of a girl sitting at a table with Trudie Adams. The girl wanted me to find her but I didn't know who she was. She told me that she was a victim of the backpacker murderer and she was slain around the same time as Trudie.

Ten days after receiving that vision, I was flicking through the Sunday papers and came upon a page featuring photographs of missing persons, for the upcoming Missing Persons Week. The girl whom I'd seen with Trudie was right there on the page. Her name was Toni Maree Cavanagh and she went missing with a friend named Kay Docherty somewhere in Wollongong around 1979. It is interesting to note that Toni Maree had reddish-blonde hair, a lighter shade than Anja Habschied's. I felt sure that these two girls were both additional victims of the backpacker murderer. I knew that he had been killing for a long time and there were many victims still to be found. I rang Detective Crea the next day and advised him of what I thought had happened to the girls.

I had another vision, in which I was shown where Toni Maree is buried. There was a cliff in the bush and the only way down was by a ladder. It was like a rope ladder but with metal chains to hold on to and metal bars for steps. At the bottom of the ladder, there were a lot of people moving around and I felt a connection to the cult – I wasn't sure, but it might have been where they met. I got a sense that it might have been part of an old walking track, because the ground was well worn, as though many people had passed through the area. I felt there were bodies here and that Toni Maree could be close by. Even though I had never been there, I also felt a very strong connection to a place called Wombeyan Caves, which is south-west of Sydney and which turned out to be included in Task Force Air's search area. It may have been in very close proximity to the caves. It turned out that the ladder wasn't permanently attached to the rock wall, as I saw a man removing it when he came back up to the top.

*

I arranged with my girlfriend Wendy, who had come with me to Galston Gorge, to visit the Belanglo State Forest. She didn't want me to go by myself.

The night before, I'd had terrible visions of my car breaking down in the forest and then being chased. I kept seeing my poppa, who was warning me not to go and telling me that something would happen. When I rang Wendy and told her about my vision, she suggested that she drive, as her car was newer.

When we reached the turn-off to the Belanglo State Forest, both of us began to get the creeps. We drove in, and the scrubby trees gave way to gum trees. I kept receiving visions of the eyes watching me again and had a very bad feeling that someone was waiting for us. It was about three in the afternoon and the pair of us got such a strong feeling not to proceed any further that we quickly turned around and went home.

I was woken up in the middle of the night with the message that I was so lucky that I didn't go right into the forest as someone was waiting for me.

A few weeks later, I was relaxing out in the backyard when I started to see a vision of a man climbing under a rock and getting into a cave. It opened into a huge cavern. The cavern split into two room-like areas. In one, there were rows of steps carved into the walls and floor – it looked like an amphitheatre. People were sitting and watching something.

At the place where the cavern split off into two rooms, there was a white letterbox with a green lid. I felt that there was something important in this cave; the police must find this spot. I then very loudly received the name 'Morton Cave'.

I rang National Parks and asked if there was such a place as Morton Cave. The man laughed and said that the Morton National Park was full of caves that joined up with the caves at Hilltop and the Wombeyan Caves. I described the area with the metal ladder and he said that there were a lot of old abandoned mines in that area and I could be describing any number of areas in Morton National Park. I asked him how close it was to Belanglo State Forest and he said that if you had a four-wheel drive you could drive from the forest to Wombeyan Caves by using the fire trails.

I felt now that I was definitely on to something. I had been told by a friend of mine that there was a large coven operating at Hilltop. Apparently, people knew it existed but they didn't want to talk about it. I called Detective Crea and told him about the cave but frustratingly I did not know exactly where it was.

Ivan Milat's murder trial began in late October 1994. Claire had been making phone calls to Colin, saying that she was desperate to ask me a few questions. Colin told her that I was too scared to speak with her directly. She asked Colin why I was so frightened to talk to her. On the occasions when we had spoken, she had told me that *they* knew that I was seeing what was really happening and that *they* were coming for me. I thought to myself: *why wouldn't I be scared?* He agreed to pass on her questions to me instead.

I thought that one of Claire's questions was interesting: where did they put the head of Anja Habschied? Where did *they* put the head of Anja Habschied?

I plucked up the courage to call Claire myself, because I wanted to ask her about the woman with long, brown, curly hair whom I kept seeing with the man I think is the murderer. She sometimes had her hair down, with the side pulled up into a half-ponytail on the top of her head. I told her that the vision of this woman seems to come more from a past era and that I felt she might have driven a little lime-green car. I also told her that the woman told me she knew what the perpetrator was doing and that it was wrong but he would kill her if she gave him up. Claire, however, wasn't able to enlighten me about any of this.

One thing I was unsure of was whether this woman was alive or dead. At the time, I was used to these people talking to me only when they had passed, but I did not feel any conviction either way in this case. My psychic ability has developed a great deal between then and now, however, and I am now of the opinion that she was alive. These days, I can feel the difference in the energy or vibration of the people in my visions. A living person's energy feels lighter and a dead person's heavier or lower, especially if he or she has been murdered, and this woman's energy felt light. Even back then, I was able to tune in to living people's thoughts; I just didn't fully realise it at the time.

I had one further and final phone conversation with Claire. I went to a local shopping centre, because Claire had told Colin that her phone was bugged and I also didn't want her to get my phone number. I told her about the last vision I had relating to the case. This vision, which came to me in November 1994, was of the back of a house. I could see a lawn and two people under a tree. The house was at the back of the property. A man went underneath it and crawled under its external steps. He had to wriggle in the dirt to get into the confined space underneath them; then he shoved a metal case like a movie-film canister up into one of the steps. I said to Claire that it was very important to solving the murder case that the canister be found. Claire replied that it couldn't be Ivan's house, as you couldn't get under it like that. I told her that if the police didn't catch everybody involved in the murders, in years to come they could start murdering people again, and Ivan would still be in jail.

After I got off the phone, I tried to ring Detective Crea, but he wasn't available so I asked for Detective Coman. When I told him of the phone call I had just had with Claire, his tone of voice changed and I sensed that he was quite angry with me. He said that if I didn't watch myself,

I could be called in as a witness at the Ivan Milat trial. Detective Coman said that of over one and a half thousand psychics who had been ringing in with information since the beginning of the case, I was one of the last few to still be in contact with the police. He said that I was already in too deep – and, with that, we ended our conversation.

From that moment on, I decided that I didn't want any further contact with Claire. I definitely didn't want to be going to court as a witness, because just getting the visions was causing enough friction in my family.

*

My experiences with Claire and the backpacker-murders case as a whole had given me a big wake-up call. I had let myself get too involved. I only hoped that, by passing on the information, I had helped provide the police with valuable clues and that now my last few years of sleeplessness would end. It was a wake-up call, too, in the sense that it had made me realise how true my visions were.

I still feel that Ivan wasn't the only perpetrator, though I do feel that he was one of them. To this day, I still see the faces of the victims who I believe are linked to the backpacker murders. I feel that there are at least another fifteen to twenty lost souls waiting to be found. My only hope is that someday at least some of these people will be laid to rest and their families will finally have some closure.

Chapter 9

I Meet My Spirit Guides

In November 1994, a twenty-two-year-old model and escort, Revelle Balmain, went missing in Sydney. Revelle's spirit came to me in a vision after I watched a news story about her. This young woman had decided that I was a good person to make contact with, so she began to be around me constantly. I could feel that she was dead.

As the weeks went by, the story began to build in the media. She had still not been found and her parents had made a plea for anyone with information about her to come forward to police.

After weeks of deliberation, I decided to contact the police officer in charge of Revelle's case, Detective Mulherin. Contacting the police was a very difficult thing to do, as I didn't want to go back to the horrifying visions and lack of sleep I had experienced with the backpacker murders.

Detective Mulherin was a little dismissive at first – I am sure that the poor man thought I was just another nutcase – but after numerous phone conversations he asked me to go to Hurstville Police Station and he would interview me about the information I was receiving and the visions I was seeing.

On my arrival at the police station, I got my first impression of what a criminal would feel like. As Detective Mulherin escorted me into the interview room, my body was filled with dread. Instead of feeling like I was trying to assist with Revelle's case, I felt more like I was guilty. Detective Mulherin listened to what I had to say and admitted that some of the things I was seeing were quite plausible. Over the upcoming months, I would keep a diary of any information I gathered and would send it on to him.

One morning, I read a newspaper story about Revelle and contacted the journalist who had written it. She asked if I would like to make contact with Revelle's family and I told her that if the family were open to speaking with me, then I would help them if I could. The journalist passed on my contact details to the family and it was up to them if they wanted to call me.

Shortly after, I did hear from Revelle's mother, Jan Balmain, and I described to her what I had seen. I had a very strong vision of Revelle lying on a leather lounge in a room with peach-apricot-coloured walls. She was wearing a silver and turquoise bracelet and her long blonde hair was hanging down over the arm of the lounge she was lying on. Jan said that the room I was describing was in fact at her home. It confirmed to her that I was really in touch with her daughter.

The most difficult of Jan's questions to answer was whether I thought Revelle was dead or alive. I said that I didn't really feel it was up to me to say, as I wasn't exactly an expert on psychic matters at this time. Jan then described a dream she had recently had about her daughter, and said that she felt that Revelle was in fact deceased. I confirmed to her that this was also what I felt. We spoke for some time and Jan asked me if there was anything that might help me to get more of a connection to Revelle. I told her that holding a personal item of Revelle's might work. This ability to discover facts about an event or person, whether alive or dead, by touching inanimate objects associated with him or her is called psychometry, and I had recently learnt it from Patricia and her psychic learning circle. Jan said that she would put me in touch with a family friend named Carol who had a number of items of Revelle's.

Carol contacted me and brought a variety of items that belonged to Revelle for me to try to work with. The most significant was a well-loved brown teddy bear. That night, I decided to go to bed holding the bear to see if my visions would start to unfold.

It didn't take long to make contact with Revelle. I started to see through her eyes. I felt that there was a man with his hands around her neck. I got the shock of my life as I awoke with the sense of a man standing over me and the feeling of being shaken violently by hands tightly clenched around my own neck.

This was one of the strongest connections I had with Revelle; I actually felt that I became Revelle for that brief moment in time. The rawness in my throat and the lack of oxygen felt very real, and it took some time for my throat to recover from the pain.

This experience made me realise that I was able to channel the victims as well as talk to them and see them. This was a huge breakthrough for me, as I hadn't been able to make a connection in this way with the victims of the backpacker murders. I soon realised that my psychic abilities were improving and I was beginning to be able to control them more than I had in the past.

*

One evening at the psychic learning circle run by my very special friend and most gifted psychic medium Patricia, we were all sitting in our usual positions and Patricia began by saying a beautiful opening prayer that asked any spirit beings who wanted to join in with our work to make their presence known. Unbeknown to me, Revelle had followed me to the circle and she abruptly made contact with the group. I hadn't told any of the members of the circle that I was working on Revelle's case, so it was quite a surprise to everyone when she appeared as clearly as if she were still alive. She stood in the middle of the group with her hands on her hips, asking us all what we were going to do to help her.

Revelle's main message was that she was very frustrated that she hadn't been found yet and she wanted her family to know what had happened to her. Her energy became quite strong and she wouldn't let the group continue the circle. She made it very clear that she wanted help and she wanted it NOW!

One of the members of the group became quite angry with me for bringing Revelle to the circle. I didn't even know that she had accompanied me, so I was hardly able to stop her from coming.

Patricia told Revelle that she needed to go into the light so she could be at peace. Revelle just threw her head back and laughed, and said that she wasn't going anywhere until her body was found. She then abruptly disappeared.

Patricia advised me that it was probably best to ask the spirit world to stop me from seeing these types of visions as they were becoming too distressing for me – and also for the rest of the group. She thought that I should work more with getting control of my gifts than being bullied by lost souls. This was a very hard decision for me to make, as I felt that each victim was coming to me for a reason. I felt that it was my responsibility to do what I could to help them.

Patricia explained that my soul development was more important at this time, so I did listen to her and tried not to focus on cases as much as I had been. To this day, I still struggle with this.

I decided I should work more on my psychic ability, so I could be more in control of it. I rang a very gifted medium I had been told about, named Margaret Dent, and tried to make an appointment for a psychic reading, to see if she could pick up what exactly was going on. Margaret's secretary informed me that she was booked up for months in advance. The secretary took my name anyway and told me she would ring back if there was a cancellation. Fortunately, she rang me back within a few days to say that a slot had become available. I was very happy to receive the call but I also realised the dilemma I was now in: I needed desperately to see Margaret but I had to do so without Warwick finding out. I knew that he wouldn't agree with me spending good money on a reading, even though I knew it would be worth every cent.

Warwick had become quite irritated with me working on Revelle's case and if he knew that I was, as he saw it, wasting money on having a reading, we would end up having an argument. I knew that Warwick had every right to be annoyed with me but the visions would not stop coming.

When the day of the appointment finally arrived, I was extremely nervous and excited at the same time, as Margaret Dent was renowned for being one of the most gifted mediums in Australia and I was going to meet her.

The reading was very interesting, to say the least. Margaret asked me what it was that I had come to see her for, and I told her about my visions of Revelle. Margaret's tone changed from being quite open and friendly to cold and curt. She informed me that she was also working on the same case with the police. She asked me what I was seeing and I described my visions to her.

Margaret then showed me a picture of a man dressed as a sheik and told me that he was the main suspect. I looked at the picture and felt absolutely nothing. I told Margaret that I didn't get a feeling the man in the picture had anything whatsoever to do with Revelle's disappearance. She told me that I didn't have enough control of my abilities. According to her, I wasn't tuning in to the right information, as it didn't match with what she was seeing.

I felt very disappointed and thought that I must just have been kidding myself that I was able to pick up information on Revelle's case. The strange thing was that in the back of my mind I still knew that I had been in contact with her and wondered how I could have got it so wrong.

Margaret told me not to be too disappointed and advised me to contact a colleague of hers named Peter who worked very similarly to herself. He would be willing to work with me on a one-on-one basis to help me learn how to control my abilities.

Just as the reading drew to a close, Margaret said to me that one day I would be doing readings for people just like she did and that I would be very busy. She also told me that I would work on further police investigations in the future. With that comment, I laughed, told her that I didn't think so and thanked her for her help. (Margaret was right, even though I didn't believe her at the time.)

Margaret also asked me to read a copy of her book called *Conversations with the Dead*, as she thought it would help me understand things better. I couldn't read the book fast enough; I found many comparisons in it to my own life experiences. One of the interesting things I noted was Margaret's reference to how her spiritual work took a toll on her health, which I could really relate to.

I look back now and realise how such a brief meeting with Margaret Dent helped me with my own journey and I truly appreciate the help that she gave me. Unfortunately, Margaret crossed over to the spirit world in February 2005.

After this meeting, I followed Margaret's advice and rang her colleague Peter and we arranged to meet. Peter and I began to meet weekly for one-on-one psychic-development classes. During this time, I progressed quite quickly and I began to get control of the visions I received from Revelle.

Almost daily, I would add to my diary the visions I saw about Revelle. I kept close contact with Carol, the Balmains' close family friend, and we met several times to conduct searches in areas that looked similar to my visions. I gave Carol a copy of my detailed diary in case she recognised any of the areas that I was recording my impressions of.

It was comforting to meet a person as passionate about finding Revelle as myself. Carol was in constant contact with the police and she was endeavouring to arrange for me to accompany them to do a search for her.

I could feel that Revelle was extremely impatient to be found. I felt at times that she was taking over my head and I found it hard to separate her from myself. Peter asked me to stop working on her case. He felt that continuing with it was holding back my psychic development. I tried to explain to him that I felt compelled to find her and I didn't want to give up before she was found.

This was a very trying time for me as I certainly wanted to advance and have control of my ever-expanding gifts, but at the same time I needed to finish what I had started with Revelle. Against both my husband Warwick's and Peter's advice, I continued working on the case.

*

Carol contacted me one morning, extremely excited, to tell me that a new detective was working on her friend's case: Detective Mark Smith, from Cronulla Police, in southern Sydney. Carol gave me Detective Smith's number and said that he was interested in speaking with me. After a number of phone calls, I finally met with him at Cronulla Police Station, and after a few more weeks a police search was organised at the old Bunnerong Power Station, at Botany, which was in the process of being dismantled. It fitted the description of a place I had been seeing in my visions. Not much of the old power station was left at the disused site; only tunnel-type areas still existed on the steep hillside.

A few days before the search, I came down with the flu, and I was extremely ill on the day of it. I knew that because of the weeks of organising and the fact that the police were finally taking me seriously I had to do it no matter how bad I was feeling.

When I arrived at the power station, the police rescue team were already there. I felt like death warmed up and I couldn't seem to make contact with Revelle. I was silently cursing myself for not listening to Warwick's and Peter's advice. The last thing I wanted to do was go home to hear Warwick saying 'I told you so'. (Don't you just hate admitting your partner is right at least some of the time?)

The search area was located on a high embankment overlooking the site where the power station had once stood. On the top of the hill were circular openings that had large metal caps on them. When the caps were removed, the openings looked quite similar to the opening of a mine shaft. Some of the shafts would drop to twenty metres in depth to the ground below. Before the rescue team were able to begin their search, they tested the area for any residual gases that might have built up in the shafts. All of the team wore oxygen masks just in case. Then the first members were lowered by rope into the now-disused ventilation shafts rising up from where the old power station once was located. The team progressively searched each tunnel and any nook and cranny they could get themselves into.

As the day wore on without any sign of Revelle, I became more and more alarmed that I had wasted the police rescue squad's time. I felt extremely unwell because of the flu and felt even worse to be such a failure. My mind was running wild, going over and over the visions I had seen during the last twelve months. I couldn't believe that I could be so off with them. I knew that the location of Botany was right, because in my vision I could see the shipping-container terminals and the sea in the background, which was exactly what I was seeing from my current location. I had visions of a cemetery that was located by the sea, again situated near the shipping-container terminals. To the right of the location we were searching was a cemetery overlooking the sea.

In the end, I just had to admit defeat. I went over to one of the officers in charge of the search, apologised for wasting his time and explained what a failure I felt. Tears began streaming down my face and I felt embarrassed that he was seeing me in such a state. He was an extremely nice man and told me not to worry. Revelle had been missing for over a year and sometimes a murderer may come back and move the victim's body to a new location. I guess we will never know if he did.

Out of the blue, the police officer began talking about Margaret Dent and told me he had gone to see her. He said that he was very open to the type of work I did and said that, the way he looked at it, at least in Revelle's case we knew that Revelle's body wasn't at the location and it was now an area the police could tick off and dismiss in the future. He also said that the rescue team would use this experience as a training exercise. Then he gave me a hug and handed me his business card in case I needed to contact him in the future.

After our conversation finished, I decided to call it a day and headed home with my tail between my legs. I didn't need to say anything to Warwick when I returned: he could see from my face how shattered I was. That wasn't enough to stop him from giving me a lecture about my stupidity and how our family should be more important to me than running all over the countryside looking for a woman I didn't even know.

Feeling rejected, and with my ego badly bruised, I quietly went to bed to hopefully get some sleep. I had only just closed my eyes when Revelle appeared. She had quite an attitude and began telling me that I had let her down and I still needed to find her. At this time of the night, I didn't want to even hear her name, let alone have her nagging me. I told her to go away as she had let me down by not making contact while we were doing the search. She didn't respond to me and suddenly disappeared.

Over the next few weeks, I still received visions about Revelle. I rang Carol and passed on the information but in all honesty I just wanted to put the case behind me. Over the years, I have still had contact with Revelle's family.

Unfortunately, to this day, Revelle's body hasn't been found. I have, however, been able to pass on messages to Revelle's mother and sister to reassure them that she is with them, even if it is in spirit. Revelle's a very strong lady and she will endeavour to help her family to find justice for her disappearance.

The one thing I had to come to terms with was that I might not be able to solve every case I received messages for. The one thing I did realise was that I might be a messenger for the spirit to make contact with the family and to let them know what had happened to them. I began to realise that the biggest hurdle I would need to overcome in the future was to not blame myself for failing and instead to look at what help, if any, I could offer to the police and the family members.

After the disappointment of this case, I vowed not to work on any police cases in the future. I have since learnt that you should adopt the saying 'Never say never', because, as you will see in the proceeding chapters, I just couldn't help myself; I felt compelled to help others.

*

I continued to attend Patricia's learning circle, where I developed the psychic skill of psychometry. This would turn out to be one of my gifts, and was to be one of the most important tools I would work with in the future.

Each week in the circle, we would hold an item from one of the other members in the group and would relay what we saw. At first, I disliked being asked to do this, as some of the messages and symbols I received didn't make any sense to me. I was worried that I would sound silly if I said what I could actually see.

Patricia patiently explained that the message wasn't for me; it was for the wearer of the item. She reassured me that no matter how strange the information seemed, it would make sense to the owner.

With her encouragement, I began to openly relate the messages and symbols I was given from spirit verbatim to the wearers of the items. To my amazement, the owners couldn't believe how accurate the messages were. The encouragement I received from the others in the circle was wonderful and soon I didn't even think about what I would say; I just let the information flow.

I was on my way and the new journey I was discovering was very exciting. I felt very privileged that I had such a wonderful teacher and group to learn with. After a number of months, I became very proficient in psychometry and then a new sensation started to come through.

Sometimes while I was sitting in the circle, I would feel a warm–hot sensation go through me and get quite dizzy. I would then feel that a presence had arrived and, if I closed my eyes and let go, it would take over my senses and begin to talk through me. At times, this was a very unsettling experience, as I didn't like the feeling of being out of control.

On one particular occasion, I felt like my soul was shooting out through the top of my head and the spirit energy was stepping in. I didn't feel very comfortable with it. Patricia reassured me that I shouldn't be frightened, but if I didn't feel comfortable I should let the spirit energy know. She told me to just talk to the energy, which I felt was male, and tell him that he was welcome to work with me but he was to pass on the message instead of channelling completely through me.

After I did this, my new acquaintance and I had a wonderful time working together. I was to later realise that I was now working with my spirit guide, named Running Horse. He is an American Indian who lived prior to white settlement in America. I found his choice of me as an acquaintance quite funny, as I had never had a particularly strong affiliation with American Indians. I am more of an angel and fairy person, but that hasn't stopped him working very strongly on my spiritual journey.

As time progressed, Running Horse became a very strong part of my life. Yet his presence in my life was not something I could speak about openly to family and friends. How could I introduce an invisible friend (or figment of my imagination) to those close to me? They most surely would have thought I was losing it. I certainly knew that my husband wouldn't understand that I had this new 'man' in my life, albeit a dead man from another lifetime away.

I decided that I would need to keep my new-found teacher a secret from the outside world and just be happy with the knowledge that I was never alone. It was kind of exciting, to be honest. Imagine having the feeling that no matter what happens in your life, you always have someone to look after you 24/7.

The one thing I did find difficult, though, was that from this time onward, I constantly heard voices and received messages and signs from spirit trying to guide me in the right direction. At times, I would feel different energies within me, some male and some female.

Occasionally, I would challenge these spirit guides, as I don't like being told what to do. Sometimes, I would make a decision and my guides would tell me it was the wrong one, but then my stubborn streak would come out and I would do exactly what my guides had warned me against. Yes, you guessed it: I was the one who was wrong!

I realised after making enough mistakes and banging my head constantly on brick walls that maybe, just maybe, if I listened, then these beautiful, patient beings would actually stay around.

Well, I am happy to report that we all work together as a beautiful team.

Now, when I look back on the beginnings of my journey, I can see how far I have come. In the scheme of things, I think spirit had this planned all along.

Chapter 10

Near-Death Experiences

In 1995, almost a year after my son Blake was born, I started to dream about a little girl. This little girl was a very happy child with straight, light-brown hair and very big, hazel eyes. Every time I went to the clothes line and hung out the washing, I would hear two lovely old ladies from the spirit world telling me about my future daughter. They would say to me, 'She's on her way, dear. It won't be very long now.' After all of the problems I had falling pregnant, I was thankful for the two beautiful children I already had, so to be told this delightful little girl was on her way was a bit of a surprise.

The spirit ladies, who called themselves Joyce and Margaret, were right, as a number of weeks later I did fall pregnant and, you guessed it, it was a girl.

During the time of my pregnancy, I still attended the psychic-development group. Katie, who was part of the learning circle, is a very gifted spirit channeller. One evening when I went to the learning circle, Katie began to channel a spirit who had decided she had some messages for me. The spirit announced, in the voice of a young girl, that she wanted to talk to the lady with the baby. Patricia asked the spirit who she was talking about, to which the spirit replied to Patricia that she wanted to talk to the lady over there and then pointed directly at me. I sat quite nervously wondering what she could possibly want with me. The young female spirit said, 'I play with the baby and I talk to the baby, and when you go to hospital, I will be there with you.' I nearly fainted. Who was this spirit and what did she want with me and my unborn child? I was absolutely terrified. I certainly didn't want any strange spirit hanging around me when I went to hospital.

It was only later, when members in the group told me that they felt the spirit was that of the child I had miscarried, that I felt more settled. A number of the group said that they always saw a little girl with white-blonde wavy hair and big blue eyes by my side. They said that they hadn't mentioned her in the past as they thought I knew she was there. The appearance of the little girl they described was similar to that of my first child, Ryan. By this stage, she would have been about four years of age if she had survived, so it all started to make sense.

From this time onward, the cloud around me began to clear. I realised that I would just have to be patient and believe I was guided by a bigger and greater force that I couldn't always see but could most certainly feel.

*

Two months before my due date, I was rushed to hospital with a form of gastroenteritis. I became dehydrated and began vomiting and passing blood, and as a result I went into early labour.

My baby would need to be placed in a humidicrib, but there were none available at the hospital at the time, so they gave me a Ventolin injection to stop the labour and a pethidine injection for the pain.

While I was being given the injections, I could feel myself leaving my body. I kept telling Warwick to shake me as I could feel myself floating towards the ceiling. Warwick thought that I was joking, so I started yelling at him, telling him he needed to shake me or I was going to go. The nurse started to give me oxygen and asked me to calm down.

The next thing I remember was that I floated up to the ceiling and went through the roof, leaving everyone in the room behind me. I was suddenly up in the sky, floating amongst the clouds. I looked down towards the earth and I could see my husband with my two boys and my new baby daughter (whom I hadn't given birth to yet) looking up towards the sky.

I felt great sadness to think that the four of them were all there together and I wasn't a part of their lives. I saw Warwick pointing up and telling the children that Mummy was up in heaven. It was a strange feeling – a kind of detached feeling – but at the same time very peaceful. The main thing that stuck in my mind was that Warwick wasn't dressed in the clothing of today; he was dressed in a First World War soldier's uniform and the children were dressed in clothing of the same era.

I heard a popping sound and realised that I was back in the hospital room and could see everybody fussing around me. I could hear voices telling me that I would need to be transported by ambulance to the Paddington Women's Hospital, as the hospital I was currently at didn't have the right equipment. The nurse left the room and returned with two ambulance officers and then I was taken down in a trolley to the ambulance.

The trip in the ambulance was another interesting experience. With me in the back was the nurse and an ambulance officer, to begin with. Then, a man with dark-black hair and sickly yellow-coloured skin, and wearing glasses with thick black frames, suddenly appeared and sat beside the nurse.

I tried to speak with the nurse to let her know that the man wanted me to give her a message: he was looking after her. As I had an oxygen mask on my face, the nurse found it difficult to understand what I was trying to tell her. I lifted the mask and told her about the man with the glasses and she burst into tears. She said that her foster father had died two weeks prior, due to suffering jaundice (which turns the skin yellow). I told her that he wanted her to know he was all right and that he loved her and would always be with her.

The rest of the trip she sat quietly sobbing and I felt sad for her loss. When we arrived at the hospital, I was rushed upstairs to the delivery suite and said goodbye to the lovely nurse who had accompanied me. Even though I was experiencing my own difficulties, I still felt peace that the gift with which I had been bestowed had in some small way touched another human being and made a difference.

The nurses checked to see how far my labour had progressed; I was still dilated. The doctor administered another injection for the pain and told me to try to rest and not to worry as I would be monitored throughout the night. If I did progress any further with my labour, all of the necessary equipment was available, the staff assured me.

Warwick stayed in the room with me for the night, sleeping on a mattress and bedding that the hospital provided for him. I, in the meantime, was bombarded with many visitors. The memories I have of my night in the delivery suite are like something out of a horror movie. The hospital, which had been operating since 1901, had a lot of history and, as I found out, a substantial number of spirits.

While trying to sleep and settle down, I constantly saw things flying around in the room. When I finally would drift off to sleep, I would be woken up by many faces trying to tell me their story and asking me for my help. At the time, all I could think about was my unborn child and her well-being; the last thing I really cared about was who wanted to give me a message. The night seemed to last forever and I couldn't wait for the first rays of sunlight to appear in the room. I was totally exhausted when morning arrived, while Warwick was quite oblivious to all of the nocturnal goings-on. He actually seemed quite refreshed, whereas I just wanted to get out of the room we were in and go home as soon as possible.

Much to my dismay the next day, even though I was no longer in premature labour, I was told that I needed to stay in hospital for up to a week until the virus passed. As the doctors were not sure what had caused me to become so ill, and the hospital couldn't afford for any other mums-to-be to catch whatever it was I had, I was told that I would be put into isolation.

Being kept isolated from the other patients and staff made my stay at the hospital even more challenging. The faces that floated around and appeared before me when I was in the delivery suite were nothing compared to what happened next.

My first evening in isolation, a very mysterious nurse came into the room to check my blood pressure and temperature. She asked me when my baby was due and I told her how I had been rushed to the hospital in early labour the night before. I spoke to her about the nurse who escorted me in the ambulance and about how her dead foster father had made an appearance. We spoke for some time about my belief in the afterlife and how I had experienced floating through the roof of the other hospital and looking down at my family. I spoke with her about all of the spirits who were hanging around the delivery suite and how I had found it hard to sleep with all of them waking me up constantly and talking to me. Quite out of the blue, the nurse said that I needed to find the Rosicrucian Society. When I asked her what on earth she was talking about, she said that we shouldn't speak too loudly but that if I found out about the Rosicrucians, then all would come to light. The nurse then abruptly got up and left the room and I never saw her again.

In the morning, I asked the nurse on my ward for the name of the mysterious nurse that I had spoken with the night before. The nurse looked at me strangely and said that she was the only nurse on the ward during the night. I described what the mysterious nurse looked like: she had short, light-brown hair and very kind blue eyes, a very soft, gentle voice and she was only of a slight build. The ward nurse said that there wasn't anybody of that description working at the hospital. I know I really spoke with the mystery nurse and I felt her hand when she took my blood pressure. I guess I will never know who she was and if she was a real person or a spirit.

Each night there was a challenge, with all of the lost souls floating around in the wards coming in to visit me. The spirits floating around in the hospital all knew that I was on the premises. I was too frightened to go to sleep.

The fact that my unborn baby was fine was the best news I could receive. When I was finally told she and I were healthy and that I could go home, I couldn't get out of the hospital quickly enough.

When I returned home, I contacted the Rosicrucian Society and was sent a book about their courses. As I was due to become a mother for the third time, I didn't have time to attend. However, I did find the information about their teachings very interesting.

Six weeks later, my darling daughter Shannon Brooke (Brooke for the girl I had lost, who would have borne this name in life) was delivered alive and well at Hurstville Community Hospital. I met Dr William Fenton again when I stayed in the labour ward, but his visits were relatively sedate compared to those I experienced at Paddington Women's Hospital, which moved premises to Randwick the next year, 1997.

*

When Shannon arrived, a lot of strange things began happening in our house. It seemed that my lost daughter, Brooke, was very jealous about my living daughter, Shannon. I thought back to the night at the learning circle when the child spirit told me that she would be with the baby and play with the baby.

One day, I was working in my office at the back of the house and Shannon was happily bouncing in her bouncinette. I had stored a disassembled nappy table on top of a cupboard and suddenly a number of the poles fell down, narrowly missing tiny Shannon in the bouncinette. I quickly moved Shannon and removed the rest of the things on the top of the cupboard. I realised how lucky it was that the poles had missed her, and I was determined that after that I would be more aware. Yet I had a strong feeling that an external force had caused this accident.

A couple of weeks later, I felt Brooke's presence in the room stronger than ever before. A cut-glass container on my dressing table flew off and landed on the floor, again almost hitting Shannon in her bouncinette. I felt that Brooke had moved it.

My mother was with me this particular time and I expressed my concern that Brooke was there and was responsible. Mum thought that I was just imagining things.

I rang my living guardian angel Patricia to see if she could assist me with the strange goings-on in the house.

My brother-in-law's mother, Nancy, had given me a beautiful, handmade caramel-coloured heritage teddy bear with a big pink bow around its neck when Shannon was born. Nancy had asked me what I wanted to call it and I replied that I would call it Brooke, after the daughter we had lost. When Patricia came to help me with Brooke, she wasn't aware of the teddy bear with the same name. Patricia told me that our daughter Brooke was a bit reluctant to go into the light, and called my nanna down from the spirit world to help. It was only when Patricia promised Brooke a caramel-coloured teddy bear with a big pink bow around its neck to accompany her that she was happy to go into the light with Nanna.

I must point out that, from my experience, when a spirit goes into the light it doesn't mean that their loved ones will never see them again. It only helps them on their spiritual journey and enables them to come back and forth when and if they like, to be with their living family on earth. I truly believe this to be the case for Brooke, as while my children have been growing up Brooke has been spoken about and acknowledged on numerous occasions by all three of my children. They have talked about her as though she was alive. Some spirits, however, are under the mistaken impression that crossing over into the light means they won't be able to make contact with their loved ones any more, so they refuse to go.

As time progressed, Shannon was more and more aware of spirit and she would be very animated while playing in her bouncinette. She would seem to play with her invisible visitors. At times, I would be in the kitchen and she would be giggling, gooing and gaaing, and when I would come in to check on her, she would be lying there holding her arms up as if she wanted to be picked up.

At first, I worried about what Shannon was seeing, but she seemed to be so happy that I thought whoever she was making contact with was a positive addition to her life. My gut feeling was that my beautiful Nanna and Poppa and my Great Auntie Ett and her sister, Brooke, were the most likely spirit visitors.

It is hard being a psychic mother because sometimes the vibration that my children are picking up is not on the same frequency as mine and I find it frustrating not to be able to see exactly what the children can see. Children are most psychic up until ten or so years of age. As my children have progressed in age, they have become less vocal about their spirit sister.

Shannon has always had the ability to see and play with the fairies, and would always talk about the little coloured lights that were whizzing around the house or in the garden. I would find it quite disconcerting when she would tell me there was one on my shoulder. I would ask her exactly where and point to where I thought she could see it and then she would tell me that I had squashed it. I was worried I had hurt the poor thing, not to mention that I hoped I didn't have squashed fairy all over my shirt!

When Shannon was about four years old, she was playing in the front yard with our rabbit M&M and asked me to take a photograph of her with the rabbit. When the film was developed, I got a surprise to find a blue swish of energy on her and the rabbit. At first, I thought that it was a double exposure and checked the negative. To my amazement, it wasn't a double exposure at all. When I showed Shannon the photograph and asked her what she thought it was, she said, 'Oh, Mummy, don't you know?

That is what a fairy looks like.' This was my first experience with taking spirit-energy photographs.

Shannon still has her fairy friends around her and sometimes when her karaoke machine is plugged into the television, the camera on it picks up little energies moving around the room when she is singing. I feel blessed that my beautiful daughter has so many delightful friends around her, both living and in spirit.

*

I don't know why I have had so many near-death experiences (NDEs), such as I had when I went into early labour with Shannon, but what I do know is that I am blessed to have been able to visit the other side and come back and talk about my journeys.

I don't feel that death is a frightening experience. To me, a lifetime can be measured like sand in an hourglass. Some of us are fortunate to be born with more sand than others. Sometimes, I feel that it would be wonderful if we knew how much time was in our hourglass, as I am sure we would utilise our days here on earth in a much more positive and fulfilling manner if so.

The most vivid NDE I've had was after having a major operation. It was the last resort to fix the reproductive problems I'd been suffering with for many years.

Weeks prior to me having the operation, I knew that I was going to die. The night before I was due to go to hospital, I made a will just in case something happened. My husband thought it a sign that I was really losing it, but he humoured me enough to help me get it done.

When the nurse came to wheel me down to theatre on a trolley, I started to cry. All I could see were images of my beautiful children's faces looking up to the sky. When my specialist and anaesthetist asked why was I crying, I told them that I was a psychic and that I had a number of visions that I was going to the light during the operation. They both looked shocked. I asked them to keep an eye on me and to make sure that I came back.

When I opened my eyes in the recovery room some hours later, it was so crowded with spirits it was like I couldn't breathe. I told one of the nurses that her grandmother was with her and that she wanted her to know that she was all right. Her grandmother then told me to tell her that she was pregnant and was going to have a beautiful baby girl. The nurse came over to me, quite surprised, and asked me not to mention anything to the staff as nobody at work knew that she was pregnant yet. She asked me how I knew. I said that her grandmother was right beside her, nursing the baby.

As the doctors couldn't get my pain under control, I was transferred to the High Dependency Unit. The nurse in charge of the unit, Julie, was beautiful; she kept coming in to check on me. She told me that if the pain became too much, all I needed to do was press the button taped to my left hand and the machine would automatically administer a dose of morphine in my drip. I told her that was good to know but I thought I should inform her that I was going to go to the light tonight. She stopped dead still and asked me to repeat what I had just said. I repeated, 'I am going to the light tonight.'

She stood there with a big smile on her face and said, 'Not on my shift! I don't want to fill out all that paperwork.'

Over the hours that followed, I pushed the button to administer the morphine for the pain. I told Julie that my skin had started to feel funny and I could see worms crawling under it, all over my body. Then I started to scream as I could see devils floating all over the room. Meanwhile, the pain was just getting worse and I was so tired but I couldn't sleep. Julie told me that she would stay with me to monitor me.

Suddenly, I had this feeling of flying and I was quickly rushing up and out of my body. I felt so free and I wasn't in pain; I felt great. I began to feel a shaking sensation and that I was floating into a black-purple haze. I wasn't frightened; I felt very calm.

I seemed to enter a black tube, like a fun-park waterslide. I felt so out of control; I was swishing this way and then that. It was like I had lost all gravity and was quickly floating through a black void. I could see a little white pinhole of light at the other end.

Abruptly, I came out of the black tube and I felt that I was flying out into the universe. There seemed to be planets and stars floating past me at a speed that I had never seen before. At times, everything would slow down and I could see what looked like beautiful planets in the universe. I felt like I was an astronaut flying through space – the only thing was, I didn't have any spacesuit or oxygen tank attached. Some moments, the vibration was so strong that I felt like my body was going to break apart.

I then went back into a black-purple swirl, with the pinhole of light steadily approaching me. The light was getting bigger and bigger, and I could see other people going there ahead of me.

I didn't feel at all scared. A beautiful feeling of calmness and love surrounded me. I had forgotten about being in the hospital bed and about the family I had left behind. All I wanted to do was get to the light at the end of the tunnel; it was drawing me to it and I deeply wanted to see what was there.

Suddenly, all of the speeding movement stopped and I was completely surrounded by a blinding light. When my eyes readjusted, I could see lots of people just smiling at me. A being came forward and asked me to follow her. I went with her and before me was a beautiful meadow.

Between myself and the meadow was a very long waist-high hedge with a gate in the middle of it. People were queuing up to go through the gate, and lots of others were already in the meadow. The female being I had met took me to the back of the queue. When it was her turn, she opened the gate, walked through and then closed it behind her. I felt upset that she had closed the gate and not asked me to come with her. A number of other beings came to the gate and stood with her. They said that I wasn't allowed to pass through it because if I did I would have to stay with them. I didn't think that was a problem, as they all looked so happy and calm. I thought I should be with them.

I could see a big rainbow that seemed to have brighter and clearer colours than what we have here on earth. The grass seemed to be so much greener, everybody seemed to be so happy and the love I could feel was so incredible. I thought that if this was heaven, then I wanted to stay. The first female being that I had met asked me to turn around. I did as she asked and then she told me to look down. As I did this, I could see my husband and my three children pointing up to where I was, and they were saying, 'Mummy is up there.' With that, I felt myself falling very quickly. I woke up with a jolt, in total agony, back in my hospital bed, feeling like I wanted to be somewhere else. If I had just experienced what it was like to die, could I go back? My life at that moment didn't seem to be worth living.

Julie, my lovely nurse, came over to me and shook me violently. I asked her to stop it as she was making me feel sick. She told me that she needed to keep me conscious because when she went to leave the room to attend to another patient my heart had stopped, setting off an alarm on the heart monitor. I had had an allergic reaction to the morphine and my breathing had stopped.

Julie said she was glad I had warned her that I was worried about something happening to me. She said that at first she thought I was exaggerating because of the after-effects of the anaesthetic, but she later realised that I wasn't joking and in fact there was a real danger that what I had warned her of might come true.

A couple of nights later, at about 1.30 am, all of the phones through the entire floor began to ring, and they continued to ring nonstop for about half an hour. I went up to the nurses' station and asked them what was going on, as it had woken me up. One of the nurses said that it was a regular occurrence on the night shift and they thought it was the work of a man called 'Old Charlie' who had died at the hospital from alcohol poisoning about ten years ago. They said that when Old Charlie wanted some attention, he would play tricks with the phones. Two of the nurses asked me if I would go with them to talk to him and ask him to stop being a nuisance.

When I went into the room he was known to frequent, which had four empty beds in it, he told me that he was lonely and that everybody walked past his room without paying him any attention. I told him that I would try to help him in the morning if he would just stop mucking around with the phones and let me get some sleep.

In the morning, I went into his room, which was still empty. I spoke to Old Charlie and told him how wonderful it would be for him if he would just go into the light. He told me he was frightened, as he didn't think that he was good enough to go up to heaven. I told him of what I had seen a couple of nights earlier. I told him of the warmth and love that I felt, and how in some ways I wished that I had stayed. I told him I would ask his guardian angels for a bright light to be brought down to him in the middle of the room and explained that it should look like a stairway coming down from above, surrounded by the brightest light he could possibly imagine. I then asked Old Charlie if he could see what I was talking about. He told me he could see it and it was getting brighter and brighter. I told him to go over to the light and that all of his loved ones would be waiting for him. He turned to me and smiled – and, with that, he was gone.

It was a very nice feeling to be able to help this lovely old gentleman. I told one of the night-shift nurses that he had gone to the light. She said she was pretty sceptical but if it stopped the phones from ringing in the middle of the night, then she would be happy. The phones in the hospital settled down from then on.

After a couple of days, I still wasn't feeling much better and my doctor came to visit me. Luckily for me, he was quite open-minded. He said that he had heard from the nursing staff about the things that had been going on while I was in hospital. He told me he was glad I hadn't gone to the light, but he had heard that I had some strange sort of experience when my heart stopped. I told him that since returning from my NDE I seemed to have the ability to see inside my own body. I said that I could see a big black spot over the area of my left ovary.

The doctor checked the area where I could see the black spot and confirmed that I had a blood clot. He jokingly asked why, if I could see it, I couldn't focus on it and dissolve it. I just laughed at him and told him that he was the doctor and he was the expert in that area.

Two days later, things seemed to be going well, so the doctor told me that I could be discharged. I advised him that the black spot I had mentioned was still there. He said not to worry, so I returned home.

But I was home for only three days when – as I suspected I might – I became very ill, suffering with fevers, weakness and a lot of pain. I rang the doctor and was immediately admitted back into hospital.

While I was there again, the anaesthetist came to pay me a visit to ask me what I had seen and experienced when I was under the anaesthetic. He explained how worried he was during the operation as in his entire medical career he had only two other patients tell him that they were going to the light prior to their operation, and both of those patients had died on the table.

Chapter 11

Scream Test

In August 2000, I was driving in the car listening to the radio and an advertisement came on asking for people to volunteer for a new Channel Ten TV program based on the paranormal. It was a reality show called *Scream Test*; I was a little concerned about the name but thought it might be interesting to see what they had in store for the contestants.

Along with about sixty other hopefuls, I was selected to audition. This took the form of a ghost tour of Windsor, west of Sydney. There, the producers noticed my gifts and selected me as one of the twenty contestants for the series.

At five different haunted locations, four contestants would spend time alone detecting paranormal activity using technical equipment, recording their own reactions and observations using a video camera, and competing in challenges. One of the four contestants at each location would be chosen as a winner and would go on to compete in the grand final, at another haunted place.

I was nervous but very excited about the challenges ahead. I kept receiving flashes that we would be filming our segments in the style of the *Blair Witch* movies, though I have never seen them. (Horror movies only increase the negative visions that come to me.) I didn't know why I was receiving this message but it was very strong. When I rang and told one of the producers of my concern, her end of the phone went deathly silent. This was enough confirmation for me that I was right.

The day finally arrived and I caught the train to the studio. All I was told was that I would be staying overnight in an unknown destination on my own. I wouldn't be able to use my mobile phone or contact my family. When the three other victims – as I was soon to start thinking of us – arrived, we were shown how to operate our video cameras and other equipment, and were put into a van and driven to our unknown destination.

I was being shown more flashes of what I would need to face. In my heart, I was hoping I was picking up the messages incorrectly, but as we got closer to our destination I received even more visions of where we were going. My hope was that it wasn't Maitland Gaol but in my gut I knew I was right.

When the van finally stopped, we were taken to a McDonald's restaurant to wait for what seemed like hours. Darkness finally came and we were led into a smaller van and asked to sit in silence. Our watches and mobile phones had to be surrendered to the producers and we were each given a black bag to put over our head. After a long wait, the van started up and we drove for a while. When it stopped, we were escorted from the vehicle, the black bags were removed and our destination was revealed: we were standing at the entrance to the now-disused Maitland Gaol.

Maitland Gaol, a very impressive, fortress-like sand-stone building, was the longest continuously operating correctional institution in Australia. Opening in 1848, it housed some of the country's most hardened criminals before it was closed in 1998. On the grounds of Maitland Gaol, sixteen men were executed by hanging between 1849 and 1897, all for rape or murder.

My stomach sank. I would be fighting all of my worst fears, not to mention the ghosts whom I knew would make their presence known.

The producers wired the four of us up to heart monitors, which would beam our heart rates back to them in the filming van. Then we were split up and told that none of us would cross paths for the rest of the night. We would each be taken to a different location, where we would watch a video giving us its background, then we would be plunged into total darkness with just a video camera and our ghost-busting kit, which included an electromagnetic-field (EMF) tester, compass, temperature gauge and a notepad and pen. The only time we could have our camera lights on was while we were filming; if we used the camera lights for any other reason, we would be disqualified. When we had specific challenges to complete that required us to read or use a computer, we would be given a kerosene lantern. Each of the locations we were taken to was wired with infrared cameras so that the filming crew would know our each and every move.

My first destination for the night was the 'suicide cell' in B Wing, which had housed the most feared or longer-term inmates. Cell 46 was a 'one out' cell – also known as a solitary-confinement cell – which prisoners were frightened of being locked in as it was well known for a number of suicides that took place there. The cell was extremely small – all it contained was a toilet and a bed.

I decided to make the most of a bad situation and thought that I might as well make friends with whatever ghosts were in there with me before any of them thought that I could be a new victim. I began to hear a man crying and the sound was coming from the bed. I knew full well that it was a spirit making his presence known, so I asked him what the matter was. He told me that he had killed himself in the cell as he was put in jail for a crime he didn't commit. He told me that his name was John and he had been involved in an armed robbery on a bank, as the driver of the getaway car. One of the others involved had shot the security guard but John was the one who got the blame. He had been given a life sentence, and suicide seemed for him to be the only way out.

He kept telling me he just wanted to be with his family; his little girl was only two when he was caught and she would be grown up now. I told him that if he listened to me, I could get him to the light and then he wouldn't be trapped in the cell any more. It wasn't as good as being brought back to life but it was better than feeling like he was trapped in his own hell, stuck in the prison cell forever. At least then he would have the opportunity to visit the family and see how they were.

Suddenly, the energy in the room changed and I felt someone grab my legs from under the bed. Whoever he was, he was trying to pull me towards him. I knew that John was no longer with me and that this spirit was very dangerous. I felt my heart just about jump out of my chest and my heartbeat was a very heavy thudding in my ears. I tried to calm myself down and take control of the situation.

Then I heard a dreadful moaning sound on my left-hand side. Now, for me, this was a little strange, as I only hear spirits and ghosts in my right ear, due to my tinnitus, which is at the frequency that allows spirit to come through. The moaning sound was coming in on my left ear, which meant that the producers were making this particular sound, to scare me.

Running Horse told me I was correct, so at least I didn't have to worry about the moaning sound as well as the new arrival that had tried to pull me to the bed. Suddenly, there was a loud banging sound at the cell door and it flew open. By this time, I was absolutely terrified, but thankfully it was the crew, who had come to collect me to take me to my next location.

I was led downstairs and through a black, boarded-up area. While I was walking, I felt myself being grabbed from behind. I felt that I had two spirits, one on either side of me, picking me up by the neck and trying to strangle me. I started coughing and choking, and the producers asked me if I had had enough or did I still wish to continue?

Being the determined (or stupid) person that I am, even though I was terrified, I thought *I haven't come this far to just chicken out and quit.*

I was seated at a table facing the wall in what would have been an exercise area for up to ten cells. The cells were empty and the doors were all open. An apparition appeared in each of the two cell doors closest to where I was sitting. One of them kept yelling profanities at me and telling me what he would do to me if he could get his hands on me. A guy in the doorway of Cell 7 told me that he had been compared to the Boston Strangler as he was in jail for a number of strangling murders.

Then more voices joined in. It started to sound like the buzzing of bees, with the whole area filling with yelling and continuous voices. I could hear banging and scraping noises. It sounded as though there was a riot going on all around me. I looked up to the other floors and the jail was full of prisoners leaning over the railings and yelling at me.

I started to feel that I was being urinated on from above and when I looked up I could see it actually happening, but when I felt my hair it was dry. I have to say that I had never felt such strong psychic impressions before in my life. I began to doubt my sanity, as what I was experiencing was so real and yet it was only a vision.

Finally, time was up and I was taken to the next location. It was becoming harder to be strong but I tried my best. A big obstacle was that I wasn't allowed to speak with the crew members when they escorted me around, unless they asked me questions. I wanted to tell them what I had gone through but instead I had to suffer in silence.

While being taken to the third location, I had to walk over the jail's courtyard. I had the most dreadful feeling, like hands were grabbing my ankles and trying to pull me down under the concrete. The crew asked me what I could feel and, when I told them, they said that all of the executed prisoners were buried beneath where we were walking and that they were buried standing up. It was thought that if a person was buried standing up, his soul wouldn't be able to go to heaven.

I was next taken to C Wing, which held serious offenders and inmates who had to be protected – from themselves and other inmates – because of the horrendous crimes they had committed.

On entering the cell, I was made very aware that the current occupants did not want me there. I could hear two female prisoners talking to me; they told me that their names were Margaret and Therese. Therese was pure evil. She told me she was in jail for killing her newborn baby. The psychic images she gave me were horrific: she said she killed the baby by hitting his head on the wall and throwing him down the stairs. I felt quite ill to think I was in the presence of one so evil.

Margaret told me that she was in jail as she had stabbed her husband, who was a drunk and who constantly bashed and abused her. Margaret was a nice lady and I felt sorry for her. She told me she was happy that I was in the cell because it stopped Therese from hurting her. She said that Therese constantly bashed her and the guards wouldn't move her.

One of the show's producers, a woman named Lee, asked me what my psychic impressions were of the cell.

When I told her that I could see and hear female prisoners in there with us, she was sceptical, because the wing had been known to house male prisoners. She radioed to the filming van and asked someone to check whether it could be possible. Lee then confirmed with me that the area had also been used as a female cell in the past and admitted that even she had had no idea.

Before Lee left me alone to complete a challenge using a computer in the room, she left a kerosene lantern on the floor. As Lee locked the door behind her, Therese told me that she was going to tip the kero on me and set me on fire. At first, I thought she was joking, then the lantern started to move ever so slightly. I began yelling at Lee to come and get the lantern out of the cell. I was beginning to get hysterical when she finally turned around and came back. Lee told me that she thought I was making it up, but when she got closer and looked through the bars of the cell, she could see a female standing behind me. She hastily unlocked the door and put the lantern on the other side of it.

Therese said that moving the lantern out of her reach wasn't enough to stop her. There was a chair in front of the computer and when I went to sit down she told me it was her cell and she wanted to sit there. She made it move to let me know that she was in control, but I eventually accomplished the challenge I'd been set.

Margaret was lovely and she helped me to keep Therese away. I felt very sorry for her, being trapped in a hellhole with such a bad spirit, so when my time was up in the cell Margaret came with me. I told her that when I finished filming I would show her how to go into the light so she could find her peace.

My next location was Cell 12, in the oldest wing of Maitland Gaol. It was where Charles Hines, the last man to be executed there, was housed and where those condemned to death spent their final hours. The prisoners were permitted to have a priest visit to give them solace and they were provided with a Bible.

On entering this cell, I smelt a sickly sweet odour of death that seemed to linger in the air, and I felt a sense of sadness and despair that this was the end for any prisoner who entered these walls. On top of this, though, there was also a sense of peace. It was the only area so far where I felt that I was safe.

I soon had to leave this cell, however, to perform my next challenge. When I approached the cell door, which the producers had closed behind me, I could hear loud footsteps pacing up and down just on the other side and was very nervous about opening it. I tried to leave, but something (or someone) was blocking it. After I made a number of attempts at running at the door, it opened.

I was now out in the open, facing numerous other cell doors, most of which were open. I could see a spirit – a man with red hair and a beard – leaning in the doorway opposite me. He didn't say anything to me, but his size and presence were enough to put me on edge.

To complete the challenge, I needed to open the combination lock on a big chain that locked the cell next door to the execution cell. I was concerned that the guy with the red hair would lock me in there, so before I entered it I put the lock in my pocket. At least this way I knew I was able to get out.

I had been given a pager at the beginning of the evening

and while I was waiting for the crew I got a message on it telling me that I was one of only two contestants still standing. I wondered what had happened to the other two.

A short time later, the crew arrived to take me to the final location: the watchtowers on the outer perimeter of the jail. When we approached, I saw guards running along the walkway between two of the watchtowers. I heard gunshots, then a man fell to the ground in front of me. I could see this image so clearly that I thought it really happened. When I asked Jonathan, one of the producers, what had happened, he had no idea what I was talking about. I told him what I saw and I think he thought I was going crazy.

I was led up some spiral stairs to the top of one of the watchtowers and given my final task, which involved answering a quiz. Part of the information I needed to answer the questions was over in the next watchtower, so I would have to go across the walkway, get what I needed and return. I was again terrified, as I am scared of heights.

I ventured halfway and felt that someone was waiting for me on the other side, so I quickly ran back. The producers sent me a message on my pager that I had to get to the other side. I managed it but didn't get all of the answers, because my time was up.

I was upset to think that I hadn't finished all of my challenges and was worried that all of my efforts had gone to waste. I told Jonathan how upset I was and he told me not to worry. It was only when I was taken back down from the tower that he told me the other contestant had pulled out some time ago, and I was the winner. I couldn't believe my ears.

I was relieved that this draining night was over and happy to have won that episode – the only problem was that I would be in the final, competing against the winners from the other episodes. That meant I would have to go through a similar ordeal once again.

On returning to the filming van and meeting up with the other contestants, I was told by the nurse how worried she had been about me, as in the suicide cell the heart monitor showed that I had flatlined a number of times. I knew that my heartbeat became very erratic, but I'd just thought it was because I was terrified.

One contestant, Sophie, had pulled out on her first location. Joseph, who was the sceptic amongst us, said he had some sort of experience that he was not willing to discuss; he couldn't wait to leave the jail. Janine, another psychically gifted person, lasted up until the third location before she decided she had had enough.

It was about two in the morning when we were taken to our motel. I thought that my ghostly experiences were over for the night, only to find out that they were just beginning.

Luckily for the others, their rooms were all next to each other. I somehow drew the short straw and had a room away from everyone in the main motel complex. I tried everything to open the door but the key wouldn't undo the lock. I asked one of the film crew to help me open it, as it was well and truly stuck. One of the girls tried and the door finally flung open and she fell inside on the floor. I asked her not to leave me by myself, as I could see a man in the room. She told me she had seen enough for one night and that she would 'leave me to it', whatever that meant.

I felt deeply traumatised by the ordeal I had gone through and the last thing I needed was a ghost or ghosts spending the rest of the night with me. I had a shower to wash off all of the negative energy I felt I was covered in and got into bed. I turned off the lights and decided I would watch a movie. *Robin Hood* with Kevin Costner was on, so at least I had something to distract me.

I fell asleep watching the movie, only to wake up with the feeling of not being alone. I could smell the most disgustingly sweaty odour and then I could see this creepy guy beside me in the bed.

I jumped up in fright, hoping I was only dreaming, but when I turned on the light I could still see him. I yelled at the man to leave the room and he unwillingly disappeared. It was about five in the morning by this stage, so I decided to ring Warwick and tell him where I was and what I had experienced. The phone went to message bank and I left a message.

In the morning, I met up with the others, who told me how scared they all were during the night. Sophie and Janine ended up sleeping in the same room, and Joseph said that he didn't exactly have a great night either. When we were put into the filming van to return home, we all talked about our experiences, except for Joseph. He seemed like a broken man. There was a huge change in him from the man I had met the previous day. Every time we discussed our experiences, he would just look away and cry and say that he didn't want to talk about it. I wondered what he had experienced to have brought him to this. Well, I suppose I will never know.

It was only when I got home and listened to the message I had left on the answering machine that I realised how affected I was by my experiences. It didn't even sound like me: I had sworn profusely during the message, which I don't normally do, and my voice had taken on more of a masculine tone. It was very creepy to think I could have brought one of the inmates home with me. I didn't quite feel myself, and I have to be honest and say I felt like I was out of control. There was something different about me. A red mark started to appear on the left side of my neck that hadn't been there before and I felt constantly angry.

During this time, we were renovating and to get to the toilet I had to pass an open doorway leading into the garage, which was always dark. When I attempted to walk past, I could hear a spirit calling out to me, to frighten me. I felt that he had followed me back from the jail.

Poor Warwick had to put up with my constant fear of the dark – I was even more frightened of it than I had been before. I began sleeping with the bedside lamp on and Warwick became increasingly angry as the nights went on. He told me that he wanted the person I was before I went on the show to come home, because the person I had become was driving him mad. I was beginning to question myself and thought that *I* was going mad.

*

As the grand-final night of *Scream Test* approached, I became increasingly nervous about going through the stress again. Being the stubborn and determined person I am, though, there was no way I was going to pull out. I think Warwick was just hoping for the whole bad experience to hurry up and be over.

The five finalists were all taken separately in taxis to begin our journey to the secret destination. I was given a vision of the old quarantine station at Sydney's North Head, and indeed that was the direction in which the taxi headed.

At Manly, on the north shore of Sydney Harbour, we were each given a black hood to put over our head and then escorted into a water taxi. For some strange reason, the producers didn't want us to work out where we were going, so they took us out on the harbour and spun the water taxi around in circles about five or six times. With the spinning around and the smell of diesel very strong in the air, I began to feel like I was going to be sick.

When they took us to a wharf and we disembarked the water taxi, our black hoods were removed. I wasn't surprised to find that we were at the quarantine station. I had been there before and I believed it had an enormous amount of history to be shared with the public and an immense amount of personal tragedy that needed to be told so that the souls of those who had lost their lives could be released and laid to rest.

The producers told us they had given each of us a character whom we were to become for the night. The character was based on an actual person who had been held in the quarantine station in the past. Mine was a woman called Rebecca Ritson. Over the course of the night, we were to find out as much as we could about this person and tap into the way he or she would have felt when detained there.

My biggest fear in returning to the quarantine station was spending time in the two most frightening locations

– the morgue and the shower block – all alone in the dark.

It was to the shower block that I was sent first. There, all passengers arriving on a quarantined ship had been forced to shower in water containing the antiseptic carbolic acid, which burned the skin. In the shower block, the crew started making fake sound effects, which was really hard to take. I couldn't hear myself speak to the camera as the noise was so loud. It sounded like every shower had been turned on and every toilet in the place flushed.

After overcoming the sound effects, I decided to listen to the poor lost souls who were trapped in there, including a number of females who told me that they had to bathe in the shower cubicles daily and were extremely upset that their beautiful hair had begun to fall out. They told me of the lack of dignity while bathing as there were peepholes in the cubicle walls that quarantine staff would look through to ensure that they disinfected themselves well enough before leaving the cubicle.

While I was sitting in one of the shower cubicles, I felt an extremely cold breeze and sensed someone walk in front of me. I had been given an instrument to test EMFs in the area and it went up to an extremely high reading – 99.4 – for a few seconds and then dropped back to zero as the spirit walked past.

When I was taken to the next location, a dark room in the Asiatic area of the quarantine station, I saw that there were a number of headstones laid down on the floor. My task here was to identify the headstone of my assigned person for the night. My kitbag contained a newspaper clipping, a wooden cross, a nurse's hat, some bandages, medical equipment wrapped in a grey fabric cover and iodine in a bottle. The newspaper clipping was a story about Archbishop Kelly, who was denied admission to the quarantine station in 1918 to administer the last rites to a nurse. I received a very strong impression that my assigned person was a nurse and that she gave her life saving others.

Confusingly, the only headstone I could find that matched any part of the name I'd been given read: 'Memory of Eliz. The wife of Thos Ritson who died Oct 27th, 1841. Aged 30 years.' Not only did Elizabeth not tally with Rebecca, I'd also already begun picking up messages from Rebecca, not Elizabeth.

When the quarantine station was operational, passengers displaying any sign of illness would be taken straight to the hospital on arrival. The hospital staff scrubbed the walls and floors of the wards with disinfectant, changed the bedding frequently and cleaned themselves before and after duty, but unfortunately some of the nursing staff succumbed to illness and a number lost their lives, including Rebecca.

My next location was the hospital. When I was locked alone in there, I felt Rebecca very strongly. I also felt the matron of the ward, Matron Pamela, who I sensed ran the ward with an iron fist. When I sat down and turned on the video player to watch the video describing the history of the hospital, Matron Pamela made it very clear to me that I was in the room to work and not sit on my backside watching a video.

When the video was over, I was in darkness and I immediately began filming my video diary. In one corner of the room, there was a walking frame with a broomstick leaning against it. The broom was thrown about a metre from where it originally stood. Through the darkness, I could see the matron coming towards me. She had her hands firmly on her hips and was saying that she had had enough of my idle chatter. She told me to get up and do my nursing duties, administering potions and prayer to the patients. I was frightened of the matron and when she came up close to me I decided I had better do what she said, or suffer the consequences.

The room had six beds and I was told by the matron to go to the last one on the left-hand side. As I approached it, the headboard began to bang very loudly. All I could think to do was run into the corner and hide. Luckily, I managed to compose myself enough to hear what to do next.

My spirit guides told me to sit on the bed and talk to the lady in it. I took their advice, and the lady told me her name was Mary and that she had been in the bed for years and was too frightened to go into the light because the priest hadn't administered her the last rites.

Mary asked me to pray for her. She wanted me to recite the psalm 'The Lord is My Shepherd', but I was so frightened that I couldn't even remember the words. I told her that I could remember 'The Lord's Prayer' and that would have to do.

As I was saying the prayer, I was overcome with emotion and began to cry uncontrollably. Next thing I knew, there was a man standing at the end of the bed telling me that he was James, Mary's husband, and that he was waiting to take her into the light.

The whole room seemed to light up. Mary squeezed my hand and thanked me, then she got out of the bed and walked over to her husband. They both held each other's hands and disappeared into a bright white light, and then the room was thrust back into darkness. This has to be one of the most beautiful occurrences I have ever witnessed and I feel blessed to have been a part of this experience.

I proceeded to talk to each lady in the ward, going from bed to bed. Each of the women called me Nurse Rebecca and I felt that I had been taken back in time. My feeling was that I was able to see life at the quarantine station through Rebecca's eyes. I felt that her spirit channelled through me and took control of me.

My next location was the morgue. I dreaded going in there, as on other tours I had done of the quarantine station I had felt quite freaked by being in that particular part of it. In the morgue's examination room, there is a large concrete slab with drainage channels, which were used to drain the blood of the deceased person during an autopsy. I decided to just stand in the corner with my back to the wall so that I could see what was going on.

It wasn't that bad at first, but then the doctor walked in. He was a cold and cruel man. He kept touching me on the head. I got a very cold feeling from the top of my head down to my right ear and then I felt an uncomfortable pulling sensation on my scalp.

I kept feeling I was being pushed towards the concrete slab where the autopsies were performed. There was no way I was going anywhere near that slab. As I do psychometry, when I touch an object I can see what has happened in the past, so I definitely didn't want to touch the slab and see all of the horror.

I was already feeling extremely panicked when the crew

caused a bucket in the examination room to blow up and topple over. They had placed a dummy's hand inside the bucket and it fell out onto the floor. Being in total darkness and then seeing a hand glowing in the dark was enough to scare anyone. I went over to the hand, then chickened out and went back to the corner. The doctor came over to me and my right hand went totally numb; I felt like he was trying to cut it off. He told me I shouldn't worry about the hand that fell out of the bucket, as when he did autopsies bits and pieces fell on the floor all the time.

The doctor started talking to me as though I was Rebecca. He told me that I was too soft-hearted to be a nurse; I got too involved with caring for the patients. He then reverted to talking directly to me and told me how he had made Rebecca help him perform an autopsy on her fiancé, William, and how weak she was that she couldn't stay in the room to finish the job.

My final location was the autoclaves: two big vaults over five metres long, in which items were disinfected. They each had a large, round handle on the front that was turned to open and shut the door, like something you would imagine on a submarine.

The room was dimly lit and the two doors of the autoclaves were open. All I could see were two dark, cavernous openings that I didn't feel very comfortable to be near. By the time I was taken to this location, I was totally exhausted. After spending what seemed like hours at the quarantine station, I really didn't care what the ghosts – or the crew, for that matter – did to me. I focused on my next challenge, which was answering questions on a test. Then I moved on to my final challenge: to fill out my log book.

The log book contained questions about my assigned person and what I thought her life was like. While I was filling it in, my answers seemed to be coming from somewhere else. I began to feel that I was not writing my own thoughts but actually doing automatic writing, one of the tools used in mediumship. It is believed that, during automatic writing, information is channelled from a spirit regarding their life or their death. (It can also be used to channel messages from higher beings, for help or guidance.)

What I discovered while writing my answers was that I was picking up on not just one person but three. The TV crew had failed to tell me that my assigned character was actually an amalgam of three different people – Annie Egan and Rebecca Thomson, both nurses who died on the job, and Elizabeth Ritson. All three of the spirits decided they wanted their stories to be told through me. I ended up writing a six-page story in my A4 log book and ran out of time before I could finish.

The crew came to get me, we all said our goodbyes and we were escorted home in taxis. None of us knew who the winner was; we were told that we had to wait until the program aired, in early 2001.

I arrived home at eight in the morning, having spent the last twenty-six hours without any sleep. I just wanted to clear my head and get some rest, so I had a shower to wash off the negative energy that I felt had become attached to me and went to bed.

I had just started to drift off to sleep when my head began to fill with visions of the spirits I had met the previous night. I soon realised they had followed me home and they seemed to think they had some unfinished business.

At first, I tried to ignore their presence, until the banging and creaking in my bedroom got the better of me. In our bedroom, we have Warwick's grandma's antique dresser, which has little brass drop handles. The spirits thought it very amusing to make sure that each one of the handles banged, until I finally got out of bed. The impression I received was that I needed to tell their stories and they wanted me to do it *now*. I found myself drawn to my office, suddenly positioned in front of the computer to begin writing the stories of my new acquaintances.

Elizabeth Ritson left Liverpool, England, on 10 July 1841 on the ship *Ayrshire* with her husband, Thomas, and their two children, John, seven, and Anne, five. There were three hundred and four passengers and thirty crew. During the voyage, five adults and seventeen children died of typhus.

Elizabeth tried to keep her family separate from the others so they wouldn't catch the disease, but seasickness was a major problem for her and, nearing the end of the journey, she became very weak and couldn't hold any food down – that was when the typhus got the better of her.

Unfortunately, on docking on 25 October 1841, Elizabeth was so ill that she was immediately admitted into the Quarantine Hospital. Her family were not allowed to be with her and she died two days later, at the age of thirty.

Thomas was so completely devastated that he couldn't care for the children, who were sent to the orphan school at Parramatta. Elizabeth told me that she was quite distressed that Thomas had deserted the children and that he should have tried to keep the family together. Thomas passed over in his forties. He was a broken man who turned to alcohol for his sorrow, and he died a lost soul with no family.

Elizabeth hadn't gone into the light because she had unfinished business. She also said she was upset that her headstone had been removed, as in England a graveyard was a sacred place. At the quarantine station, people desecrated her gravesite by walking over it. She obviously wanted her story to be told and hoped that I might be able to help her. I hope that by my doing so here, this poor woman might now be laid to rest and join her beloved family.

Annie Egan, formerly of Emerald Hill, in Melbourne, was a nurse in private practice in Sydney when she volunteered to nurse First World War servicemen from the *Medic* who had been quarantined with Spanish influenza. Annie hadn't married, as far as I can tell. She had lost the love of her life to war, so she was more concerned about saving the troops that returned home. A Catholic, she thought more about caring for others than she thought about herself. She gave her life in the same manner.

She became infected on 26 November 1918. In Annie Egan's last days, she pleaded for a visit from a priest to hear her confession but her pleas were refused by the authorities, keen to prevent the spread of the deadly flu. All that the priest could do was send a message to her that he would hold a requiem Mass for her soul.

Annie died on 5 December 1918 and was buried with full military honours by the quarantined servicemen. At the request of her relatives, Annie's burial service was conducted by another Catholic nurse, whom I feel could have been Rebecca Thomson.

At a Mass held for the nurse in St Mary's Cathedral on 6 December 1918, Archbishop Kelly denounced the authorities' 'impious refusal' of a visit from him. Changes were later made in parliament so that doctors, who treated the body, and clergy, who helped the soul, could visit the quarantine station to bring solace to the dying.

Rebecca Thomson was another strict Catholic nurse at the quarantine hospital. She knew Annie Egan very well and they were close friends. They both had the same dedication to looking after others and a strong relationship with the Church.

The love of her life was William, her childhood sweetheart. Rebecca became engaged to him before he joined up and left for the First World War. William, an excellent marksman who was very excited to volunteer for service, refused to marry Rebecca before he left, as he didn't want her to be a young war widow if he didn't return.

In William's absence, Rebecca volunteered to be a quarantine nurse as she felt it was her duty to help others. As the clergy were not always allowed into the quarantine station in times of need, Rebecca, a cheerful and well-liked woman, took it upon herself to offer prayer and solace to the sick and dying.

She waited eagerly for William's return from the war, as all she wanted to do was settle down and have a family. She was excited when there was news that the war was finally over and that William was coming home.

When William arrived, he was put into quarantine due to an outbreak of pneumonic influenza on the ship. On arrival, William seemed to only have a slight sniffle and cough. Unfortunately, within a day of being quarantined he became desperately ill. Rebecca looked after him the best she could but, at the end of the week, on 11 November 1918, poor William passed away.

The love of Rebecca's life had been taken from her and her whole world fell apart. Matron Pamela told Rebecca to snap out of it as there were others to care for, so, under her instruction, Rebecca got back to work. She took her job even more to heart than before, believing that she hadn't prayed enough to God, because, if she had, He wouldn't have taken William from her. I feel that she actually wanted to become a nun, as nobody would take William's place.

Rebecca worked very long hours and had little rest. In January 1919, she caught the same disease as William, pneumonic influenza, and died.

After I finished writing the ladies' stories, an overwhelming feeling of calmness came over me and I was finally able to get some sleep.

*

The next couple of months seemed to drag while I was waiting for the program to air on Channel Ten.

The Maitland Gaol episode was the first to be aired. I hadn't realised how frightening it would be to watch what I had experienced during the filming. I began to suffer with horrible nightmares after seeing my episode. All of the terrible memories of being locked up in the jail came flooding back. The spirits that had followed me home were still in my house and they were enjoying every minute of making me suffer. I began to drive Warwick mental again with my fear of the dark and my desperate need to sleep with the light on.

I didn't win the grand-final episode, but in my heart I knew that I had learnt more about myself in filming the program than I had in a whole lifetime. Filming *Scream Test* was a life-changing experience. I had faced a number of my biggest fears and I had a new-found quest: to see if I could capture images of spirits and ghosts on film.

I don't know whether Warwick would always agree that *Scream Test* changed things for the better, but it has certainly made me a stronger and more determined person than I ever was. If someone asked me whether I would do it again, I would answer them by saying, 'Bring it on!'

Chapter 12

Justice for Mary Seretis-Joiner

Back in 1994, I had begun giving psychic readings to friends and acquaintances. It wasn't until several years later that I started to do psychic readings for the public. A lovely woman named Yana had come to me on a number of occasions, as her father had passed and I was able to make contact with him. Yana and I had known each other for a couple of years when, one evening, she rang me sounding quite alarmed. She asked if I would mind trying to help her find a close girlfriend of hers who had gone missing.

Yana's friend, Mary Seretis-Joiner, had last been seen on 8 October 2000, leaving the RSL club at Brighton-Le-Sands, a southern suburb of Sydney. She had had a disagreement with her husband, Patrick, at her cousin's wedding. Patrick had told Yana that Mary had driven off in her car, a late-model VW, and had not been seen since. Patrick said he was concerned for Mary's safety. I asked Yana if she could please bring some personal items of Mary's for me to tune in to and advised her that jewellery would be the best type of thing.

When Yana went to Mary's house to ask Patrick if she could borrow some of Mary's jewellery, he told her that Mary didn't wear much jewellery, so he gave her some of the badges Mary wore on her work uniform. Mary was a Qantas customer-service officer at Sydney airport.

Yana brought me the badges and I tried to tune in to them. When I first held them, I heard Running Horse and another, female, voice telling me that there was much more jewellery than this. From that moment on, I felt that Patrick was trying to hide something. I wasn't sure if it was because he didn't believe in mediums, or if it was because he didn't want me to see the truth behind what had happened to Mary.

Initially, I couldn't tell whether Mary was dead or alive; the images I was picking up were a bit all over the place. What I did see was that Mary's car had left the wedding and that the vehicle was heading south, towards Wollongong. I felt that the vehicle had gone through the Royal National Park, in the Sutherland shire of Sydney. This seemed a little strange, as it wasn't the main route you would take if you were driving to Wollongong from Brighton-Le-Sands, where Mary was last seen.

I could see a woman in a small, dark place; I felt that she was in the foetal position in the dark. I said to Yana that I didn't know if she had checked in to a motel and was upset and had kept the curtains drawn, causing the room to be dark, but this seemed to be the best way to describe my vision. Yana replied that Patrick thought Mary had gone to Wollongong and was probably staying in a motel until she sorted things out.

While holding the badges, I kept hearing the words that there had been a breakdown. I told Yana that I wondered if this meant that Mary may have had a mental breakdown. I could feel pain in my head and wasn't sure if it was because Mary had a migraine due to the stress of the argument or because she was lying injured somewhere.

I told Yana that I felt concerned for Mary's safety, as something just didn't feel quite right. I could see that there had been problems between Mary and Patrick. I was seeing a lot of strange images and at that stage things weren't quite making sense, so I told Yana I would need to keep the badges overnight in order to work out the strange messages I was receiving.

I told Yana that if Patrick was interested, I would be able to speak with him and give him a reading also. Yana said she would ask him, and left.

I didn't have very much to work with except for the badges Mary wore on her work uniform. Yana hadn't given me any photographs of Mary, so I had no idea what she even looked like, except for the vague psychic images that I was seeing in my mind.

I decided to call it a night, as Yana and I had spoken for about two hours and I was feeling quite drained. I thought that if I held the badges when I went to sleep, they might give me a better connection to Mary and I would be able to receive more information.

During the night, I had a very vivid dream that actually felt like it was real. In the dream, the doorbell rang and I went to the front door and opened it. There was a woman standing at the screen door looking deathly pale. I had never seen this woman before but I felt that she was at the door to tell me something. She was about a hundred and sixty-five centimetres in height, of a slight build, and she was dressed in what looked like a work uniform – a light-blue patterned blouse, a navy-blue skirt and black shoes. The strange thing about what she was wearing was that, on the collar of her blouse, she had the badges I had been holding all night.

The mystery woman had dark, almost black hair, pulled tightly back off her face in a ponytail. Her hair was meticulously neat and she had lovely brown eyes. What I remember most was the red lipstick she was wearing and that her eyes were hauntingly sad. I felt that she wanted to tell me something but she didn't utter a word to me. In the dream, I just stood at the door looking at the woman and I could feel her pleading for me to help her.

In my heart, I knew that Mary had made contact with me and she wanted me to know what had happened to her. I also knew from this dream that Mary was dead.

On awakening, I had a feeling of dread. I was worried about how I was going to tell Yana that her friend was dead. And the next thing I needed to establish was how it had happened.

That morning, the local paper arrived and, while flicking through it, I noticed a story about the missing woman, Mary Seretis-Joiner. The story had a photograph of the woman I had dreamt of during the night. That confirmed that the woman I knew to be dead was indeed Mary.

I rang Yana and told her about my dream. It was a very difficult moment when I told her that I thought Mary was dead. Yana and I agreed that we should meet up again and see what other information I could gather on Mary's disappearance.

Yana spoke with Patrick and told him of what I had picked up. She said that he was devastated by the news and that he would do anything he could to help find out what had happened to his wife.

A couple of days later, at a police media conference broadcast on every TV station, Patrick made a plea for anyone with any information about Mary's whereabouts to come forward. He was so emotional that he broke down in front of the cameras. While watching this, I felt extremely ill. This was the point at which I truly began to believe that Patrick was responsible for Mary's death in some way. It wouldn't have been the first time that a person making such a televised plea turned out to be the one who did the deed. In my heart, I hoped that I was wrong, but deep within me I knew I was right. I knew I was about to open Pandora's box by assisting with this case; what I wasn't sure about was whether or not I would be able to cope with the outcome.

That night, I rang Yana and told her I felt that something wasn't right about the media conference. I told her that I felt suspicious about Patrick but just couldn't put my finger on it. I asked her why, if Patrick was so concerned about Mary, he didn't ever take up my offer of help.

Yana admitted that Patrick was acting strangely. She said he was always interested in any information that I relayed to her after each reading but he still declined to make any personal contact with me. I asked Yana to be very careful about what information she passed on to him, as I felt that Patrick was the one who had murdered his wife. She told me that each time she spoke with Patrick, he was becoming more and more unnerved by the information I was receiving from Mary. Then, one day, Yana rang me and said she felt that Patrick was beginning to crack.

Yana, who was in contact with the police officers in charge of the case, told me that they were open to speaking with me about what I had picked up from Mary, and she passed on the names of two detectives.

The detective I spoke with was Paul Connery from Cronulla Police. He was a very nice guy and he was actually receptive to what I had picked up. I felt quite at ease speaking to him, which made my job a lot easier. I find that if the detective on the case is open to the kind of work I do, then the spirits work with me much better. All I hoped was that Mary would help me to give the police enough information to find her body and catch her killer. I began to write down the messages from Mary so I could pass them on to the police.

Mary kept giving me images of driving through the Royal National Park but she never seemed to get to a destination in the Wollongong area. I got a strong feeling that Mary's car could still be in the park, abandoned somewhere. I at least knew that her car had travelled through the park after her disappearance. I strongly felt that she had injuries on the right side of her head, as I felt very strong pain on that side of my head whenever I tuned in to her.

Mary began to show me things through her eyes. I could see that she and Patrick had had an argument after the wedding. I felt strongly that she was on the coast somewhere; I could smell the sea air and I felt wind and rain on my face. I could see that there were local native bushes close to where they had their argument. Mary told me that she had a type of vegetation in her hair and she showed me what type of leaf it had. It was from a coastal banksia – I recognised it because I have the same type of tree at the front of my property. When I tuned in to Mary, I could hear gravel or rocks crunching beneath my feet and I could see the city skyline in the distance from where the argument took place. I could see that Mary and Patrick were yelling at each other but I felt that the area was so remote that even if she screamed no one would be able to hear her.

I could see it was a place that fishermen frequented. I was getting images of people fishing at the location. I could also see that there were rocky outcrops that the sea would wash against and that, at the time the argument took place, the area was deserted. I began to be shown Mary's last minutes, as if I was watching as a bystander.

What I am about to relay is really quite sickening. I could see that Mary and Patrick were leaning or sitting on the bonnet of the VW and that Patrick was yelling right in Mary's face. He then got up and turned towards her. He took a firm grip on both of her arms and began to shake her violently. I heard her telling him that she had had enough and that she wanted to leave him. She was very distraught about having to leave her cousin's wedding and said she couldn't stand the thought of letting her family down.

Patrick became even more angry at this statement. He told her that he thought she loved her family more than she loved him. I then saw Patrick hitting Mary violently on the right side of the face and head. I saw her putting up her hand to stop the blows but, at this point, Patrick was out of control. I then saw Mary's tiny frame crumple and fall to the ground. I felt that she hit her head on a rock. I saw Patrick pick up a rock that was lying on the ground and begin hitting her on the side of the head with it, and then he began to kick her. There was blood everywhere and I could see Mary's body lying motionless on the ground. When he was finished, I saw him cast the rock into the rough seas.

In the vision, Patrick then dragged Mary by the legs towards the boot of the car. I felt that she had drag marks across her back and that her hair was a sticky, bloody mess. Her shoe fell off and Patrick hastily picked it up. He then opened the boot of the car, pulled out a tarp or blanket and lined the inside of the boot with it before putting Mary's body inside and angrily throwing the shoe in as well.

At this point, I felt, Mary was still alive, despite how badly she had been beaten. Images flooded into my mind of Mary lying battered and bruised, locked in the boot of a car, with little air and no means of escape. I felt that her head injuries were so bad, though, that she would never have recovered. The whole right-hand side of her head was fractured and bleeding. Her body looked like a bloodied and bruised rag doll.

Patrick coldly closed the car boot as though nothing had taken place.

I saw that darkness was fast approaching and Patrick

was worried about what he was now going to do with the car and his wife's body. I felt that he contemplated pushing the car off a cliff into the sea to conceal Mary's fate, but then he panicked and began driving.

I now understood my prior visions of Mary in a foetal position in a small darkened area: she wasn't in a hotel room; she was in the boot of her own car.

The vision abruptly changed and I began seeing things through Mary's eyes; she had just realised she was no longer attached to her body and that she was floating. I now had a bird's eye view of Mary's car with Patrick driving, travelling through the Royal National Park along a tarred road. The car seemed to be heading south, towards the Stanwell Tops area, then the vision suddenly stopped.

A couple of days later, I rang Ian, my brother-in-law, and asked him if he would come for a drive through the Royal National Park to see if I could find a bush track that I thought was related to Mary's murder. Ian, quite unperturbed, said he would come so that I wasn't out there alone. We both decided it would be good for me to have a witness if anything actually came to pass. To be honest, I think back now and wonder what the two of us would have done if we had found Mary's car, or her body for that matter. I don't think either of us really thought about the consequences. I honestly am happy that I didn't personally find Mary's body, because from the psychic horror I was witness to I don't think I would have coped with finding her in real time.

I drove us through the Royal National Park and, whenever an area looked similar to my visions, I turned off and investigated. There were a couple of locations that could have suited my visions as they had gravel roadways, were out of the way and close to the coast, and there were coastal banksias growing. We drove as far as Bundeena but nothing proved to me that I had found the exact spot. Feeling very disappointed with myself, I decided to call it a day. I was beginning to feel that I had let Mary down.

That night, I tried to sleep, only to find my head filled with visions of Mary and Patrick's life. I felt strongly that Patrick and Mary had a very unhappy marriage. Mary showed me glimpses of violence and arguments between Patrick and herself. I also got the strong impression that Mary's family didn't like Patrick very much. I felt that Mary was a very gentle and conscientious person; she kept telling me that all she ever wanted was to be happily married and to be loved. I felt that she was a very well-liked person, but I didn't get the same feeling about Patrick. I felt that he was a very jealous and controlling person, who treated Mary more like a possession than a partner. Patrick loved the feeling of being in control. I had the feeling that Patrick had committed acts of violence in past relationships.

Being a medium can be a very hard thing to live with, because at times you are privy to intimate details of people's lives, which aren't always pleasant to see. The hardest part is that you may know what has gone on or is going on but you can't prevent the outcome. It can be quite unsettling – a feeling of helplessness would be the best way to describe it.

*

Two and a half weeks after Mary Seretis-Joiner's disappearance, Patrick Joiner sent a letter to police stating that Mary was dead and her body was indeed in the boot of her car, as I had seen in my visions. He admitted to police that she had died after he'd hit her during an argument but insisted that he had not meant to kill her, that it was an accident. He informed police that her car was in Abercrombie Street, in the inner-city suburb of Redfern.

I have always felt that the car was left abandoned in the Royal National Park for some time prior to it being moved into the inner city. When the police found the car, it was unlocked, with the keys in the ignition. If a car as new as Mary's VW was left unattended for two and a half weeks with the keys in the ignition in Abercrombie Street, Redfern, it would surely have been stolen or at least noticed by the locals.

The news of Patrick's arrest was the news that Yana and I had both been waiting for. To say the least, we were very relieved.

The two detectives on the case made contact with me again a few days after Patrick's arrest. We met at Cronulla Police Station and we decided that if I visited Mary's house, I might get more information about Mary and Patrick's life and what took place. We walked around Mary's property but didn't go inside the house. I was very drawn to the garden shed in the backyard, as I felt that something had been hidden in it.

Mary was very distressed that her beloved dog was missing from the property. I later found out that Patrick had given the dog to one of his family members.

The police informed me that since Patrick had turned himself in, Mary's family had gone through the house and thrown out anything pertaining to him. I was very alarmed by this statement, as I felt that they had unknowingly removed evidence that could help to make sure he was put behind bars for a very long time.

While I was being driven around in the car by the detectives, I felt like I had a direct line to Mary. She was showing me, I felt, that Patrick's past relationships had ended due to his violent and controlling behaviour. I felt that he may have had a police record for violence at that time and that he may have lived interstate in the past. I was shown the map of Australia, and the state of Victoria kept jumping out at me. From this vision, I felt that he may have been married or in a permanent relationship with a woman from Victoria. I felt that if the police were able to access records from the Victoria Police, they would be able to bring up a file about Patrick concerning his violence.

After visiting Mary's place, the detectives asked me where I wanted to go next and I asked them to take me past Cronulla Leagues Club. I could see that, after leaving Mary's cousin's wedding party at the Brighton-Le-Sands RSL Club, Mary asked Patrick to call into another club because she thought she would be safer being in a crowded area.

After passing the Cronulla Leagues Club, I asked the detectives to take me to Cape Solander, which is part of the Botany Bay National Park. As we drove into the park, I asked if we could go to the left-hand road leading up to Cape Solander. When we parked the car and disembarked, a number of things seemed to make sense. There were coastal banksia plants growing, the road was made up of gravel and dirt, and you could see the city skyline from where we were standing. The area was known for its fishing and the ocean lapped up wildly on the rocks in a strong, stormy breeze. We spent some time at the location but did not find any evidence and decided to call it a day. It was pouring with rain and we were all drenched and cold so we returned to Cronulla Police Station.

Although there were a large number of psychic matches to my visions when going to Cape Solander, it later came to light that it was not the site of Mary's murder. Mary was actually murdered in the Royal National Park, at Bundeena, where I'd initially been looking for her body. From Bundeena, which is the next bay around from Cape Solander, you can also see the city skyline. Coastal banksias are native to the area and fishermen do frequent it.

It was during Patrick Joiner's murder trial that the messages I had received about a breakdown finally made sense. The court was told that, on the night Mary went missing, Patrick called NRMA for help because he had run out of petrol on the F6 Freeway heading towards Wollongong in Mary's VW.

That Mary and Patrick had a troubled marriage and that Patrick had a history of violence were also borne out in court when Mary's brother Steven testified that he knew his sister's marriage was violent and had offered to help her leave Patrick. He said that Patrick had beaten her in the past and he had seen the resulting bruises on her arms, back and head. Mary had refused his help because 'she was pretty proud' and wanted to make her marriage work.

To everyone's relief, Patrick was sentenced to eighteen years in jail for the murder of his wife. Nothing will bring Mary back, but at least Patrick has been brought to justice and he has been stopped from hurting anyone else again.

*

In 2005, I took the train to Town Hall, Sydney, to go to the Mind Body Spirit Festival at Darling Harbour. I probably only catch a train to the city at most three to five times in a year. On my way home, I got to the platform and sat on a bench to wait until my train arrived. An older lady of European descent came up and sat beside me. I had never met or seen this woman before. She started up a conversation, telling me that it was the anniversary of her daughter's death. She then started telling me that both her daughter and her husband had died and she only had one child still living, a son whose name was Steven.

At first, I didn't get the connection, then I suddenly saw Mary appear. Our train arrived and the woman and I got on; she sat down beside me to continue her story. She told me that she was so heartbroken because her daughter, Mary, had been murdered.

I told her that I knew all about Mary and that I had assisted the police with Mary's case after Yana sought my help in solving her disappearance. Mary then gave me messages to pass on to her mother. The most important things she wanted her mum to know were that she was with her dad and that the two of them were doing their best to take care of her from spirit.

People often ask me if I believe in coincidences. I always say no. I believe that everything happens for a reason, and spirits go to great measures to orchestrate such meetings as I had with Mary's mother.

Chapter 13

Searching for Evidence of Spirit

The positive influence that participating in *Scream Test* had on the direction of my life in fact came out of an initial disappointment. I had experienced and seen so much paranormal activity in both Maitland Gaol and the North Head Quarantine Station but it was apparent on watching the shows that hardly any of it was visible to the viewers. In addition, in a voiceover during the program the producers said that none of the contestants captured any photographic or video evidence to prove that spirits really do exist.

I always feel that when you are frustrated or disappointed with something, you should use that negative energy and turn it into a positive. My *Scream Test* experience was the perfect driving force to help me find proof of ghosts or spirits. I felt that if spirits could make their presence known to me in such a strong manner, then it had to be possible to capture some form of tangible evidence on film.

I set myself a new challenge to prove the sceptics wrong: I would do everything I could to get a photograph of a ghost or spirit. I believe that when we die, we leave a residual energy or essence of our self behind. This energy can also be explained as our life force, soul or spirit. From my experiences with the other side, the energy we leave behind, if strong enough, can be seen, felt, heard, smelt or even photographed. Our eyes generally can see the energy in our peripheral vision, but a camera can capture the energy directly in front of it.

After filming the *Scream Test* grand final at the quarantine station, I had become good friends with Darren James, the winner of the episode at the Parramatta Female Orphan School. Darren was on a similar quest to mine: to prove that ghosts really do exist. Six film and television students from Macquarie University were making a documentary looking behind the scenes of what Darren experienced when he filmed his episode. I was invited along to take part in the investigation process at the orphanage and to see if I could capture the image of a ghost on film.

Parramatta Female Orphan School was built in 1818 to house children of convicts and abandoned or orphaned children. Initially, girls of five years or older were sent to the orphan school, but the minimum age was lowered to two years due to the high demand. It was also opened up to orphaned boys. The orphanage became the Rydalmere Insane Asylum in 1886, and the building is now part of the University of Western Sydney.

The original entrance to the orphan school was via a stairway that led up from the Parramatta River. When the orphanage was operational, the orphans were transported by boat along the river and led up the stairs to their new home. The crew decided to film from the viewpoint of the children on arrival at the orphanage. We began at the bottom of the stairs that led up from the riverbank to the grounds.

While the crew were setting up the camera gear, Liz, our sound recordist, was testing the microphone. Liz asked Suzie, another member of the crew, to ascend the stairs and stop at the top. Whenever Suzie stopped, Liz would hear another set of footsteps following right behind her.

At first, Liz thought she was hearing things but after four attempts she realised that there was possibly a ghost following Suzie up the steps to make his or her presence known. Darren and I joked and said that we already had our first proof. Liz quite sceptically said she would wait and see what had happened by the end of the day before she decided whether or not she believed in ghosts. Well, Liz was in for much more than she expected . . .

After shooting at the steps, we commenced exploring the building, one side of which was for the accommodation of boys only and the other side for girls only. When I entered through the kitchen area on the boys' side to access the adjoining bathroom areas, I could hear young boys laughing at me. I looked up, and part of the ceiling was missing and the rafters were exposed. I could clearly see two very cheeky boys sitting up on the rafters, pointing down at me and laughing. They were between the ages of nine and eleven; they were dressed in pants with patches on their knees and they both wore white-cream, button-up, collarless shirts and braces. As soon as they realised that I could see them, they instantly vanished.

I took three photos in this area and when I had the film developed (this was before I had a digital camera), I was very amazed by what I'd captured. One of the photos looks like a vapour of smoke, the next looks like white droplets falling from the ceiling, while the last one looks like waves of light exiting to the side of the picture.

In the actual bathroom, I became quite frightened and felt that I wasn't alone. The feeling that I picked up was that a lot of abuse had taken place in this area. I could sense the spirit of an older boy who was very solidly built. He was approximately thirteen or fourteen years of age; he had short, straight hair and squinty little brown eyes and a freckled face. He told me that he frequented this area and that he was in control here. He was a very angry and hateful individual and I felt that he was one of the orphanage's bullies.

I asked him why he was here and he told me that his parents were dead and that nobody loved him. He had been abused by one of the older boys in the past and thought it only fair that others should suffer the same fate. I felt very sorry for this lost spirit as he hadn't even realised he was dead. He told me that he was sent to the orphanage in about 1865 – and here I was talking to him in the year 2000. How sad it was for him to be trapped in a time warp of sadness, abuse and misery.

I told him I could send him to the light, where he could be at peace and be with his dead parents. He sadly informed me that if he left the orphanage, he had nowhere else to go and challenged me that if God really existed, like he was taught at the orphanage, then why wasn't he already in heaven? With that statement, he disappeared.

At times, it can be very hard to work with spirits, as they move about so quickly and freely. The other thing to remember is that even in death we all have free will, so if a deceased person doesn't want my help, then I have no right to interfere.

Investigating in another area upstairs and on the other side that was part of the girls' rooms, Darren and I felt a presence in the toilet and, to our amazement, a big, red ball of light was captured on one of the video cameras. It rolled across the floor and circled around the outside of the bottom of the toilet bowl and then just seemed to evaporate into nothing.

While we were filming upstairs, I could feel the presence of the mental patients who had been here when the building was used as the Rydalmere Insane Asylum. Our sound recordist, Liz, said she could hear a loud moaning sound coming through her headphones, so she pointed the boom mike towards the sound, only to have the microphone wrenched out of her hand and then to feel two strong hands firmly grab her by the arm. The hands tried to pull her through a broken window. Liz turned a pale shade of grey and turned and ran. I have never seen anyone run as fast as poor Liz did to get out of the room. She refused to go back into the building for the rest of the day. Another member of our film crew became quite sick while we were filming and she also didn't want to return to the haunted buildings.

When I got home, I couldn't wait to get my photos developed. I took my film to the local photo lab but I had to wait twenty-four hours until I could get the photos back. I couldn't believe my eyes when I opened up the packets: out of the forty-eight photos I had taken, six had captured images of spirits. It was so exciting – I actually had my first images of ghosts on film! I had also disproved the fallacy that ghosts only come out during the night, as I had taken all of the photographs at Parramatta Female Orphan School during the day.

Through a bit of experimentation, I discovered that if I used a flash and a faster ASA setting on the camera (ASA is a measure of film speed or light sensitivity of a camera film set by the American Standards Association) – e.g. 400 ASA or greater – the spirits seemed to reflect and show up better on the photographs. It is not totally impossible to capture an image of a spirit without the use of a flash, but it certainly helps; the results I got without the flash were sometimes disappointing. Spirits tend to use energy to make their presence known. For instance, they have a habit of using electrical energy to turn appliances on or off. So it isn't any wonder that spirits use the energy from a flash or light to show themselves to the living.

Capturing a ghost on film for the first time was one of the most exciting things I have ever done. My journey had begun. Now I wanted to try to capture as many images as possible. I decided that I needed to test my theories even further. My aim was to visit as many haunted locations as

I could, including those featured on *Scream Test*, to see what tangible evidence I could capture myself. I would go armed with a video camera, which I had won on the program, and a still camera and see what eventuated.

I revisited the Parramatta orphanage on numerous occasions. On one of my visits, I was walking around the outside of the main building and could hear children giggling and laughing. I could hear someone calling me and asking me to come over to a missing air vent in the wall, close to the ground. When I looked into the hole where the air vent was missing, all I could see was the empty space under the floor of the building. I set up the camera on a tripod, pointing the lens at the hole in the wall.

At first, nothing showed up on the viewfinder. Thankfully, I was patient, as a few minutes later a blue image appeared in the picture frame. Suddenly, a strange smell began to come out from the hole and I had an overwhelming feeling of nausea come over me.

I began to speak to whoever or whatever was inside the underground floor space. I was able to hear the voice of a small boy named Ben, who told me that when he was naughty, as punishment he would be lowered through a hole in the floor and locked down there. He told me that he could be locked under the floor for hours and often missed out on his dinner. He said that he suffered with stomach upsets and nausea, so I now understood why I felt so ill when I tuned into this little lost boy. The area was about one metre high, with a floor space of around one metre by three metres.

A girlfriend of mine named Jackie had accompanied me on my visit. Luckily, she understood my psychic gifts so at least she was open to me talking to an invisible boy inside a hole in the wall.

The little boy was quite happy that I could see him on camera and he did everything possible to make his presence known. My camera suddenly started to have a mind of its own. It began to go in and out of focus, even though the setting was on automatic. It was beating similarly to the rate of a heartbeat and it didn't respond to anything I did to it.

I asked Ben to stop doing whatever he was doing, but then I realised that he could respond to me through the camera if I asked him questions requiring a yes or no answer.

When I asked him if he was affecting my camera, it kept rapidly going in and out of focus; when I asked him if it was caused by something else, it stopped. After asking him a number of questions, I discovered that the little boy had been at the location for over a hundred years and that he was frightened to leave.

After a while, the camera ceased moving in and out of focus and a larger image appeared in the viewfinder. A very bright blue-white flash of light appeared from around the corner of the foundations. The small male spirit seemed to cower in the opposite corner of the underground space when this much larger and stronger spirit arrived.

This larger male spirit wouldn't speak to me; he seemed to be too arrogant to answer my questions. After about five minutes, this presence left the area, once again showing up as a very distinct blue-white flash of light on my camera.

I asked Ben why he had been frightened and he told

me that it was the man who had locked him under the floor in the first place.

Over the following weeks, I made numerous visits to the hole in the wall and I have captured many images of the spirits under the floor space. Parramatta orphanage has always been an area where I know I can make contact with spirit.

*

The Burnside Homes are a group of twenty-two buildings in North Parramatta, Sydney, that were used to house and care for destitute children. A Scotsman named James Burns, who was the co-founder of Burns Philp and Company, established the homes in 1911. They were an extremely well-run cottage system. Each had its own identity, and great efforts were made to make the children's lives as close as possible to those in an ordinary home.

When I was a teenager, my mother used to work at the War Memorial Home at Burnside. The building my mother worked in was used to care for underprivileged boys who came from single-parent families or families in need of financial support. I remember going in the car with my father and waiting while he went to pick my mum up after work. The building reminded me of a castle, as it is two storeys high, with a big tower at the front entrance. The tower has an open verandah and when I would wait in the car, I would always feel that somebody was watching me.

One Christmas, my family was invited to the home for a Christmas party. I wasn't particularly excited to be spending the evening in such a haunted-looking place. The family my mother worked for lived on the premises and they had a number of children. My brother, Michael, was having a lovely time with the other children and they were exploring the house like it was an adventure.

Michael and the others went up into the tower to see the beautiful panoramic view of the area. I ventured up the first five steps of the ladder and then, because of my terrible fear of heights, I chickened out. Feeling quite embarrassed, I retreated and left the others to enjoy the view. I went back downstairs to join the adults and sat patiently waiting until it was time to go home.

It wasn't until some twenty-two years later, when I had embarked on my journey of spirit photography, that I returned to the house on the hill at Burnside Homes.

I visited the area with a tour group I had organised and we were privileged enough to be able to investigate the home after dark with a guide named Sandra who worked at Burnside Homes. I felt that the home had been quite a happy place and I didn't feel that it was an area where there had been tragic deaths due to mistreatment or illness of the occupants. In all, it didn't seem overly haunted like some of the other locations I had visited.

When I arrived at the tower, I did feel quite uneasy, though. I wondered if it was just because of my fear of heights and the memories of getting to the ladder and not having the courage to proceed up it when I was a child. I was extremely determined that this time I would get to the top, and when I got there, the view was spectacular. I didn't feel too happy about standing near the edge but I had at least got to the top of the tower.

After a few minutes, we descended the ladder and the group gathered outside the building, in the car park. While Sandra gave us a talk about the history of the area and surrounding buildings, I had the strongest urge to look up at the tower and take a photo. The feeling of being watched that I had experienced when I was a child sitting in the car waiting for my mother returned and I knew that this time the group was being watched. When I had my photographs developed, I had captured an image of a person in a hooded cloak standing on the tower looking down at us. This remains the clearest image I have captured of spirit to date. The interesting thing is that, after we had left the building, the property had been locked up securely and there was no living person inside . . . or was there?

*

Monte Cristo, a house built in 1884 by Christopher William Crawley on a hill overlooking the beautiful historical town of Junee in New South Wales, has had a very traumatic past. Little wonder it is dubbed 'Australia's Most Haunted House'.

The strongest presence is that of Christopher's wife, Mrs Elizabeth Crawley. After Mr Crawley's death in 1910, Mrs Crawley was often seen dressed in black in the chapel at Monte Cristo. She died in 1933 at the age of ninety-two, from a heart attack due to a burst appendix.

There have been at least three deaths on the second storey of this beautiful homestead: a maid was pushed to her death over the balcony and her ghost is often sighted by visitors; a woman died giving birth on one of the beds;

and Mr Crawley died in what is now known as the Boys' Bedroom, as a result of blood poisoning from an infected carbuncle that he got from wearing starched collars.

Also within the main house, one of the Crawleys' baby daughters slipped out of her nanny's arms, fell down the stairs and died of her injuries. The nanny claimed that the baby was pushed from her arms.

The Stable and Coach House at Monte Cristo was once used as sleeping quarters by a stable boy named Morris. One day, Morris took ill and was too sick to get out of bed. His boss thought that he was faking his illness, so he set fire to the boy's bedding, but poor Morris was so ill that he couldn't move and he was burnt to death in his bed.

A man named Ralph Morris, who was mentally retarded and the son of the housekeeper, was kept chained up in shackles at the Caretaker's Cottage for forty years. After Ralph's mother passed, he was sent to an insane asylum, where he died shortly afterwards.

The most recent death at Monte Cristo was in 1961, when caretaker Jackie Simpson was murdered by a fifteen-year-old boy who had watched the movie *Psycho* several times. The poor caretaker was shot to death in his cottage.

Young children dressed in sailor suits are often seen in the gardens surrounding the property. On the top landing, a woman dressed in period costume has been known to walk back and forth. It is thought that there are up to ten spirits inhabiting the property.

In October 2001, I went to Junee, four hundred and eighty kilometres south-west of Sydney, to see the famous haunted house for myself. I was joined by a group of twelve enthusiastic friends who, like me, hoped to capture evidence of spirits and spend the night in the most haunted house in Australia.

I travelled with my friend Darren James and Josh Martin, from ABC's *Stretch TV*. Josh, who came with us to film a program called *Haunted House*, is a fun yet sceptical television journalist who thought it would be interesting to see whether any ghosts would make their presence known on camera.

We were met by the very accommodating Olive and Reg Ryan, who have owned the property since 1963. It had been abandoned and vandalised before they bought it and the Ryans have lovingly restored the property to its former glory.

Reg kindly escorted us through his very stately home but, on entering some of the rooms, I received the distinct feeling from elsewhere that I wasn't at all welcome. I could certainly feel Mrs Crawley's presence and I didn't get the feeling that she liked me. I thought it would be even more interesting to investigate the property at night, in the dark.

Josh, Darren and I then decided to look through the property to work out the best areas to position the cameras for the night. We first investigated the main homestead. I was very happily going from room to room taking photos, until I entered the drawing room. I said to Darren, 'Wouldn't it be funny if Mrs Crawley made her presence known while we were taking the photos?' Suddenly, an icy breeze entered the room and my camera completely jammed – to this day, it hasn't worked. Luckily, I had a back-up camera.

I knew I was in for an interesting night. I went upstairs to look through the bedroom and got a very uneasy feeling that I wasn't alone. When I got to the top of the stairs, I felt very strongly that someone was behind me and I had a strange sensation that someone wanted to push me back down them. I held on very tightly to the balustrade because the overwhelming feeling of dread was too strong to ignore.

I decided to take a walk along the verandah on the second storey and again felt that I wasn't alone. I felt an even stronger presence behind me, willing me to look over the edge. I felt quite alarmed at how strong the feeling was to comply. Fortunately, because of my fear of heights, sanity prevailed and I held on to the wall of the house to walk along the verandah, in case anyone decided I should get a bit of a shove over the edge.

I walked over to the room that Mrs Crawley had converted into a chapel. On approaching the door, I heard a loud voice in my head tell me I wasn't welcome there, as it was Mrs Crawley's private domain. I heeded the advice.

We left the main homestead and decided to look through the stable area. On our approach, I could smell the strong odour of something burning. I could very clearly see a young boy standing before me with a sooty black face. I was surprised that Darren and Josh couldn't see him, because he was as solid as a living person to me. I took a picture of the stable window and a carriage that was stored in the stable. When the photograph was developed, a smoke-like vapour had been captured exiting the window.

We then progressed up the stairs of the stable loft. They are quite narrow and there isn't a balustrade to hold while climbing up. When I neared the top, I strongly felt that someone from below had hold of my foot and was trying to pull me off them to the floor below. It is quite a big drop from the top of the loft to the floor and the thought of falling was a little frightening. When I got to the top of the stairs, I had a very strong feeling of shortness of breath; the heat was stifling in this area.

I couldn't wait to leave, so we pressed on to the ballroom, Darren and Josh walking ahead of me. In the ballroom, there are doors leading off to the side, and the boys went through them a few minutes before me. When I approached the open doors, both of them abruptly banged shut in front of me, catching my hand. When I went to open them, they became stuck. I knocked and Darren had to come to let me through, as they had mysteriously locked themselves. Both Darren and Josh thought that this was extremely funny and joked that things could only get better.

Josh positioned motion-activated infrared cameras in the drawing room, chapel and stables. The plan was to check the cameras throughout the night and move them to different locations if the activity was better somewhere else.

We then all gathered for dinner before commencing our ghostly adventure. After dinner, we went out onto the courtyard at the back of the old homestead. While standing there planning where to begin filming with some other cameras we had brought, a display of lights began in what were to be our bedrooms for the night.

All of the group were out in the courtyard and yet someone or something was going between our rooms and turning the lights on and off, like a disco. At first, we thought that one of the group was playing tricks, so my friend Matt went upstairs to see who it was. When Matt came back down, he said that there wasn't anybody up in the rooms we were staying in. Reg and Olive were downstairs in the front part of the homestead watching television, quite oblivious to the light display we were all witnessing.

While we were discussing what had happened with the lights, we all saw a man wearing a top hat and tails in the old servants' quarters on the ground floor. A light went on in the quarters and then abruptly went off. We all saw the man walk across to the adjoining room, and the light in that room went on and then quickly turned off.

I went into the first room to investigate who he was. As I entered, I tried to turn on the light to see for myself if he was still there. The light switches in this part of the house are the type with a pull string that hangs from the ceiling. When I pulled the cord, nothing happened. I tried again and still nothing happened. I then shone a torch on the light fitting, only to see that there wasn't a light bulb in the socket. I went to the next room and discovered the same thing.

Then, a very loud bang came from the kitchen behind the servants' quarters, so I went to investigate. The bang went off again so loudly that I thought something had been dropped or thrown at me. I could hear loud footsteps pacing in the kitchen and when they began to come in my direction, I decided it would be best to get myself out of there as quickly as I could.

Some of the group were still outside the building watching all of the commotion and they were all very amused. They remarked that I looked as white as a ghost when I came out. The boys were certainly right: things were just getting better and better.

I left a voice-activated cassette recorder near where the poor, unfortunate disabled man had been chained to the wall. My aim was to see if any electronic voice phenomena (EVP) got recorded on the tape. The way this works is that spirits can make noises using energy or even by moving items. They have been known to come through people's TV sets, radios, mobile phones or on tape-recording devices. They leave ghostly voices or screams to remind the living they exist. Indeed, when I returned to the area later in the evening, the tape had recorded the sounds of a chain rattling and a man moaning. It was very eerie and haunting.

To our disappointment, when we checked the motion-activated camera in the drawing room, none of the spirits of the house had bothered to make their presence known to the camera. We began to think that they weren't interested in coming out to play on this particular occasion. It was only when we all decided to call it a night that things began to get exciting – for me, at least.

In the morning, Josh reported that he had slept like a baby, and Darren didn't have any incidents to report. I, on the other hand, had been woken up constantly through the night. I was sharing the room with a girl named Kelly and in the morning she wondered why I had been in and out of the room for most of the night, which I certainly hadn't.

At one stage, I had been woken up by a woman dressed in period clothing: a long, black dress with long sleeves and white cuffs and a white, lacy collar. She'd had an extremely stern look on her face and had given me the impression that I wasn't welcome in the house. I'd rolled over and gone back to sleep, thinking I must have been having a dream about Mrs Crawley.

On waking in the morning, I had felt chilled to the bone and couldn't stop shaking. The weather had changed during the night and a very icy wind had blown in from the south. I had looked down at the bed and my blankets had been neatly folded back twice, leaving me covered by only a sheet.

I'd decided I needed to have a nice hot shower to get rid of the chill I was experiencing, but before I'd been able to get to the bathroom, the heavy velvet curtains that divided the guest area from the Ryans' living quarters had flown completely open as if someone had been about to walk through the passageway.

When I'd looked to see who was on the other side, I'd been surprised to find that no one was there. Although a strong breeze had been blowing outside, there hadn't been any draught whatsoever that could have caused the curtains to blow up and open like they'd done. My first impression had been that I was back in the presence of Mrs Crawley.

When I'd got into the shower and turned on the hot and cold water, the steaming hot water had begun flowing through the shower nozzle, but just as I'd put a large dollop of shampoo into my hair, the water had turned dead cold. I'd had the hot-water nozzle turned on as far as it would go and I'd now started to receive only a trickle of freezing-cold water. To my disgust, I'd had to finish showering in a freezing-cold shower and had ended up being colder than I'd been before I'd got in. I had quickly got dressed and gone downstairs to meet the others for breakfast with my teeth loudly chattering.

I told Darren and Josh about the shower and all the rest, and they laughed and said they thought that Mrs Crawley had it in for me.

After breakfast, Olive Ryan asked me if I would mind doing a reading for her and I told her I would be delighted to. She led me into what is known as the Breakfast Room so we could conduct it in private. Just as I tuned in and began the reading for Olive, an icy chill came into the air and I strongly felt an icy presence on my right-hand side. I tried desperately to ignore Mrs Crawley but the more I did so, the more uncomfortable I began to feel.

Olive asked me what was wrong and I told her that I felt Mrs Crawley was in the room. Olive then told me about an unnerving discovery that had taken place in the room we were sitting in. One morning, when coming down to start breakfast, she found her family's kitten in the kitchen with its eyes gouged out and its stomach torn open. Olive said that there was no sign of intruders and to this day the family still do not know what happened to it.

With that thought firmly in my head, I tried to continue with the reading. I began to get a message about Olive's mother and I asked Olive if her mother was all right. Olive replied that, as far as she knew, her mother was fine. I told her that I'd got a very strong message that her mother wasn't well and that Olive would be going to see her very shortly.

Just as I finished saying this, the chandelier above the table we were sitting at began to vibrate and an overwhelming feeling of nausea took over me. I felt like I was going to vomit and I just had to get out of the room as quickly as possible. Olive knowingly said that there are areas in the house that have that type of effect on people.

I asked if we could sit outside in the garden and Olive willingly agreed. As soon as I left the house, I began to feel better, so we continued the reading. While we were sitting in the garden, I didn't feel Mrs Crawley's presence at all. I felt very relieved to be away from her negative and controlling energy.

Olive is such a warm and gentle soul. I asked her how she coped with living in such a haunted house. She replied that owning the house was her husband Reg's dream and they had spent a large part of their lives restoring the place to its former glory. The house is certainly one of the grandest and most beautiful properties that I have been privileged to stay at, but I certainly wouldn't be able to cope with the negative energy surrounding it.

Just as the reading drew to a close, Olive excused herself to answer a phone call. She came back quite shocked and told me that her mother had taken ill and that she would need to fly up to Queensland as soon as possible to see her. I couldn't help but think that Mrs Crawley had struck again.

During our long road trip home, Darren and I asked Josh if he was up to going to our next location: Maitland Gaol. Josh just smiled and said he would leave us to it.

*

As Maitland Gaol was the most frightening of my *Scream Test* locations, my return there to capture evidence of ghosts or spirits on camera was to be one of the most emotional elements of my plan. It took all of my courage to be able to go through with it.

I still had the very noticeable mark around my neck that had appeared after my *Scream Test* experience at Maitland eighteen months earlier. The mark wasn't always visible – it was only when I had paranormal activity around me that it would suddenly appear, usually after doing a reading for a client. At times, the mark could look like I had been strangled or choked.

After lots of organising, Darren and I were able to persuade the university crew with whom we filmed at Parramatta Female Orphan School to accompany us. The moment I arrived at the gates, all of my bad memories began flooding back. It took an enormous effort to walk through the gates knowing what hideous spirits lay inside. My biggest concern on returning was whether I would be physically attacked, like I was the last time I visited the place.

We were met by our guide for the day, who had been an inmate of the jail in his earlier days. I decided it was best to visit the prime locations in the order that I had the last time, so I could face my fears and demons one by one.

Cell 46, in B wing – the suicide cell – certainly looked a lot less threatening during the day. I could still feel that there were presences in this room but I didn't feel that any of them were going to attack me like the last time. Instead, all I could feel was the sadness and despair that the prisoners of the past would have felt. On the ground floor of B Wing, as I passed the threshold of where the spirits had grabbed me by the throat, I could hear them taunting me. A rough male voice whispered into my ear and said, 'Welcome back, bitch. We've been waiting for you!'

As I heard these words, I felt the hairs on the back of my neck go up. I questioned myself about what on earth I was thinking to return to this location. I breathed deeply and tried to remind myself that I was in control and not the ghostly presences who had been hanging around me for the past eighteen months.

The crew asked me what I was feeling and asked me to point out the areas where I had experienced most of the ghostly activity. I pointed to the last cell and told them what greetings I was hearing from the spirits in the area. The others couldn't hear anything but they all admitted that they were feeling a drop in the temperature of the area.

As I approached Cell 7, near the left-hand-side back wall, I could see the spirit who had taunted me eighteen months prior, standing with a smug look on his face in the doorway. He was telling me exactly what he would like to do to me and acting quite tough. I told him that he didn't scare me any more and that I had nothing to fear from him. He began bragging about the others he had got rid of and likened himself once again to the Boston Strangler. I told him that I wasn't interested in his bragging and he just stood angrily in the doorway with a very evil look on his face.

The crew asked me whether I wanted to enter the cell and I told them that I wasn't exactly keen on the idea. But, I thought, if it was a way of possibly ridding myself of the recurring red marks that appeared on my neck, then so be it.

As we entered the cell, the spirit stood firmly in the doorway. What he didn't realise was that we could all walk through him with little resistance. He wasn't too happy with that experience and proceeded to tell me what he wanted to do to all of us.

After entering the cell, all of the fear I had carried with me for so long diminished. The cell didn't feel at all frightening – the feeling I picked up was of confinement, sadness and depression. I could still hear the spirit inhabitant of Cell 7, but he didn't have the same bravado that he had when I first arrived back in the area.

He seemed to mellow but then told me again about the people he had murdered. I again told him that his bragging about what he had done wasn't making an impression on me at all. So he sat down on the bed with his head in his hands. Even though I felt his sadness, I wasn't going to succumb to feeling sorry for this nasty spirit. I left the cell and immediately felt like I had taken back control of my life. This particular experience was a major breakthrough for my sense of self.

Next stop was C wing, which was the area where I had experienced the female spirits of the past. I was greeted by my friend Margaret, who was the spirit who had protected me the last time I was in the jail. I felt relieved in one way that I had met up with her again, yet I felt saddened that she still hadn't progressed into the light. Thankfully, the evil spirit named Therese whom I had encountered last time wasn't anywhere to be found. The clues from the *Scream Test* challenge were still very visible on the walls and I immediately felt like I had travelled back in time to the night I was locked inside the cell. But this time I felt extremely calm and in control. It was as though the more cells I entered, the more I felt composed. It was quite a liberating experience, after feeling so out of control during the filming of the show.

Nothing had changed in the execution cell since my last visit. To the left of it was the cell where I had encountered the tall prisoner with the red hair. He was still there when I approached his cell. He didn't attempt to talk to me; he just stood in the doorway watching me. I asked the prison guide about the history of the cell and he told me that when he was serving time in the prison, a man fitting the description of the spirit I was seeing was a prisoner there.

On entering the execution cell, the same sweet, sickly smell appeared as before; the sense of sadness and despair was extremely heavy in this room.

We then went to an area that I hadn't visited during *Scream Test*, the maximum-security cells in 5 Wing. This section had housed inmates such as Ivan Milat and George Savvas. In 1997, these two prisoners had planned an escape from the jail but were stopped by prison officers. Savvas was found dead in his cell after reportedly hanging himself, the day after the escape was planned for.

We walked down a hallway and, when we reached the end, the door of the cell where George Savvas was found hanged suddenly swung itself completely open, then just as suddenly swung shut. Now, I should explain that the doors in this area are extremely heavy to swing open by yourself, let alone for the door to do so of its own accord.

Some of the crew thought it would be quite funny to be locked inside a cell by themselves for a few minutes. I told them all not to be stupid, but they were grown adults so of course they didn't listen to me. Well, it didn't take too long for some of them to turn a pale shade of grey, and they soon wanted to get the hell out of there. Funny, I'd told them not to play with these types of energies.

We were able to visit the watchtowers only at night, so we had a break from filming and returned after dark. Our plan was also to revisit some of the areas of the jail we had been to during the day, to see what transpired in the dark. The building seemed so much more gloomy and foreboding as we approached it that night.

We experienced quite a few frustrations, such as batteries going flat even though they were fully charged and our lights not working at all. We filmed as much as we could by the light of our torches and the cameras' built-in lights but, to be quite honest, our efforts were in vain. However, when I had the film developed from my still camera, I discovered that I had managed to capture a few images during the day that provided very exciting evidence of ghosts or spirits.

The watchtowers were one of the last areas that we visited and they were still very creepy. I felt like someone was up on one of them looking at me and when I had the photograph developed a hazy image of a spirit appeared in the frame.

We visited some other areas during the night, the chapel being one of them. A number of us sat quietly and the only feeling I received was that of peace and solitude. It didn't feel frightening and for me was probably one of the only areas in the jail where I felt safe. I don't feel it was specifically because of the connection to the church but more that this was a place where the prisoners reflected about what they had done and, in some cases, had a feeling of remorse.

This trip remains one of the hardest things I have ever done, but at the end of the weekend I felt like I had finally faced my demons and regained control of my life. The day afterwards, I was surprised to find that the red marks around my neck had vividly reappeared, but from then on they gradually became fainter whenever they came back, until finally I was rid of them once and for all.

Me at five.

Me at eight with my brother, Michael, and my poppa.

Me at twenty.

Me at forty.

Some of the early photographs I took using a non-digital SLR camera at 400 ASA with a flash at the disused Parramatta Female Orphan School (which became the Rydalmere Insane Asylum). The darkness is due to the windows being boarded up. With my eyes, I could see two little boys sitting in the rafters watching me, but the camera captured something very different. Left: Spirit energy leaving the room. Right: Two photographs of a strange energy that seemed to float down from the ceiling, invisible to the naked eye.

The War Memorial Home at Burnside Homes in North Parramatta, where my mother worked. I had always felt that the tower was haunted, and when I returned to visit the site some years later for a ghost tour I captured the image of a hooded person looking down from the tower. This photograph was also taken with a non-digital SLR camera at 400 ASA with a flash.

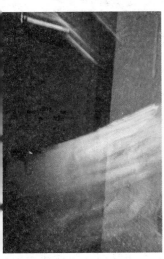

A spirit energy leaving one of the cells at Maitland Gaol. Again, this was taken with a non-digital SLR camera at 400 ASA with a flash.

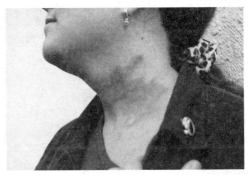

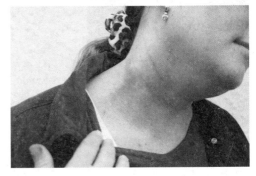

While I was locked in Maitland Gaol, I was attacked by two of the spirit inmates. I felt that I was being strangled. These marks came up a few days later and would reappear whenever I was in the presence of paranormal activity. It took me eighteen months to work up the courage to return to the site to rid myself of the spirits that had followed me home. These photos were taken the day after my return visit.

Forensic investigator Scott Coleman, Detective Steve Rose and me taking a break at the Niamh Maye search area. (Courtesy of Anne Maye)

This photograph of Niamh Maye was taken shortly before she disappeared. She was wearing the same clothes on the day of her disappearance. (Courtesy of Anne Maye)

Left: This is the angel that Niamh guided me to in the Salvation Army store.
Bottom: The view above the search area at Blowering Dam, taken by Niamh's mother, Anne Maye. I was aiming for the triangular area that had been logged.

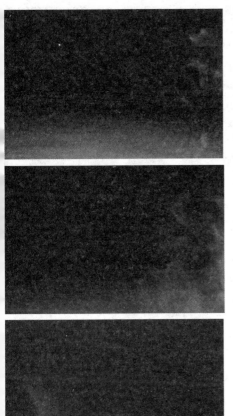

During a ghost tour on Friday 13, I visited the Antill Park Country Golf Club, at Picton, with Rowena Gilbert. While we were walking around the site, I became very drawn to the lower car-park area. I could feel energy building up around us, so I began to take random photographs in the direction I was drawn to. To my surprise, I initially captured a couple of orbs, and over the next round of photographs strange ectoplasm began to show up. The final photo, when lightened, revealed the presence of a ghostly figure. After I took this photograph, my camera batteries went completely dead. (All three photographs were taken on a digital camera at 400 ASA with a flash.)

Orbs joining the tour group in the very haunted, now-disused Redbank Range Tunnel, Picton (also known as the Mushroom Tunnel). This tunnel is renowned for the strange lights that are often seen moving up and down inside it at night. (Taken on a digital camera at 400 ASA with a flash.)

Brendan Thompson wearing his beloved Wests Tigers football gear. (Courtesy of the Thompson family)

A smiling Mitchell Davies. (Courtesy of the Davies family)

Jack Parker and his best mate, Matt Lye. Both boys died in a fatal car accident when they came off the road and hit a tree at Picton. (Courtesy of the Parker and Lye families)

The Claremont Hotel (formerly called the Continental Hotel), Claremont, Western Australia – the last location in which Jane Rimmer was seen alive.

A location at Henderson that I feel could be connected to Sarah Spiers. This area is close to power lines and a power station.

Left: A memorial cross was placed among the arum lilies where Jane Rimmer's remains were found, at Woolcoot Road, Wellard, a southern suburb of Perth.

Right: Ciara Glennon's remains were off a bush track that joined Pipidinny Road, Eglinton, and were obscured by a very large grass tree, which I had seen in my visions.

Power lines running along Pipidinny Road, near where Ciara Glennon was found.

Directly across the road from where Jane Rimmer's remains were found are more power lines. I believe they could be relevant.

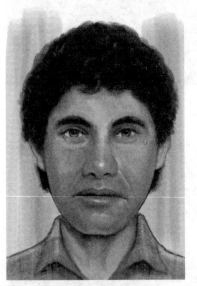

Terry Dunnett's composite images of the man I feel is the Claremont serial killer. The image on the left is how the perpetrator looked at the time of the attacks and the one on the right is how he looks now, both based on the visions I have received. (Supplied and drawn by Terry Dunnett)

Chapter 14

Desperately Seeking Niamh Maye

In 2001 and 2002, I worked with my dear friend Alan Levinson, who owns and runs a company called Haunted Sydney Tours. His tours of Sydney are quite different to most, as the vehicles the tourists are escorted around in are converted Cadillac hearses called Elvira and Morticia. My role was to give readings to each of the passengers during the evening and inform them about the spirits I was picking up in the haunted locations we visited on the tour.

One evening a couple of weeks before Easter in 2002, after returning home from working on a tour, I went to bed and drifted off to sleep, only to have a vision about the hearse Elvira. In the vision, I was sitting in the vehicle's front seat beside Alan and we were stopped at traffic lights. While we waited for the lights to turn green, another hearse drove up and stopped beside us. The strange thing about the other hearse was that it was a convertible and the top was down. During the dream, I thought how unusual it was for a hearse to be a convertible and have its top down, but I supposed that in a dream anything is possible. Due to its top being down, I was given an extremely clear view of its occupants.

Sitting in the front passenger seat was a pretty young woman and in the driver's seat was a man whom I could only describe as cold and frightening. He had black hair, dark eyes, olive or tanned skin and a very dark presence. The young woman looked between seventeen and nineteen years of age and had a lovely, gentle face. She had light-brown, shoulder-length hair and her eyes were hazel-brown. She was of a slight build and was dressed in a T-shirt and cargo pants.

The young woman looked over at me and smiled, and my immediate reaction was a strong sense that she needed to get out of the car and away from the driver. I don't know why I felt this; I just did. The young woman sat in the car beside the man quite oblivious to how I felt about him. Next thing, the hearse drove off at the lights and disappeared in front of us, and that was the last I saw of them.

The vision woke me up. I felt that it wasn't really a dream, that it had really happened. I wondered if it was some sort of message. I took note of their appearances in the vision in case anything came up about them on the news.

To my surprise, two weeks later on the nightly news

there was a story about the disappearance of a young woman by the name of Niamh Maye who was last seen on Easter Saturday in the Batlow area, in country New South Wales. It was reported that Niamh was seen with a man who was driving a hearse.

They showed a police officer speaking about her disappearance at a media conference – it was Detective Gae Crea, whom I had worked with on the backpacker murders. I have enormous respect for Gae as he is one of the first police officers who actually took my visions seriously. I instantly felt that there was some connection between the dream that I'd had and the fact that he was in charge of the case.

A rush of emotions went through me, as I knew immediately when I saw her face on the TV screen that the man in the hearse had killed her. I also realised that when I'd dreamt about the missing woman, she had still been alive. I felt guilt, dread and anger. My immediate thoughts were: *why did I dream about this girl if I couldn't save her? Why didn't I do something about the dream before now? If I had, then maybe she would still be alive.*

Being a medium can be a very rewarding vocation but at times it can be hard to cope with the responsibility of having knowledge but not being able to do anything about it. I have come to realise that I am only the messenger and it is not my place to save every person that I get a vision about. I think some outcomes are predestined – however, that doesn't take away my frustration and pain when I feel that I haven't done enough to help someone in need.

I had to snap myself back to reality and realise that I couldn't hold myself responsible for these things. My next line of attack was to contact the police so I could at least help them to find her. As I had experienced negative police officers in the past, I had reservations about becoming involved in this case and questioned whether I should contact Gae or just let sleeping dogs lie.

It took all of my courage, but I made contact with Gae. He was wonderful and listened to all of my information. He asked me if I was open to speaking with Niamh's parents and, as I felt we had nothing to lose, we set up a time to speak on the phone.

Initially, I felt nervous about speaking with the poor girl's parents. I had concerns about what questions they would ask me and I hoped they would be open to working with someone like myself. My fears were instantly put to rest, as Niamh's parents, Brian and Anne, are the most beautiful, open-minded people.

Anne Maye arranged to send me some personal items of Niamh's to work with. I received two necklaces, one a silver Celtic-type pendant on a leather thong and the other a dainty necklace that had little jewels dangling from it.

The first thing to ascertain was whether Niamh was in fact dead or alive. As soon as I held the jewellery, she appeared in front of me and I could hear her talking to me loud and clear. From this moment on, I knew that my earlier suspicions were correct: she had already passed. I can somehow feel the difference between someone who is dead and someone who is alive when I hold the person's jewellery. A deceased person has a heavier energy or feeling than a living person has, and of course a living person isn't going to stand in front of me in spirit and begin to communicate with me.

Over the next few months, Niamh would make many visits to me, relaying lots of information. In one particular vision, she told me that the perpetrator was moving north, to Queensland. From the scenery I was being shown, I felt that the area was in or around Brisbane. I kept seeing the number 2, which I thought meant two weeks. Niamh showed me him striking again and then told me that if the police weren't quick enough, he would commit suicide.

This vision really upset me, as it meant that after all of the work the police and I had done on this case there was a chance that the murderer might kill himself before he could be caught. I frantically rang up Detective Crea. The police had a 'person of interest' for the case and Gae confirmed that this man had moved to Queensland two weeks prior to our conversation. Unfortunately, as there wasn't enough evidence to charge him for Niamh's disappearance, the New South Wales Police hadn't been able to stop him moving interstate.

The person of interest indeed did reoffend, just as Niamh had shown me in the vision. He was arrested on 18 October 2002 for the bashing and rape of a woman in West End, Brisbane. He wasn't handcuffed while in custody and he broke free from the arresting officers, then jumped from a multi-level car park to his death.

The only positive aspect of this outcome was that he couldn't strike again. The unfortunate side was that only he knew what had happened to Niamh.

*

Niamh came from a large, very close-knit, loving family in Armidale, in northern New South Wales. At the time of her disappearance, she was on a working holiday, picking apples in Batlow, near Tumut, in southern New South Wales. She was working to save money to help pay for her university studies; she had hoped to get a degree and work in film and television.

Niamh was last seen in a hearse with the person of interest leaving a camping ground at Jingellic, where she had been with friends during Easter, to return to Batlow. She had a bus ticket to take her north from Batlow to the train station at Cootamundra. When he was interviewed by New South Wales Police before he committed suicide, the person of interest said that he gave Niamh a lift to Tumut, north of Batlow, and dropped her off on the Gocup road to Gundagai, as she was en route to Sydney and planned to hitch-hike the rest of the way to the train station to save the bus fare. He said she had a train ticket to Sydney and had arranged to meet her sister there for the Easter long weekend.

It took a further twelve months before the police felt that I had provided enough evidence to do a search in an area Niamh had shown me through visions. I was very nervous about the whole thing and I hoped that I wasn't wasting their time. I knew in my heart what I was seeing and hearing, but to actually go and find an area that I had never been to before in my life and identify it from my visions was quite confronting.

I enlisted the help of an old and trusted friend, Donn Groves, who is a clinical hypnotherapist. Donn is very experienced and in the past he had worked with another medium who worked with police in similar circumstances. Donn and I felt that if I went under hypnosis and contacted Niamh, we could try asking her for a description of where she was and how she got there.

The session was very successful. We made contact almost immediately. Niamh was mostly worried about her family and wanted me to relay to them that she hadn't run away. She wanted to let her parents know that she definitely hadn't hitch-hiked, which was reported on the news.

Niamh kept asking me if I could help her to get home, as she needed to be with her mum and dad. I felt that she still wasn't sure she was actually dead. She did show me that she had been murdered and where she was buried, but it was like she was looking at what happened as an observer, not really being part of it.

She showed me that a person she knew had given her a lift in a black hearse. There was a large social group of workers who picked apples at Batlow and this man was a part of that group. He was in fact the man I had seen driving the hearse in my initial vision. She told me that she had worked with him and that she felt sorry for him. He was a bit of an odd bod and had had many family problems. Having a kind and gentle nature, she felt that she should try to save him.

She started to describe surroundings to me. One particular thing she mentioned was that he took her past black-and-white cows in a paddock. Under hypnosis, I could hear the cows mooing in the distance. She also said that she wasn't in the direction that everybody thought she was – she was actually in the opposite direction.

I saw her trying to get out of the car and run away and the perpetrator chasing her. Somehow, he got her back in the car and they drove down into the forest. She told me that they had passed a big electricity substation and then turned right.

I could see a pine forest with many roads leading in various directions. I felt that there was accommodation for the forestry workers near where she now lay. She said that there was a smell of pine needles and a musty, stale, wet smell. She told me that she was very cold and had a constant feeling of being wet. She said that her hands and feet were tied and that she was wrapped up in something blue. I felt that it was her tent, which was also known to be missing.

She said that people riding horses had passed by where she was and that I would know the area by the hoof marks on the ground. She told me there was a dam above the area that she was buried in and that she had been to the spot prior to her death with the perpetrator, on a so-called 'picnic'. Now, she told me, she thought that it was a dry run and that he had her murder planned all along.

She was very angry that she could have been so naive, as she did have gut feelings that there was something dark about this man. She had moments when she felt extremely frightened of him. She said he had a strange obsession with death and that he loved to sleep in the back of the hearse to see what it felt like. He had told her that he fantasised about what it would be like to have a real corpse in there. She told me that his wish had come true as, after he killed her, he had actually placed her in the back of the hearse.

She also told me that since her murder he had returned

to the scene to see if she was still there. She kept telling me that I must look for something that was blue, as it would lead me to her. She said that she was on the edge of a forest and that a triangle would lead the way.

I knew what this meant from one of numerous photos her mother had taken and sent to me. In Niamh's last conversation with her mother before she went missing, she had told her that the man with the hearse had wanted to go to a forested area named Blowering Dam in the next few days for a picnic, but she was reluctant to go. Anne had subsequently gone out there and taken a panoramic photo from a vantage point above the forest. It showed a triangular logged area that was close to a permanent camp for forestry workers. There was a dam right next to this. Niamh told me that she was at the bottom of the triangular area and that I should go nineteen trees across and twelve trees up, and then I would find her body. She said that the forestry trucks would drive past below her location on a road heading off to the left. She said that she would lead me there by me causing an orb to hover above the site when I took a photograph of the area.

She then showed me how the man had killed her: I felt a coldness on my neck and then felt blood running down the back of my throat. I found that I had a difficult time breathing and talking, as I could feel all of this air rushing in through my neck. It felt like my throat had been cut, and my voice became very soft. The only way I could talk was by holding my throat. A friend of mine, Dion Isaacson, was filming the hypnosis session. He told me afterwards that at this point I clutched my throat quite tightly and by doing so I got my hand caught up with the lapel microphone I had on. He said that for some time all he could hear was my pulse, almost deafening him through the earphones he was wearing.

Niamh gave me a few other details and then I could feel her energy withdrawing. I felt extremely drained. When I experience the feeling of what happened to a victim, I do feel the pain they went through, but it isn't quite as severe as if it actually happened to me. It is more like a psychic impression that fades after I break contact.

Dion made a copy of the video of the hypnosis session for the police. This was to give them an idea of the information that Niamh had passed on, to help us work out where to focus our search.

When I travelled to Tumut the following week and met Detective Steve Rose, he admitted to me that he was very sceptical about what I was trying to do but said that he would keep an open mind and that it was worth a try. Charmaine, a girlfriend from Sydney, accompanied me for moral support during my stay in Tumut. Dion also drove down, to document anything that might come to light during our search. Niamh's parents also joined us for the search and it was a privilege to finally meet these wonderful, loving people in person. All of our previous work had been done over the phone, with the Mayes being in Armidale and me in Sydney.

During our initial meeting, I felt a pang of guilt in my heart that I hadn't saved their daughter for them. I told them this and they said that some things just weren't meant to be. Brian and Anne are very spiritual people and they said that their faith keeps them going and gives them hope.

I felt that the focus of our search should be to get to the triangular logged area of Blowering Dam that Anne had photographed from above. The police gave me a large map and asked me which direction we should travel in first. I told them I wanted to head south, as Niamh was telling me that was where we would see the black-and-white cows.

Eight of us set off on the search for Niamh. I travelled with Charmaine and police officers Steve, Gae and Mick in the police four-wheel drive. Dion drove down in his van with his camera equipment and Brian and Anne drove down in their own vehicle.

When we got into the police four-wheel drive and began driving, we went some distance up the road and passed the black-and-white cows, like I had indicated. Steve commented that this was the only area in the district that had this breed of cow.

As we drove along, Niamh would tell me to say 'Go right here' or 'Turn left'. We followed her directions and ended up going deep into the forest.

We got to the place where her mum had taken the photo, with the triangular section below us. The problem was that there had been very heavy rain a few days earlier and the roadway had collapsed, so we had to look for an alternative access. Having never been here before in my life, I again asked Niamh which direction to take. The road she directed us down went past an electricity substation – which was familiar to me from some of my visions – and she said we had to turn right when we reached it. I felt that my visions and connection to Niamh had really been validated.

We descended the mountain and arrived at the triangular section of forest. There was a forestry camp below us, plus logging trucks passing below and to the left. My spirits soared, as I truly felt that this was it. I was going to be able to help Niamh return home to her parents.

When we stopped the vehicle where Niamh had indicated, I ran from the car and quickly began to count the pine trees in order to pinpoint her position. I hurriedly looked to see if I could spot any blue items. All I could find were blue bird feathers. *Maybe this is what I am looking for?* I wondered.

I truly felt that Niamh was with me, but I also had a dreadful feeling that the perpetrator was watching. As we searched and the day wore on, I could hear the perpetrator telling me that I would never find her and that she belonged to him.

I relayed this fear to the police and Steve produced a photograph of Niamh and their person of interest, who called himself Jack, in homage to the actor Jack Nicholson. It was taken only about half a kilometre down the road on which we were all standing. It seemed we were really close to finding this beautiful lost girl.

We searched for the rest of the day in the area I had pinpointed and, yes, we found the proof of horse hoof prints. There was also a dam next to where we were searching. The forestry camp was below us and the area that I felt Niamh could be buried in was covered in pine needles and smelt damp and wet.

My heart sank as the sun began to set and her body still had not been found. We decided to call it a day. I felt a total failure. How could I be so wrong? How could so many details from my visions be so close to reality, yet we were still so far from finding her? The police officers were supportive and said not to worry, we would try again tomorrow.

We again went to the site the next day and searched but still didn't find any sign of Niamh or her belongings. The whole time I was in the forest, I could hear the evil laughing of Jack. He kept telling me that he had won and that I would never succeed.

On the approach of darkness, we had to call it a day. This time, I had to return home to my family in Sydney. I was so despondent that I had failed.

A week later, Detective Steve Rose contacted me and said that our search had produced their first lead in the case. A witness, a forestry worker, had come forward after hearing about our search. He confirmed that the hearse had been sighted near the electricity substation and that it had turned right from there, like Niamh had told me.

I hadn't found Niamh, yet valuable information had come out of the search.

*

A few nights after returning home, my computer in the upstairs lounge room turned itself on. My husband awoke and told me off for leaving the computer on when I went to bed. Only thing was, I hadn't even used the computer. In fact, I hadn't used this particular computer for months.

I got up and turned it off and went back to bed, only to be awoken by the computer booting up again about half an hour later. Again, I got up and turned the computer off, and, yes, you guessed it, the computer turned itself on again. I got tired of turning the stupid thing off, so I unplugged it from the power point and returned to bed, vowing to sort the problem out in the morning.

The next day, I plugged the computer back in and it started doing the same thing.

Niamh started to communicate with me. She told me that it was her way of getting my attention. She was letting me know she wanted to talk by turning on the computer. I rang her mum, Anne, and told her what was happening. She offhandedly asked what type of computer it was. I told her it was a Macintosh LC 630. Anne said that Niamh had the model before that one and thought that she may have been responsible for turning my computer on.

After I got off the phone, I asked Niamh to turn the computer on if she wanted to make contact with me. I waited three or four minutes and then, to my surprise, the computer turned itself on. I even got my video camera out to film this happening, and again it happened.

I began asking her questions and said that she could answer yes by turning the computer on or no by leaving it off. To my amazement, she did answer my questions.

Over the next six weeks, she kept turning on the computer to get my attention. It was unsettling when I was asleep and she would turn it on to get my attention in the middle of the night. I had to tell her that I was going to unplug it at night and plug it back in during the day so she could communicate with me then. Sometimes, spirits aren't aware whether it is night or day, so they are not governed by our earthly time limits.

*

I spoke further with Niamh's family and the police, and we decided to do one more search for her body in the same location, in case I had missed anything – only this time a team of volunteer police officers from across the extensive Cootamundra Local Area Command would conduct the search. The photo that Steve had shown me of Niamh with Jack – which was found amongst Jack's possessions – was taken in Jack's hearse on the road adjacent to this site, so it must have had some significance.

I travelled to Tumut with Niamh's parents and on the way we witnessed the most beautiful sun shower that I have ever seen in my life. It was pouring down with rain while the sun was shining brightly and the brightest double rainbow that any of us had ever seen appeared over the valley below us. We all hoped and prayed that this was a sign we were going to find her.

After arriving at Tumut, we met up with two of Niamh's sisters and we all went down to the forest in the afternoon to see if Niamh could help us locate her remains. My video camera hadn't been working for some time before this trip, but I had an overwhelming feeling that I needed to take it with me into the forest. When we arrived at the location, my video camera started working again, and continued to for the whole time we were there. We stayed until dark and I also took a number of still photos of the area we would search the following morning. In a number of the photographs, an orb appeared above the spot I felt most drawn to, so I was hopeful that this was a sign from Niamh that we would find her there.

Niamh's family had brought a special remembrance candle with her name on it to the forest. Before we left, we had a little ceremony for her; Niamh's parents lit the candle and we all spoke with her, asking her to help us find her so she could return home. It was an extremely emotional moment and I truly felt that she was with us. My video camera abruptly stopped working again when the ceremony was over.

We all left the forest and returned back to town to our motel. I went to bed and desperately tried to pick up any extra details from Niamh for the search in the morning. I felt I was trying too hard, as I couldn't get anything. I had a very sleepless night and my head was filled with images of Jack's face.

The morning of the search was very nerve-racking for me. I met the twenty police officers from the search team. I could see some strange looks coming my way when I was introduced to them as a psychic/medium. All of the officers were very nice to me but I could feel that they were questioning what they were doing working with someone like me.

I travelled down to the location with Steve Rose and the police's local area commander, Stan Wall. The search location was approximately half an hour's drive out of town. The weather was fine and there was a coolness in the air.

When we arrived at the location, an officer named Scott

Coleman from the Forensics Unit joined us. This really brought home to me that we could be finding Niamh's remains. Momentarily, I wondered how I would cope if Niamh was recovered while I was present.

The search area was covered in large blackberry bushes. The team had to hack their way through them before they could even begin to search the forest floor. It was very hard going for the team but they never gave up.

The officers searched in a grid pattern, an arm's length away from each other, back and forth in the area that I pinpointed. I felt that Niamh could be wrapped in her tent, so we were hoping that one of the metal eyelets on the tent might pinpoint her location. One of the officers had a metal detector and he got a positive reading close to where I thought Niamh was. There was an air of expectation while he searched to find what had set the detector off. Unfortunately, it was only a piece of old fencing wire.

During the day, Anne and I both felt that Jack was around us, silently watching and laughing at us. The location we were searching didn't have any amenities, so if nature called the closest toilets were in the forestry camp, about half a kilometre away. I made the trek down the dirt road to the camp on my own. Nobody was at the camp at the time, but after entering the toilet block I heard the door open behind me. I could hear loud, heavy footsteps following me in and I got a feeling that I was being watched by an invisible intruder.

It was only after I mentioned how uncomfortable I felt about using the toilets down at the camp that Anne relayed she had heard the same loud footsteps and experienced the same feeling of not being alone when she had gone down there.

As the day drew on, it became clear that the police search party wouldn't find anything. Jack's energy was very strong at the camp and he was enjoying every minute of the search failing, because he is the one who knows where Niamh is. I became very worried that I was wasting everyone's time. I felt heartbroken that I had let Niamh and her family down.

Niamh's parents were wonderful. They said that at least we had covered another area and that, little by little, they were making the search area smaller. All the police officers were very understanding. They said at least we had tried. I appreciated the way they treated me with respect.

From that day on, I have vowed that I will never give up in my hope of finding Niamh.

*

I still often think about Niamh Maye. At times, it haunts me that I dreamt about her before she was murdered and I didn't prevent it. I hope and pray that one day I will find her, so she can be taken home.

It is very hard to work so closely on a case such as this because it feels as though this person was part of my family. I have such direct contact that I end up feeling everyone else's pain. I feel that this has to happen, though, as otherwise I wouldn't be able to have the empathy needed to connect with the victim's spirit.

I have shared this story with you as it shows what it is really like to be a medium. There are a lot of TV programs in which a medium or psychic solves every case. Believe me, it is not as easy as it looks. In my opinion, my job is to assist the police and to fill in the missing gaps where leads and clues may have gone cold. I would love to be able to solve the entire case but I think that would be an unrealistic expectation, not to mention egotistical on my part.

The police have told me that I have given them some amazing insights and clues connected to this case, so I will just have to be happy that at least in some small way I have assisted them.

I still keep in contact with the Maye family and I feel privileged to have been a part of their lives. Anne has told me that Niamh's favourite bird was the blue wren, so whenever I see one I am reminded of her. Sometimes, I wonder if it is her spirit coming to visit.

One day at work, I went across the road to the fruit market to buy some yoghurt for lunch and on crossing the street I felt myself being guided to walk into a Salvation Army shop that I needed to pass to get to the market.

Bewildered, I found myself standing inside the door of the shop, drawn to some little angels that were hanging on a metal tree. There were about thirty of them and they all had names printed on them. On the bottom branch, there was only one little angel, hanging there all by itself. On closer inspection, I saw it had the name Niamh printed across the front of it. Now, I have to say that Niamh is not the most common name. The fact that this little angel was there with Niamh's name on it indicated to me that she was close by. Of course, I bought the angel and that night I rang Anne and told her what had happened. Anne began to laugh, as she said that she had been thinking of me and was going to give me a ring. We both feel that, even though Niamh has passed, she is always close by.

Every Easter is a sad time, though, as it was on Easter Saturday that Niamh disappeared. I try to look at it from the perspective that as each Easter passes it brings me closer to being able to find her and bring her home.

I will never give up on finding Niamh as long as I draw breath.

Chapter 15

Advancements in Spirit Photography

I was continuing my endeavours to capture evidence of spirits or ghosts in photographs, only now I was beginning to realise how helpful the new digital photography could be. I had bought my first digital camera and was capturing amazing spirit images like never before.

The rural township of Picton, approximately eighty kilometres south-west of Sydney, is one place where I had incredible spirit-photography experiences. The town is well known for its history. Major Henry Colden Antill was given the first land grant in the area in 1821. In 1844, Antill subdivided his estate, making it possible for the town of Picton to be founded on the north side of Stonequarry Creek. Picton is a very picturesque town with many historical buildings and churches, and it is now becoming better known for its ghosts.

Liz Vincent is the well-known resident historian in Picton. She has written books about Picton's past and regularly runs ghost tours of the town. My first trip to Picton was on one of Liz Vincent's tours. It took place on the unlucky date of Friday 13 September in 2002. I thought that if anything spooky was going to happen, odds were that this was the night. And boy, what a night to remember it was.

I had arranged to meet friend and fellow paranormal researcher and photographer Rowena Gilbert in the car park near St Mark's Anglican, where the tour began. Liz's tour was fully booked, with a group consisting of sixty-eight people. On arrival, we boarded a bus that would take us to our first destination and the first course of a dinner that would stretch throughout the evening. Each course of the meal was to be at a different haunted location, which was a bit of fun.

The first course was at the haunted post office. I personally didn't feel anything at this location. (I did enjoy the pumpkin soup, though!) After we all finished, we were back on the bus, heading to our next location, the Antill family homestead, now part of the Antill Park Country Golf Club.

The beautiful homestead, set on the picturesque rolling greens just out of Picton, proved to be one of the most interesting places I have visited. I have since returned there on many occasions and I am never disappointed by what transpires.

On this particular night, we had our main course and

then we were given time to wander around the homestead to see if we felt anything. Rowena and I went upstairs and checked out all of the rooms. One in particular I couldn't enter and a man of about my height, a hundred and sixty-five centimetres, appeared abruptly at the doorway and told me I wasn't welcome in his office. This gentleman was dressed in military uniform and I believe that he was one of the members of the Antill family who had once lived at the homestead.

The room next to this was also extremely interesting, for when I entered it I could see a young woman sitting at the window staring out into the distance. This young lady was dressed in period clothes of a long, floral dress and a bonnet. She had tears rolling down her face and she told me she was waiting for her love to come home. She told me about a carriage accident on the long, sprawling driveway leading down from the homestead to the road. The lovely woman told me that two young boys were killed in the accident and that she died of a broken heart.

When I spoke to Liz Vincent about the spirits I met in the house, she said that the military gentleman was commonly seen on the top floor and was well known for ordering people out of the room or abruptly shutting the door in people's faces. Also, the lovely, forlorn young woman was a common sight to guests at the property. Liz had heard stories about a carriage accident but nothing had ever been confirmed.

As the top floor of the homestead was becoming too overcrowded with others in the tour group, Rowena and I decided to investigate the grounds around the house. We were walking around in the courtyard when I felt myself being pulled to the side of the property adjacent to the car park. I couldn't explain why I was being drawn there; a voice in my head was asking me to hurry up and start taking photographs.

Rowena and I quickly began taking photos in the moonlit car park, not really aiming at anything. I just stood and kept photographing directly in front of me and then slightly to the side.

Well, whoever it was who had told me to take the photos didn't let me down: I began to capture photographs of orbs. Because we were using digital cameras, we were able to view the orbs in our shots straight away, rather than having to wait to have film developed, as in the past. The longer we stood there, the more the energies gathered. It was as if every spirit in the area knew we were there to capture their images.

I find it extremely interesting that a number of people can all be standing side by side taking photographs at the same time and yet not all photographers will capture the same spirit image. I have had numerous experiences when I or someone with me may capture an image and the rest of the group gets no result. I like to think that the spirits have to allow us to take their photograph, and when they do it is a privilege. It seems to be up to them whom they show themselves to.

It was quite interesting that Rowena could take a shot at the exact same time as me and not have any orbs in frame when my photograph was bursting with them. The next minute, I didn't capture anything and Rowena did. It was just amazing to witness the phenomenon that was taking place in an empty car park in Picton.

I began to talk to the spirits around us and asked them to make their presence known even more clearly by manifesting themselves in a different form. The next shot I took showed a curling, swirling vapour with an orange tinge on the right-hand side of us. I showed Rowena and we couldn't contain our excitement with what I had captured. The next couple of shots turned back into orbs and then suddenly a bigger swirling vapour appeared, only this time it was blue in colour. Again, the vapour disappeared and the orbs reappeared. About ten shots later, the best image I have captured to date on digital camera appeared, this time on our right-hand side: it looked like the outline of a vapour in the shape of a person waving at us.

When I showed Rowena what I had on camera, she was amazed. I went to take more photographs and then my camera batteries went dead. I quickly changed the batteries before the spirits disappeared but the fresh batteries wouldn't work. Luckily, Rowena's camera batteries were still charged. She continued to take photographs and did capture a lot of orbs but there were no more appearances from the vapours.

In the distance, we could hear Liz letting the group know that it was time to go. She asked everyone to board the bus to our next destination, the very haunted Redbank Range Tunnel.

The Redbank Range Tunnel is a train tunnel that has not been used since 1919, when the railway route changed. Local woman Emily Bollard was struck by a train and killed in the tunnel in 1916 – there are questions as to whether it was an accident or suicide – and there have also been reports of other suicides in the tunnel in the past.

Liz escorted us to the halfway point of the tunnel. We were asked to stand quietly with our torches turned off, plunging us into complete darkness, and we were lucky enough to have Emily and friends make their presence known.

Along the roof of the tunnel, a blue shining light was moving extremely quickly towards the group. The light flitted from side to side and onto the tunnel walls. Just as it seemed to be on top of us, it disappeared. It then began to shine further back along the roof and turned on and off intermittently as if it was a strobe.

The night was completely still, with not even the slightest of breezes in the air. Suddenly, a rush of wind came down the tunnel, similar to what you would experience if you were waiting for a train in an underground station. The air had a different kind of a smell to it, too hard to put into words.

Just as quickly as the wind had sprung up, it died down. Even though I am psychic, I do question things, but on this occasion I cannot dispute the fact that I did see Emily Bollard at the far end of the tunnel, dressed in a period skirt with a button-up blouse, a shawl around her shoulders and a bonnet on her head. I didn't say anything to the rest of the group apart from Rowena, and nearly everyone in the group verified seeing the same thing that I did. Emily didn't seem to be walking – it was as though she was floating towards us, slightly above ground level.

Another spirit joined her. He seemed to be a much darker and more sinister person and was dressed in what looked like a black cape with a hood. As he neared her, it seemed he was blocking her from getting too close to us.

When this dark spirit appeared, some of the group started to panic. One poor young woman left the group and ran back to the bus, terrified at what she was seeing. I wasn't scared but I have to say that the dark spirit had terrible energy and I sure wouldn't want to be in the tunnel by myself, night or day, as it seemed to be his domain.

Liz soon told the group it was time to leave the tunnel and move on to the next location, which was called Ghost Bridge. Ghost Bridge was given its name due to three terrible deaths. A man hanged himself from the bridge, a railway employee cut his throat there and a woman, Eliza Jane Whitehall, was accidentally shot there while on a rabbit-shooting expedition with friends.

As soon as we disembarked the bus, the temperature abruptly dropped and the energy became electric. Everyone in the group began taking photos; there were camera flashes going off everywhere. Luckily, my camera recovered from the earlier battery problems and I had just enough power left to take eight more photographs. Every photograph had an image of an orb in it, which was very exciting.

Nearly everyone in the group who took a photo captured an image with orbs in it that night. At least half of the members in the group could see a misty image of a person standing on the railway line under the bridge, until a goods train came thundering along and the image abruptly disappeared. The bridge certainly lived up to its name.

Our next destination was Razorback Range, where a number of murders and accidents have taken place in the past. Bushranger John Lynch is said to have committed a number of murders along the road and then discarded his victims. The road is also well known for its unexplained fatalities.

After that, the group moved on to dessert but I was extremely tired by this time and knew that I had a one-and-a-half-hour drive home, so I told Rowena that I was calling it a day. I thought that the tour had been extremely eventful and probably one of the most exciting nights I have had with paranormal activity, except for my *Scream Test* experience at Maitland Gaol. I was surprised, though, when I discovered that my ghostly visitors hadn't finished with me yet.

Like me, Rowena had driven by herself and she had to drive back in the opposite direction to me, as she was staying at a friend's in Parramatta. Before leaving, we had decided that we would put our mobile phones on hands-free in case we needed to contact each other. Since we were both travelling alone at night, it seemed like a good idea.

We followed each other along the road out of Picton until Rowena's exit to Parramatta came up and she turned off. I drove about another kilometre down the road and things began to get very scary.

Suddenly, from the left-hand side, two very large German shepherds came out of nowhere up ahead of my car. One was all black and the other was black and tan. They were very vicious and they ran straight out in front of me. I swerved to miss them and then I heard a loud thump. I was too frightened to get out of the car in case they attacked me but I stopped and looked in my rear-vision mirror, only to find that both of the dogs had mysteriously vanished. There wasn't even any blood on the road. I quickly started up the car, just wanting to get home in one piece.

Feeling extremely shaken, I quickly rang Rowena and told her what had just happened. I asked her to stay talking to me on the phone until I got onto the highway, as the road I was travelling on became increasingly darker the further I got out of town.

Driving further and further into the darkness, I began to cross the last bridge before my turn-off onto the highway to Sydney. Suddenly, I saw a man standing in the middle of the road across the bridge. As I got closer to him, I realised that he was transparent blue. I was really freaking out by this stage. I swerved to miss him but it was too late and he jumped onto the bonnet of my car. All I could see was his face looking at me.

Luckily, I had Rowena still on the phone, so I could describe everything that was happening to me. The man turned into a blue mist and came through the windscreen of my car. At the time, I was playing the Red Hot Chili Peppers' song 'By the Way' on my car stereo, and a strange voice started coming through the speakers. Then someone behind me began to grab me by the back of the neck.

I really didn't think I was going to survive the night, so I asked Rowena to call my home in the morning in case I never made it back alive. This may sound a little extreme, but under the circumstances I was really feeling quite panicked. I called in my spirit guide Running Horse and asked him to protect me and to keep me safe. As soon as I did this, my ghostly passenger disappeared. (Pity I didn't think to do this sooner.)

Finally, I reached the turn-off to Sydney and an overwhelming feeling of calmness came over me. I could hear Running Horse telling me that I was now safe and I just needed to concentrate on driving home.

I did arrive home in one piece, of course, as you are now reading my story. I rang Rowena to let her know that I still had a pulse and we joked about what a weird night we had just experienced. I couldn't wait to put the photos on my computer to see exactly what I had captured. They remain some of my best to date.

I also rang Liz Vincent and told her of my ghostly visitors on the road leading out of Picton. Liz told me that the ghost dogs had been spotted on a number of occasions and her husband, John, had had a similar experience, but he saw only the black-and-tan German shepherd. The dog ran out at him and he hit it with his car, but when he got out to see if the dog was all right, it had completely disappeared. I have since been on other ghost tours at Picton and a number of other people have verified having the same experience.

As for the ghost man on the bridge, apparently a local man had been murdered on it and his body thrown off into the water below. That explained why his ghost was hanging around, but I still don't know why he jumped into my car and began grabbing me by the neck.

I have to say I always get quite nervous when I have to drive along that stretch of road. The sign showing that the highway turn-off is up ahead can never come quickly enough.

On another tour to Picton, my experience in the tunnel was even more amazing. The hooded man decided that he was going to target me for the night and he wouldn't leave me alone. Unbeknown to me, a lovely lady named Jackie who was on the tour took some photographs of me. One of the photos shows lights around the back of my head and the hooded figure floating above me.

At the end of the night, I was having a chat in the car park with Jackie and her family before we left to go home. We got caught up talking, as Jackie's grandmother, who is in spirit, wanted to give the family some messages.

By the time we finished chatting, there was only Jackie's car and mine left in the now-darkened car park. Jackie and her family got into the car and got ready to drive off, when my car's central locking started to misbehave. Every time I clicked to open the car, it relocked itself. I then tried to use the key, to no avail. I found myself standing alone in the car park, with Jackie and her family driving up the road.

I quickly ran after them and got them to stop and help me. After about twenty minutes of the car relocking itself, I just lost it and I told the #$%#$%% ghosts to stop playing around and open up my car so I could go home. Instantly, the doors unlocked and I was allowed to get in.

We all started to laugh, saying I should have been more forceful in the first place. Thankfully, my drive home was quite uneventful and I made it home safely.

*

Of all of the places I have visited on ghost tours, Picton has to be the most haunted, and it has produced some of my best photographic evidence of spirits. Another place of note is Callan Park, in the Sydney suburb of

221

Lilyfield, where the Callan Park Hospital for the Insane was established in 1878.

Part of the old hospital complex became the now-disused Rozelle Hospital, while the Kirkbride Block, built in 1885 and used to house and treat inmates until 1994, now forms the centrepiece for the Sydney College of the Arts. I have visited the Sydney College of the Arts on a number of occasions and have been very excited by some of the paranormal experiences that have taken place.

Initially, I was contacted by a lovely lady named Alyssa Simone, who was studying spirit photography at the college. Alyssa had heard about my own journey of spirit photography and she thought that I might be interested in doing an investigation at the college.

I met Alyssa at the college with my friend Thor, who was part of the university camera crew that accompanied me to the Parramatta Female Orphan School and Maitland Gaol. Also joining us was Robb Tilley, who is a parapsychologist and fellow researcher.

Underneath the college's print-media rooms are the now-disused underground cells that once housed some of the most violent and mentally disturbed male patients of the hospital. If you weren't told of the existence of these tunnels and cells, you would never suspect their existence. When you enter the stairwell, the area looks innocent enough, yet there is an eerie atmosphere, a strange smell begins to envelop you and you can't help but feel that you are transcending time and entering a past era. When you arrive at the bottom step, you are overwhelmed with the barrenness of the area. Lying before you is a long corridor and on the right-hand side there are a number of cells where the patients would have been held. There are small barred windows on the left-hand side near the roof that let in minimal light and ventilation. This area is reminiscent of something you would see in an Indiana Jones or Tomb Raider movie.

At the end, on the left-hand side, the corridor opens out into a large room, with a small iron stairway leading up to a door on the right. There is no running water or sewerage in the tunnels and cells, and buckets would have been used to bring in fresh water and remove waste. Some parts of the chamber are in total darkness.

I first visited during winter and the area was icy cold and damp. The energy in there was very oppressive. I felt short of breath and extremely dehydrated. I imagine the feelings I was picking up were similar to what the patients would have experienced. There were many different energies lurking around down in the chambers and I could feel the strength and the anger from some of the occupants. I felt that I was being watched from every corner and could feel draughts of air flying past me, close to my face. At times, I could smell bad breath and body odour wafting around the room, even though in real time none of the group smelt like that. (I hope not, anyway!)

I began to take photographs with a Sony 2.1 megapixel digital camera, and my feeling of not being alone proved to be correct. I began capturing hundreds of tiny orbs in the photographs; the area was bursting with activity. The orbs were moving extremely quickly in and out of frame. One moment, there were lots of orbs and then suddenly there were none.

Alyssa took us through a corridor off to the left. For some reason, the energy didn't seem so heavy in this area, perhaps because it had lighting. I felt that the spirits were all hiding in the dark. I took a number of photographs in this section and, as I expected, didn't capture any spirit images.

We left this area and decided to visit another tunnel area that led off from the main corridor, on the right-hand side. This area was absolutely pitch black, as there was no electricity. One corridor led to a blocked-off stairwell and the other door led off to two sandstone archways that were tunnels to nowhere. Both of these areas had very heavy energy. Alyssa told us that the patients were led into them during the day to walk around and exercise. I was quite uneasy, as it felt like people were touching me on the face and hands. I took some photographs and again captured a lot of orbs.

I met a young spirit named Thomas. Thomas was a pale and frail-looking young man, about sixteen to eighteen years old. He told me that he was sent to the hospital because he had suffered from polio and both of his legs were deformed and twisted to one side. He said that his mother was a wealthy woman of society and the family lived in a very grand two-storey house in Balmain. His mother was the talk of the town and she would host parties and entertain, he said. She was embarrassed about her son's deformities, so she had him locked up in the hospital to get him out of the way. Thomas was a beautiful young man with big, blue, gentle eyes and brown wavy hair. The sadness in his eyes was too much to bear. Being a mother myself, I couldn't understand how anyone could abandon their child, no matter what they had wrong with them. It was distressing to see that Thomas had to drag his body and two twisted legs along the ground to get around.

I tried to explain to him that he was now in the spirit world and that he no longer needed to stay in such an awful place. I told him about the light and that, when he crossed over, his body would be healed and he wouldn't have any problems with his legs.

He seemed happy with my explanation and agreed that he didn't want to stay underground any longer. Alyssa, Thor, Robb and I stood in a circle, held hands and tried to imagine a beautiful beam of light coming in through the middle of the roof. The more we concentrated on the light, the more the energy in the area grew. Robb and I both spoke to Thomas and told him that he was free to go into spirit. At first, he seemed a little frightened to move towards the light, but once he dragged himself forward and was surrounded by it, the smile on his face was unmistakeable.

As the area is so haunted, a lot of the other spirits began to come close because they too could see the light. We spoke to all of them and told them that they were all welcome to go, and one after another the lost spirits of the past vanished into the light. The energy in the room was electric and the feeling of gratitude we were picking up from the ghost patients was deeply moving. After about ten minutes, all of the spirits who had decided to leave had transcended to the other side. This moment was very humbling; we all felt that in some small way we may have made a difference to the poor lost souls who had been trapped in time.

We all felt speechless and drained afterwards and thought it was time to leave the underground chambers and get some light around ourselves in the form of sunshine and fresh air. I have always known how beautiful it is to stand in the sunlight, hear the birds chirp and feel the wind on my face – but, until this point, I hadn't really thought about what it would be like to have these simple pleasures taken away. I deeply felt for the patients who had missed out on all of the things that we take for granted.

Our next location was known as The Female Ward, Ward 10, which was in a three-storey building on the northern side of the hospital grounds. The bottom floor is now used to house the maintenance personnel's tools and the rest of the building is left abandoned. On entering the ground floor, I took a number of photographs and the camera soon showed that we had company. There were lots of orbs in the shots, mostly hiding behind the tools and work equipment.

Alyssa guided us up to the second floor. While I was walking up the stairs, I unfortunately met an unpleasant man from the past who nicknamed himself 'Cattle Prod'. The reason was obvious, as he kept hitting the right side of my head with what looked and felt like a cattle prod. This man was brutally cruel and I could see that the female patients were absolutely terrified of him. He attacked me a number of times during my visit to the ward and, by the end of the day, I felt that I was getting a migraine headache from all of the zaps.

We progressed up to the second floor, where all except one of the windows were boarded up. The ward was empty apart from a few bits of plaster that had fallen from the ceiling and an abandoned chair at the very back of the room below the only open window.

I found it quite different to the underground area. The energy was certainly different: it was easy to see that the vibrations there were only female. I felt quite strange, as though I had been transported to the past. I began to see the room full of activity: I could see patients wandering around in white gowns, their hair dishevelled and their faces blank. Some of them were wearing straitjackets. Suddenly, I felt that these women knew I could see them. They all disappeared from the room and I was back in the present, in the abandoned ward.

When I walked into the bath and shower room, I had to look twice as I could see a person lying in the bathtub with her wrists cut. When I had a second glance, the female in the bath was gone.

I picked up a lot of fear in the bathroom and I am not sure if it was because the patients were mistreated there or because patients had committed suicide in the area. I didn't get any spirit images on my still camera, so I was extremely surprised by the spirit activity that showed up on my video camera.

I saw some little balls of light shooting out of the walls and from the abandoned shower stalls. It seemed to me that the spirits hid inside the shower stalls when they were frightened, just like they may have done when they were alive.

I left the bathroom and began to take photographs facing towards the one window that wasn't boarded up. The whole area was completely full of orbs; I would have to say I have never captured so many orbs in the one frame as I did there. I felt that all of the ladies were gathering to see what we were doing.

Robb and I thought it would be interesting to communicate with the ladies. We asked them to change the shape of the orbs that appeared on the camera if they could understand what we were saying. I quickly took a photograph with Robb standing in the middle of frame and the orbs were all around him, perfectly round in shape. I told them that I was going to take another shot and if at all possible could they change their shape into something that would indicate their understanding. I quickly took another shot and, to my surprise, the spirits proved to me that they understood: the orbs had all turned into a diamond shape. I thanked the ladies for their help and then took another shot, in which they had all turned back into their familiar round shape once more.

This was quite a breakthrough, as the orbs had shown that they were an intelligent life force and they were able to interact with us. I actually felt that they were excited I could see them and finally communicate with them.

I was very thankful for Alyssa drawing my attention to such an amazing historical and haunted site. My next plan was to return as soon as possible, better equipped with video and infrared camera equipment, to see if I could capture even better proof of spirit.

*

Upon returning from the location, I felt as if I had brought a few friends home with me. I kept having visions of the female patients in the ward and I had a strong feeling that the ladies were very excited about my plan to return. The ladies asked me to bring with me a box of chocolates and a bunch of roses. They also asked me to bring some candles, as they were sick and tired of being in the dark.

It took me a couple of weeks to get the film equipment organised. A company called Production Toys, owned by Roger Bailey, graciously lent us most of what we needed for the day, including an infrared lens to attach to the video camera. I was joined by a friend of mine, Jackson Baker, along with one of his colleagues, Luke, who was a cameraman, and Leanne, a film and video student.

We first headed to the second floor of Ward 10, where I set up a little table with a candle, the flowers and the box of chocolates. We all went into the shower area to see if anything came up on camera. However, the female spirits seemed to be too frightened with all of us in the small room at once. I asked if the others would mind if I stayed in the shower area by myself with the infrared camera while they investigated the other areas of the ward.

Once I was left by myself, the spirits started to show up on the camera. I could also smell a strange kind of odour in the air that I often associate with spirit activity when I am filming. It is quite an earthy smell, almost like the smell of mould and wet dirt mixed together.

With my eyes, I couldn't see a thing, as the room was pitch black, but I could certainly feel that there were whooshes of air passing close to my face and swirling around me. While looking through the viewfinder, I became extremely excited, as the orbs were showing up on the video camera clearer than I had ever witnessed before. One giant orb mysteriously came out of the tiled wall, moved quite boldly towards me and then disappeared out through the opposite wall. A tiny little orb that I could only explain as looking like a flittering butterfly came from the furthest shower door. This energy seemed to be very shy and fragile, while the bigger orb showed itself off as though it was a spotlight.

The flittering orb soon disappeared and the large showy orb made another appearance. Once the rest of the spirits became used to me being in the room, it turned into an orb fest. There were orbs flying in and out of the shower doors, coming in and out of the walls and swiftly passing by me.

As my friend Jackson came in to see how things were progressing, the spirits suddenly all went past me and out into the main ward area. I spoke to them and told them that Jackson was with me and that he wasn't going to harm them. Immediately, the orbs turned around and began to come back into the room.

Suddenly, I began to hear the spirits speaking to me and my head quickly filled with names and visions. It was an extremely exciting moment when the orbs actually trusted me enough to communicate with me in more than one form.

A spirit named Mary Logan began to communicate with me the strongest. She told me that she was only nineteen years of age when she was admitted to the ward. She had been sent there because she had post-natal depression after giving birth to a stillborn child. This poor young woman couldn't understand why her family had had her locked away when she didn't really have anything wrong with her. All she wanted was to be back home with her family and loved ones, not locked up in a place for crazy people.

Another spirit, named Elizabeth, soon began to communicate with me. She told me that her husband was having an affair and he wanted her out of the way, so she was got rid of by being locked up in the ward.

Soon, the spirits were communicating with me so rapidly that I couldn't keep up with them all. One of the ladies told me that she had passed due to being pushed down the stairs by Cattle Prod when she was going down to the bottom floor. She told me that she had fractured her skull. I took this as a warning to be careful while going up and down the stairs.

I told the spirits that I was going up to the top floor by myself with the camera, if any of them wished to join me. I quickly went up to the top floor and positioned the camera facing towards the door. I took one of the candles with me, as the top floor is in complete and utter darkness.

After about five minutes, the spirits began to arrive. Through the viewfinder on the camera it looked as if it was snowing, as there were more orbs than I have ever seen in my life. I felt like every spirit in the building had come up to see what I was doing.

I sat up there for about thirty minutes in silence and just observed the spirits, which were visible both with the viewfinder and without. As they became more used to me being in the ward, they began to come closer and fly around me. Some of them shone brighter than others; some lingered, while others just quickly flew past me.

Jackson came up to join me. The spirits were used to him by now, so his arrival didn't disturb them very much.

We were both happily watching all of the spirit activity on the camera when suddenly they all began flying out the door and going back down to the floor below.

I took note of what the time was: twelve midday. We went to get some lunch and on the way I went and spoke to the facility manager, Christine, to ask her if she knew what time the patients would have had lunch. Christine said that lunch was served at midday, so this explained the mass exodus from the top floor. It seemed that the spirits thought it was lunchtime. I find that spirits are creatures of habit, just like the living. The funniest thing about this was that spirits don't need to eat any more.

After lunch, I couldn't wait to get back inside to see if the spirits were still willing to show up on camera. Luckily, they were. They were flying in and out of the room, showing up very well on the camera. By this time, they were so used to our presence that they seemed to be having a competition for who could show off the most.

We had a camera tripod set up in one corner and hanging from it was a cable. The spirits seemed to be having great fun flying in and around the tripod – one even decided to do a loop-the-loop around the cable. I told them that we had forgotten to mention their chocolates, which were waiting for them on the table. I said that if they followed me over there, they could have their gift.

As we walked up to the table, I took a couple of still photographs and I wasn't at all surprised to see an image of an orb hovering above the chocolate box. I guess that whether we are dead or alive, the taste for chocolate never diminishes. When we went to the table, I began to film with the infrared camera and captured a large number of the orbs flying up to the chocolates.

Now, I should explain that of course the spirits couldn't literally eat the chocolates for themselves, so the crew and I had the arduous task of eating the chocolates for them. In doing so, the orbs just had to touch us to get their taste of the chocolate. Luke and Leanne, the student, began to eat the chocolates first, while Jackson and I filmed. As they took each bite, an orb would swiftly fly up, touch them and fly off. This was a very interesting phenomenon; it seemed that the spirits were savouring every bite as much as the crew.

It didn't take too long for the whole box of Cadbury's Roses to disappear. After the final chocolate was gone, the spirit activity completely died down. I felt I should have brought a bigger box, as the spirits seemed to have enjoyed their first taste of chocolate in some time.

It was the most exciting day I have ever had when it comes to filming and photographing spirits. I have since returned to this site on numerous occasions, once with the team from Channel Seven's Sunday *Sunrise* program, and I have never been disappointed. Each time I return to the site, I feel I am welcomed back by the spirits as though I am a long-lost friend.

*

For those of you wishing to try spirit photography, the good thing is that just about any type of camera will do the job (although digital photography is the cheapest and will give you immediate results) and you don't have to be psychic. A video camera with night vision is an advantage, as is using a flash on your camera, day or night, as the spirits are drawn to the flash and will reflect off it.

My first digital camera was only 2.1 megapixels and the results from it are still some of my best. The lower resolution tends to pick up spirit images better. The only problem with the resolution being quite low is that the images don't blow up perfectly, as they become pixelated.

I feel it can be a bit hit and miss doing spirit photography, but the more practice you have, the better you will become. Don't always wait until you see something in front of you to begin shooting. If the area feels different – say, colder or more scary than expected – then you should take a photograph.

Haunted locations will usually reward you with spirit photography, but don't expect to get a photograph of a spirit every time. Sometimes, I am on a ghost tour and am seeing lots of activity around me. However, when I take a picture I don't capture any images at all. Just be patient (I have found that it takes three to five minutes for the spirits to gather and know that you're there) and have your camera batteries charged, with at least a couple of spares. When the spirits want to appear, they will show themselves to the person whom they want to photograph them. In the past, a group of us have taken photographs yet only one or two of the group have captured the image. Sometimes, the energy will alternate between cameras. Remember, spirits were living beings before they passed. If you are nice to them and ask them to show themselves, then they usually will oblige.

I find that windy nights or nights when there is a thunderstorm can be most fruitful, as the spirits seem to be drawn to the electrical energy around them.

At weddings or family gatherings, if you would like to have proof that a deceased loved one is present, ask them to show up on film. You may be surprised by what you see. Always listen to your children or children close to you. If they tell you that Grandma or Grandpop is visiting, grab the camera and take a shot. As I have said, children are most open to spirit up to around ten years of age.

Over the years, I have taken thousands of photographs in haunted locations, and one thing I have discovered is that it is better if you and your team wear dark colours, as it is easier to identify the spirits against a black or dark background. As I have also said, it is a fallacy that spirits only appear at night. When you think about it, a spirit or ghost is trapped in a time frame of history, so why would they only appear during the night? From my own experiences, spirits seem to go about their business just like they would if they were alive – that's why they become trapped. The poor spirits just don't realise that they are actually dead.

Don't be surprised if what you see with your eyes is very different to what you capture on camera. I have on occasions seen a very clear image of a person yet the camera has captured only the image of a moving energy that looked like a see-through tube of light.

Most importantly, always white light yourself before you begin to interact with the spirit world. If you take this simple precaution, spirits won't follow you home or attach themselves to you. To do this, all you need to do is imagine a great big bubble of white light surrounding you, or imagine turning a light on above your head that surrounds your whole body. I also use the shower: when I turn the shower on, I imagine that the water is showering me with white light to use as a force field for protection.

Chapter 16

Sensing Murder

In 2004, I was sent a renewal for membership to the Psychics Association. The funny thing was, I wasn't even a member at that time. The thing I noticed most was a bright-red piece of paper included with the paperwork. It was a leaflet asking for psychics and/or mediums to audition for a TV program that would involve working on unsolved police cases – or what are known as cold cases. I felt that this was a sign from spirit that I needed to audition.

I rang the number the following morning and told the receptionist that I was interested in auditioning. When I told her my name, she sounded very excited and said she would need to transfer me. She put me through to one of the producers, who asked me whether or not I returned my phone calls. I was bemused by her question, until she explained that in fact they had been trying to contact me the previous week to see if I was interested in auditioning. I had changed mobile providers and my message bank hadn't been working, so I had not received any of their calls.

I realised how spirit must have intervened, because if I hadn't received the Psychics Association renewal with the leaflet inside it, I probably would have missed out on the opportunity altogether.

The following day, I met producers Rhonda Byrne – of *The Secret* fame – and Drew Herriot, and did an audition in which I was given a skull ring and two black-and-white photographs and was asked to relay what I felt with each item. I received a phone call a couple of days later: I had been accepted as part of the program. I was told that I was chosen from over a hundred psychics in Australia.

For each episode of *Sensing Murder*, I would have two days of filming, the first in a studio and the second at locations associated with the crime. I would not be given any information about the case by the crew at any time and it was only when I had finished filming that I would be told the history behind the case.

Two weeks later, I was on a plane bound for Melbourne to film the first episode. Firstly, I was asked to sit before a camera and I was given a photograph of a woman in her early twenties with brown, wavy, shoulder-length hair and very big, blue eyes. She looked very happy in the photograph and she had a carefree air about her. She was standing on what looked like a jetty, with yachts and boats in the background.

Lisa, one of the producers, asked me what feelings I was picking up from holding the photograph. Once I relaxed, I began to feel that the person I was looking at was no longer alive. I could actually feel her presence right beside me and then I began to see her with my eyes.

I started to hear motorcycles and felt that I was watching a bike race. I then saw fairy penguins and felt that I was crossing over a bridge to get to an island. I recognised the location as Phillip Island, off the coast of Victoria, as I had been there on a weekend away eighteen years earlier. Phillip Island is very well known for its yearly motorcycle Grand Prix Race, so the motorbike sound helped give me another clue to the location.

I was given an audio cassette to hold and then Lisa asked me to put on headphones to listen to the voices on the tape. I could hear two females talking. They were telling a friend who was overseas that they had made the recording to tell her what they'd been up to while she was away. I felt the blue-eyed woman in the photograph was one of the female voices on the tape. She had a very cheeky, lively feel about her and at the time the tape had been recorded it seemed like she didn't have a care in the world.

I started to see a triangle; I felt that it related to a love triangle. My next psychic vision was of the victim and a female friend of hers riding horses in a paddock adjoining a beach. The impression I was picking up was that this young woman was a happy, fun-loving person who had lots of friends and was extremely popular. I could see a man with brown wavy hair, blue-green eyes and a nice smile, around a hundred and eighty centimetres tall and with broad shoulders. I got the impression that this man was the young woman's boyfriend.

Next, I was handed a black-and-white photograph of a woman who was in her thirties, with dark straight hair with a fringe; she was wearing glasses. I didn't like the feel of this woman. At first, I couldn't tell if she was dead or alive. Then I saw her standing beside the other woman and I knew that she also was dead.

When I tuned in to the woman wearing glasses, I became very aware of her worry for her children. I could see two little boys. One of the boys was about two or three years of age and the other was between four and six. I could also see a house on a property back from the road. The driveway leading up to the house was quite long and was flanked by some large trees.

This woman's energy seemed to feel quite controlling and manipulative. I felt that she was very angry and could be quite nasty, and that she didn't like the other, younger woman at all. The woman with glasses was quite old-fashioned looking and she seemed to worry more about her children than her appearance. I didn't feel that this woman was a happy person in life, although on the surface everything looked to be just perfect. The woman gave me the impression that things in her life were out of control and she was extremely distressed by not being able to sort them out. I felt that this was the other woman involved in the love triangle that I was seeing.

I could also see a dirt road and hear gravel crunching. It sounded like a car was being driven over gravel and I could see a driveway leading off to a house. I could see a car that looked like an old Kingswood with the rounded tail lights, similar to the type that was used as a taxi in the mid-eighties. I knew from the distinctive sound the car made as it idled that it had a twin exhaust.

I could see that the property was set back on the high side of the road. I felt wind on my face and smelt sea air. I was given the impression that this property could be close to a beach or a coastal area. I could also hear voices and felt like there was a party going on. I felt that whoever lived at this house owned a dog, as I could hear one barking in the background. I was suddenly at the back of the house and I could see and hear a screen door banging.

I saw a butch-looking woman who seemed to be very jealous of the victim. I felt that this masculine woman had it in for her. But I could see that the young woman was quite oblivious to this situation.

Lisa asked me what I thought the murder weapon was. I told her that I felt it was a knife and that there had been multiple stab wounds. It looked like a frenzied attack and I could see blood everywhere. I also felt as though my throat was cut. The visions I was picking up were absolutely horrific; I felt at a loss to think that one human being could do this to another.

I got a strong feeling that the person who killed the young woman was used to slaughtering animals. I could hear snippets of conversation and I could hear the words 'Killing her was like leading a lamb to the slaughter'. I felt that it was a male who killed the young woman, but I saw that the older woman and another man were witnesses to the attack.

I believed that the young woman knew the attackers,

which made it even more personal. I could see that her dog didn't attack the perpetrators, which again gave me the impression that the victim knew them. I could see that the back screen door was unlocked and the perpetrators just went straight in.

There seemed to be some type of family involvement, as I kept hearing the words 'Keep it in the family' and 'Blood is thicker than water'. I could hear the perpetrators say that they needed to protect the family and they needed to stick together.

I could see that when the attack began the young woman put up a big fight and tried to get away. I could also see that the older woman was later attacked and murdered.

I had a sudden vision of what looked like a place called Seal Rocks, which is located down a dead-end road on Phillip Island. I could see the older woman arguing with the two men who were present at the young woman's murder. I felt that the older woman was hit from behind with a blunt object; it looked like a rock or a piece of wood. The men seemingly had the intention of dumping her body at Seal Rocks, as it is well known for the white pointer sharks that feed there. I could see that it was low tide, though, so they weren't able to dump her body as they had planned.

I could see that the men panicked and needed to work out how to dispose of the woman's body quite quickly. I then could feel my head aching severely, as if part of my skull had been crushed in.

I then saw that the second victim was taken to a property with lots of black-and-white cows in the paddock. Near a barn or milking shed to the left-hand side of the property, she was wrapped up in a tarp or some type of canvas material. I then saw a big pit that already had dead animals' remains in it, at the back part of the property. It was near some dense scrub that looked like tea-tree bushes and I felt that the back of the property was right on the coastline or rocks. I felt that it was hard to access this property from the back and I saw that there were no roads leading to the property from this side. The rocks at the back of the property were similar to the black-brown jagged rocks at Seal Rocks.

I saw the older woman being dropped into the pit, still wrapped in the tarp, then I saw other animals' remains put on top of her, to cover up her murder.

After about an hour of working with the photographs, I was told that I would be taken to the location of the murder early in the morning.

The next morning, I was taken by car to an unknown destination. I was certain that Phillip Island was the place we were headed. We drove for about an hour and then the Phillip Island sign appeared and I knew that my visions were correct. I was driven to a number of locations on the island, but it wasn't until we reached the third one that I felt a strong connection. We drove up a gravel road, stopped at the bottom of a slight rise and I was asked what direction I felt I needed to go in and what psychic impressions I was receiving.

I was excited to get out of the car as hearing gravel crunching under the wheels had brought back a flood of the visions I had received the previous day. I thought, *Thank God, I am finally picking up something.* I was drawn up the hill. It was like I was being pulled by some strange force.

I could smell the salt air and I could feel the wind hitting my face. I could see paddocks below me with two horses grazing and there was a beach adjoining the paddocks, just like where I had seen the two girls riding in an earlier vision. I felt that I was very close to the house I had seen the day before in the visions, where I had felt the young woman was murdered.

I got to the top of the hill and was compelled to stop. To my left, there were paddocks leading down to the beach, which was about one or two kilometres away, and to my right was a driveway leading up to a house.

When I looked at the front of the house, I felt that something was wrong. I knew I was at the right place, but the house looked different to my visions. I realised that it had been renovated and the front of the house was unrecognisable. It was like someone was trying to hide the horror that had taken place there.

Suddenly, I was transported back to the night of the party I had seen in my visions and it was like I was watching a scene from a movie. The visions were coming thick and fast and I could see the young woman's face. I felt as if she was beckoning me up the driveway to the back of the house. She looked so sad and fragile and she wanted me to see what had happened. Unfortunately, the victim's parents didn't want to take part in the filming, so we weren't allowed to go onto the property or inside the house.

The young woman showed me a triangle again and then showed me the woman with the glasses. I once again saw the man with brown wavy hair as also being part of the triangle. Now, it all seemed to gel: I felt that he could be the husband of the woman with the glasses, and that the young woman had a crush on this man or they were having an affair.

The crew then took me to a dirt road where there was a sign pointing to Seal Rocks. We proceeded about halfway down the road, stopped and I was asked to get out.

Bingo, I thought to myself. This was the area I had seen in my vision. We were parked out the front of a house and in the adjoining paddock there were black-and-white cows grazing. The house looked very familiar to me and it had big trees in front of it, near the road. Suddenly, a vision flooded in of the woman with the glasses. I asked the crew if I could go down the road a bit further so I could stand above the Seal Rocks area. Drew said that there wasn't enough time and that they didn't think there was a need. I felt quite disappointed, as I knew that there was definitely a connection.

The woman with the glasses began to show me that she had been taken down the hill to Seal Rocks and that was where the argument and, subsequently, her murder took place.

As this vision ended, I became very drawn to the house I was in front of. The woman with the glasses showed me that this property was her home. She showed me herself being a normal mum, playing with her two little boys. I got the impression that the family still lived at this property and that they were well known on the island. I could hear the same motorcycle sounds that I had heard in my vision. I soon realised that the area where we were standing backed on to the rear of the Phillip Island motorcycle track. At the time we were there, some of the motorcyclists were doing lap practice.

The cows in the paddock started to moo, which got my attention, and I felt that there was a connection to the cows in my visions from the day before. In the distance, on the left-hand side of the woman's property, I could see a large shed. I felt that her body was buried down towards the back of the property, past the shed. Again, I wasn't given access to the property, as the family declined to be involved in the series.

After filming my impressions in front of the second property, I was told it was time to return to Sydney. I was disappointed in some ways, as I felt I needed more time at the location to pick up more clues. The format for *Sensing Murder* was quite fixed, so there were many limitations that we needed to abide by when we filmed. I find from past experiences of working on police cases that information begins to flow after I have been to the location. I find I need a couple of days to gather my thoughts and write down all of my information. It sometimes takes time for it to build, so to speak. I felt that if we had had more time, we could have unlocked even more clues.

On the journey to the airport, Lisa filled me in on the details of the case. The young woman in the photograph was Elizabeth (Beth) Barnard, whose bloodied body was found at her parents' property on Phillip Island in September 1986. Beth, who was twenty-three years old at the time, was found with her throat cut and the letter 'A' carved into her chest. It is alleged that Vivienne Cameron, the older woman with glasses, was the killer.

The allegation is that, on the night of Beth's murder, Vivienne accused her husband, Fergus, of having an affair with Beth. Vivienne and Fergus agreed to separate immediately. Vivienne was to move to Melbourne, leaving Fergus and the two children behind at their home on Phillip Island. Prior to leaving the island that night, Vivienne drove Fergus to his sister's house. Vivienne has never been seen again. Early the following morning, Beth Barnard's body was found. Vivienne's abandoned car was discovered near the San Remo Bridge on the island. An extensive land and sea search, lasting for three days, didn't find any trace of Vivienne's body.

I now fully understood the connection to the penguins, as Lisa told me that Beth worked for Fergus Cameron at the Penguin Parade. And there was further significance to the sound of motorcycles: Fergus was the owner of the track at the time of Beth's death.

*

A few weeks later, I received a phone call telling me that the next case would again be down in Victoria.

I was first given a violin in a case to hold and asked to report my feelings. I felt that this person was quite musical and she had an absolute love for her violin. She may have studied two different instruments at the same time. I began to see awards to do with her music and I wondered if she had won a scholarship or some form of accolade in her field.

From working with this item, I began to see a young woman in her early twenties. She had blonde to light-brown wavy hair and bright-blue eyes. I felt that this woman was quite an active person and she had a lovely, soft energy. I also felt that the person who owned the item was deceased.

The second item I was handed was a gold chain with a locket on it. I kept picking up an 'S' sound to do with her name. I was told by my guide Running Horse that her name was an old-fashioned one like Suzanne or Sandra.

I began to see that she had been on her way somewhere and didn't reach her final destination. Then she told me that she had been snatched.

The area she went missing from was quite deserted. I was given the impression that she was heading towards her car but something happened when she got there. She told me that she was worried about her bag and keys and then she showed me a red car. An image of another car with three or four people in it then appeared in my mind. When she was nearing her red car, this other car stopped her and asked for directions.

She showed me that there was a struggle at her car and I felt that there was blood left at the scene. I felt strongly that she was taken away from there to another location.

I could see a bridge and trees close to the area where the struggle had taken place. The bridge was like a railway overpass at a train station. A map began to appear in my mind. I was shown Melbourne and then I was shown I needed to leave Melbourne and head south, towards the coast, not far from the beach.

I felt that the attack was extremely brutal and the victim was stabbed many times, on the right side, chest and middle rib area.

I could see another car at the time of the attack that was a cream-yellow colour. I felt that a gang was somehow involved with the case as I kept being given the name the

Brat Pack. I could also see a skinny, weedy-looking man with a pointy nose and long, thin face. His eyes were dark, his hair was brown and he had a rat's tail. I kept getting the nicknames of Rat, The Rat, Rat Tail.

The confusing thing with the visions was that I was seeing a gang in one instance but when I saw the victim being attacked I only ever saw one perpetrator.

I felt that the perpetrator lived close to the location where the attack had taken place. My feeling was that he hated women, that he stalked his victims, had problems at home and was a bit of a misfit. I felt that he did manual labour or was a tradesman. I kept being shown his hands and felt that he was extremely strong and he enjoyed every moment of the attack.

It seemed that he had been a peeping Tom during his childhood and then had found it wasn't gratifying enough. He was around a hundred and eighty centimetres tall and had a heavy build with broad shoulders. He had brown hair. I saw that this person could become very frightening, as a darkness would come over him and nothing could stop him when he was in this state. I felt that he could have worn dark-coloured clothing and a balaclava when he attacked.

He loved the powerful feeling when he attacked and killed his victims; he tended to get off on their fear. The more the victim struggled, the more he was turned on. I felt that he was in jail at the time we were filming *Sensing Murder*. The message I got was that he was a habitual offender who should never be released into the public again as he could not be rehabilitated. I felt that he had attacked four or five victims.

The next impression I got was of a creek or river and I could see very tall reeds like you would find at the water's edge. I could also see ducks floating on the waterway and there was a bridge over a road that had a flood sign on it. I felt that when it rained, the water would cover the bridge, which backed onto a green house. I could hear dogs barking and I felt that these dogs belonged to one of the properties backing on to the river.

I was being told that the dogs went berserk the night that the young woman's body was dumped. I could see that the reeds were so thick and overgrown that a body could easily be concealed amongst them and it would have been possible for the perpetrator to walk on them without getting wet.

I could also see a water tower or water tank near the waterway. I felt that there were properties on one side of the waterway but not the other. As the scrubland was so thick on the other side, not many people would frequent the area. The waterway was not all that wide and was more like marshland.

The following morning, I was driven to a train station and the crew asked me to get on a train, which was heading south. Just after getting on it, I could feel the victim's presence. As we passed a station, Seaford, she made me feel like I needed to look out the window. I saw a small creek running alongside the train track. The creek was lined with the reeds she had shown me in my visions and I felt that there was certainly some significance to the creek, or it was a sign.

The crew told me to get off at Kananook station. I felt quite confused, as the young woman kept telling me that she was in the opposite direction. She kept flashing me the reeds and saying, 'That is where you will find me.' I relayed this message to the crew but they insisted I get off the train.

I disembarked and went upstairs to an overhead railway bridge above the station. The area was the exact place I had seen in my earlier visions. Suddenly, I felt like the victim had hold of my hand and she was pulling me towards the car park.

I told the crew that the victim was pulling me to the back of the railway car park and descended the steps. When I got to the bottom, I was handed a brown, sandblasted leather jacket that I was told belonged to the victim.

The victim then pulled me to the back of the car park and suddenly made me stop. She said that this was where her car had been parked. I got the feeling that I wanted to look on the ground for any signs of blood. I knew that there would be nothing to see in real time, as the clothing the victim was wearing in the visions dated the incident at least a decade into the past. However, psychically I could see a rather large pool of blood in front of me.

I stood at the scene and suddenly everything grew dark; I was transported back to the night the victim was attacked and I began to see what happened through her eyes. I was suddenly alone in a darkened, isolated car park. I could see a parked red car, with a few other cars still remaining in the car park. I felt an overwhelming sense of nervousness, that I needed to hurry to get to the car. I didn't like the feeling of being there all alone. I could hear a car coming through the car-park entrance and the lights were shining on me. The car slowed down and stopped. I could see that there were three or four people inside.

Since this experience, I have always questioned whether the people in the car were responsible for the young woman's murder. My feeling is that the gang were cruising for the night in the car park but they left her alone. I feel that the solitary man whom I had seen stalking her in the back area of the car park was the actual perpetrator.

Next stop was the victim's house. When I arrived there, I felt that her family had moved out a long time ago. On entering her old bedroom, I picked up a large amount of energy. In real time, I was standing in a room that was painted peach in colour and had vertical blinds. Then I was suddenly transported back in time and I was now looking through lacy curtains and pink-mauve walls. I was very drawn to look out the back window of the bedroom. I could see that the property backed on to a school's playing field.

Abruptly, I was standing in the bedroom and it was night. I could see that the victim was getting changed in her bedroom and I could also see a man dressed in black with a balaclava over his face. I got the feeling of being watched and could see the man watching the young woman from the school grounds. The perpetrator gave me the impression that he was a voyeur and he could have been known for being a peeping Tom.

After filming at the house, I was taken to a place half a kilometre down the same street, a bike path called Nat's Track. It is named after a seventeen-year-old woman named Natalie Russell who was brutally murdered after school one day in 1993. Natalie was riding her bike home on the track when she was attacked; fortunately, her killer was caught and is serving time.

I was told by the crew that I was able to stand at the entrance to the track to see if I picked up any vibes but there wouldn't be enough time for me to walk its whole length. I felt disappointed but I also understood the time constraints with filming a TV program.

While standing at the entrance to the track, I could strongly feel the energy of Natalie Russell. I could feel her beckoning me to walk with her to where she was murdered. I told her that I wouldn't be able to come with her. Lisa told me that it was time to leave and then the strangest thing happened.

Our car had been parked up on the footpath as the road was extremely busy. As Lisa tried to drive the car forward and down over the kerb, one of the wheels became wedged in a drainage hole on the kerb. To top it all off, the chassis of the car became stuck on the concrete block covering the drain.

I thought to myself how apt it was that this had happened. I felt that spirit was ensuring that I did get the time I needed to walk along the track. Lisa would have to wait a half an hour for other crew members, who were filming in another location, to come and help get the car out of the drain.

I knew little about Natalie's death, and certainly not the exact location, but when I got halfway down the track the most horrible feeling came over me. I felt that something very sinister had taken place on the other side of the cyclone fence, in the dense bushes. I felt that this was the site of Natalie's murder. I was taken back to the time that she was murdered. It was like a little movie playing in my head, showing me the events leading to her death. The image of Natalie's murderer that appeared before me was the same as the man I had seen at Kananook station. I felt that he had murdered both Natalie and the victim of our cold case.

It was only when I returned from walking along the track that Lisa told me the full story of what had happened to Natalie and that the person who murdered her is a man named Paul Denyer. He is currently serving a life sentence for the murder of three women, including Natalie, and the assault of a fourth victim who managed to escape. Hearing this, I felt that Paul Denyer could well have been the person responsible for our cold-case victim's murder, as in my earlier visions I saw that he had attacked four or five victims. From the visions I picked up at Nat's track of Natalie's death, the manner in which she was murdered was very similar to that of the murder of the cold-case victim. The only difference was that Natalie's body had been recovered.

I felt that the young woman whose cold case I was working on was Denyer's first victim. He was careful about the way he disposed of her body as he didn't want to get caught. But when he didn't get much publicity for her killing, he decided to be more brazen the next time he struck. He enjoyed the limelight and the fear factor. I felt that he almost wanted to get caught so that he could brag about what he had done to his victims.

Once the crew had got the car out of the drainage ditch, we drove to the airport so I could catch my flight home.

But we had time for just one more location on the way.

That morning, one of the crew, Gerrard, who was our sound recordist, had slept in and he'd had to meet us at Kananook train station instead of travelling with the rest of the crew. On the way, he had taken a wrong turn and arrived at the place that I had been describing the previous day in my interview – the reedy creek or river. He had excitedly told me that he thought he had found the spot that I was describing.

When we arrived at the location, I knew Gerrard was right. There was a low-lying bridge that crossed over a creek; there was a green house and a barking dog. The reeds were all along the river and they were so thick that you were able to walk on them without getting wet. There were ducks swimming up and down the creek. And the area was a little isolated, except for the houses backing on to the water.

When I got out of the car, I definitely felt that this was the spot that could have been used to dispose of the victim's body. We ran out of time, though, and I didn't get to look further down the river to see whether or not there was a water tower of some kind. One of the producers, Paul, thought that the police may have searched the location previously but said that if the site was viable we might be able to get the police to return with sniffer dogs.

I left Melbourne feeling relieved that we may have made a breakthrough in the case, only to be disappointed later on when I heard that the producers didn't search the site any further.

I had been right about the victim's name being an old-fashioned one beginning with 'S', but it wasn't Suzanne or

Sandra – it was Sarah. On 11 July 1990, Sarah MacDiarmid, who was twenty-three years old, caught a train from Richmond to Kananook after playing tennis with her friends at Flinders Park. Sarah got off the train about 10.20 pm and has never been seen since. It is believed that Sarah was abducted as she walked to her red 1978 Honda Civic, which was parked in the Kananook station car park. Sarah's body has never been found. An inquest was held into her death in May 1996. The coroner, Iain West, found that Sarah was dead through foul play. Nobody has been charged with her murder.

*

I had told the *Sensing Murder* producers that I was willing to go under hypnosis if need be. It was arranged that a forensic hypnotherapist who was used by the Victoria Police would be working with me for the next case.

Before I went under hypnosis, I was given three photographs, each showing a different schoolgirl. It felt to me like two of the girls were still alive. Unfortunately, though, when I held one of the photographs, of a very pretty Asian girl, I instantly felt a connection to her and I could hear her talking loud and clear. This gave me the impression that she was deceased.

She told me that she was worried about her parents and showed me that she had been taken away from her family. I could see that the perpetrator had also abducted the other two girls, and I saw that each of the victims was bound, gagged and blindfolded. I felt that the murder victim had been tied to a chair with her hands behind her back.

The perpetrator seemed to have some very strange mannerisms and I felt that he was obsessive-compulsive. I kept getting the feeling that he was a clean freak and when I tuned in to him I kept feeling that I wanted to wash my hands. I kept picking up the vision of him washing his hands under the tap.

I could see that the perpetrator was a teacher, or posed as a teacher, and that was how he was able to pick his victims. I saw that he had a black leather briefcase with what looked like exam papers inside, perhaps maths. I could see that sometimes this man wore a hat and a trench-coat-style jacket. I also felt that he disguised his appearance. At times, he could have a beard, moustache or glasses. I felt that one of his victims was murdered and the others weren't because she, unlike the other two girls, could identify him.

It seemed like the perpetrator had something wrong with one of his legs; he had a distinctive stride or limp. He was quite a tall man, of a slight-to-medium build, with broad shoulders. He had green-grey eyes that had a cold hardness about them. His hair was straight and salt-and-pepper, cut in a short, neat style. His face was long and he had drawn cheeks and small, thin lips. He could have had a gold filling in the tooth to the left of his front teeth. I felt at the time I worked on the case that he would be in his late fifties to mid-sixties.

I kept seeing electricity transformer towers; they backed on to the house that he lived in. I felt that there could be vacant land or a paddock behind his house, that the house was very close to a railway line and he lived alone. The inside of his house was extremely neat. It was an older-style fibro or weatherboard place.

We decided it was now time for me to go under hypnosis to see if I could pick up any further clues.

Hypnosis is an interesting thing to experience. While being hypnotised, I have always felt that I am in a relaxed state of mind, yet I am in another world. The experience isn't frightening; it is almost like going off into a semi-dream state.

I lay down on a couch and the hypnotherapist asked me to close my eyes and listen to his voice. He led me through a number of exercises, including a guided meditation. After that, he asked me to make contact with the victim. The victim told me that her name was Karmein. When I go under hypnosis in this type of case, I actually become the victim, so I feel and experience what they are experiencing. I picked up Karmein's pain and fear.

Karmein began sobbing because she couldn't find her mum. She was extremely sad that her family didn't know what had happened to her. She was also worried about her sisters and she wanted to make sure that they were okay. Karmein then showed me that her parents were no longer together since her death and she blamed herself for their break-up.

The hypnotherapist asked for her to concentrate on what had happened to her and asked her for a description of the perpetrator. The new information I picked up was that he was a person who wouldn't stand out if you passed him in the street; he was a very quiet, private person who kept very much to himself. I didn't feel that he was the type who'd be very friendly with the neighbours and I doubted that he had ever been married or in a relationship. I felt that he cared for his elderly mother before she passed and hadn't had much time to himself apart from going to work.

The hypnotherapist then asked Karmein, through me, to go to the front of his house and describe it. It was a light-green weatherboard or fibro house built in the 1950s or 1960s and it had an old-fashioned wire-and-timber front fence. If you were standing out the front, you would see a gate in the centre and another on the right that opened onto a driveway, which led to a garage. The front door was in the centre of the house and there were three steps leading up to a small landing in front of it. There was a window to the left that would be looking into the lounge–dining area and, on the right, a smaller window looking into the front bedroom. Between the house and the garage was a gate with a distinct zigzag pattern on it, leading out into the backyard. The garage had a light-green roller door. The house had a chimney on the left-hand side with two round, terracotta chimney pots on the top. The roof was tiled in a terracotta colour.

Karmein was then asked to go inside the house and describe the floor plan and the furniture, so we went through the front door and into the lounge–dining room. The furniture was quite old but in immaculate condition. The lounge was brown vinyl, the dining table was rectangular with white patterned laminex on top and chrome aluminium trim. Around it were chrome and vinyl mustard-brown chairs from the 1950s or 1960s. There was a fireplace with a sandstone mantelpiece.

Leading off the lounge–dining room was the kitchen, which had a large window with cafe-style curtains looking out over the backyard and the power lines. The palings on the back fence were quite widely spread apart and the land at the back of the property gently sloped away.

On the right side of the house was the first bedroom and next to it was a small bathroom; the bath and pedestal basin were light-green porcelain. Beside the bathroom was the second bedroom, where the curtains seemed to be drawn shut. I felt that this was where the perpetrator kept his victims tied to a chair. There was a large timber wardrobe and a bed with a light-green chenille bedspread. There was a lamp sitting on a bedside table. The home almost felt sterile, as it seemed to be so meticulously kept.

I could see that the perpetrator brought the victims in through a side door in the garage and the back door of the house so that he wouldn't be seen.

While under hypnosis, I felt that there was another victim, whom the police didn't realise was linked to the same perpetrator. Another young girl, named Jessica, kept coming through. She said that she was with Karmein and that he had murdered her as well. She was older than Karmein and I felt she was a runaway. She worked at a local convenience store that the perpetrator frequented.

The hypnotist asked Jessica and Karmein if they knew how they got to the perpetrator's home and Jessica gave a very good description of the roads that he had taken them on.

Karmein said that she was then tied up and blindfolded. I could hear a clicking sound in the background and I got the impression that he took photographs of the victims. It sounded like a Polaroid camera because I could hear the photo pop out. I also felt that he filmed the girls and may have kept locks of their hair as trophies. Karmein said that she put up a big fight and tried to get away but unfortunately, in the struggle, she got her blindfold off. As she was now able to identify the perpetrator, he killed her. I felt that she was smothered with a pillow, as I could feel something over her face.

I could see that Karmein's body had been taken to another location after her death. Again, I was shown vacant land and overhead transformer towers.

After an hour and a half, I was brought out of the hypnosis. I couldn't stop shaking and I was icy to the bone.

In the morning, I was taken to the Melbourne suburb of Templestowe. We were parked out the front of a house and I felt that this was where Karmein had once lived. I could instantly tell that her family didn't live there any more. Karmein told me her mum feared that the perpetrator may come back for her sisters, so after her parents broke up they had moved away. I felt the fear and terror that the family must have experienced on the night of Karmein's disappearance. In cases like this, it is hard to return to the site of the victim's death or disappearance because the trauma is trapped at the location psychically.

Karmein's home was on a corner and I was given a strong impression that the perpetrator had sat in his car and waited in the dark, watching the property. I felt that he had targeted Karmein and knew the movements of the family quite well.

The property was brick and had two big wrought-iron gates at the front. I felt that they were left open the night the perpetrator struck. I could see that he broke into the house when the parents were not at home. There were two other children in the house but he wanted only Karmein; the other two girls were tied up and locked in the wardrobe.

After filming at Karmein's home, I was taken to an industrial suburb on the outskirts of Melbourne called Thomastown. On the way, we passed houses very similar to what I had seen under hypnosis. The homes were the right vintage and they had weatherboard cladding. Most of them had chimneys and a number of them had the terracotta chimney pots I had also noted when I was hypnotised.

When we arrived at the site in Thomastown, I couldn't help but feel how lonely and deserted it was. It backed on to a large number of factories and a large paddock with a small, winding creek. The entire site had large overhead electricity towers.

While walking in this area, I felt that Karmein's spirit was close. I could see the young girl in a white nightie and I felt that her remains had been found nearby. I felt that she was already dead when she was taken to the location.

The strange thing was that though I had seen that Karmein was suffocated or strangled at the perpetrator's home before he dumped her body, while I was at Thomastown I could see that Karmein was also shot. I told the crew that I could now see the perpetrator had shot Karmein, but I said it off camera, not while I was being filmed. The crew were a little disappointed with me as they only took into account what I said on camera.

At the end of filming, I was told that the cold case was indeed that of Karmein Chan's abduction and murder. In the late 1980s and early 1990s, three young schoolgirls were kidnapped in three separate attacks by a Melbourne man nicknamed Mr Cruel by police. Two of the girls, Sharon Wills and Nicola Lynas, were abducted and eventually released. Unfortunately, the third victim, Karmein Chan, wasn't so lucky. Twelve months after her disappearance in 1991, her badly decomposed body was found in Melbourne's northern outskirts, in Edgars Creek, Thomastown – the final site I was taken to for filming. As I picked up at the site, she had been shot. There was also an electricity substation very close to where Karmein's remains were found. The police revealed for the first time in 2006 – almost two years after this episode was shot – that they believe Mr Cruel did film or photograph his victims.

Mr Cruel has never been caught.

*

A few weeks after the shoot, I was told that my footage on Karmein Chan would not be going to air. The producers had opted to focus on the clues given by two other psychics instead. I felt greatly disappointed that my information wasn't going to be used to help solve the case. Given the physical and emotional toll of going under hypnosis, I had second thoughts about continuing to work on the program, but after a number of conversations with the producers I agreed to film another case. My next one was in Queensland.

Initially, I was given a very distinctive-looking gold ring to tune in to. It was a braided gold band with a five-pointed star on top that had a diamond in the centre. Around the star was a crescent-shaped moon with six tiny pearls inside.

Once I held the ring, I could feel the strong presence of a young woman. She had long, straight, light-brown hair and beautiful brown eyes. She had a big, wide smile and she told me that she was as tall as me, a hundred and sixty-five centimetres. I could see by her hair and the way she was dressed that the crime had happened some time back. It looked like it was in the seventies, as she was wearing flared denim jeans and a T-shirt. I felt that she liked to wear platform shoes.

A second girl stood before me. She was shorter than the first girl and had brown, shoulder-length wavy hair. This young woman had a more solid build and she had a very cheeky smile, with dimples in her cheeks. I felt that the second woman was slightly younger than the other victim. I got a very strong feeling that these two women were inseparable.

The taller woman was the one who communicated with me the most. She began to show me that something had happened to her car. I felt that the two girls had gone on a holiday, as I could see they had their bags packed.

I sensed that the girls came from Sydney and they had travelled up to Queensland on their holiday. A map of New South Wales and Queensland began to form in my mind. The taller girl told me that, after reaching Queensland, their car had broken down and at some point they'd decided to hitch-hike.

I felt that initially the girls were quite at ease with the two males who picked them up. They may have met one of the men while they were on holiday in Brisbane.

Both of the perpetrators had brown hair and were wearing jeans. One of them was around a hundred and eighty centimetres tall. He was wearing a light-coloured shirt with the sleeves rolled up. He had tattoos on his upper and lower arms and had callused hands. His hair was wavy and longer than the other perpetrator's. He was clean-shaven and he had nice blue eyes (although they went ice cold when he turned on the girls). He had chiselled features and a nice smile.

The other perpetrator had a more stocky build, beady or squinty eyes that could have been green-grey. He was around a hundred and seventy centimetres tall, and he had a distinctive tattoo of a snake on his arm. He went by the nicknames The Snake, Snakey and just Snake. He looked more scruffy than the other perpetrator and he needed a shave. He had a violent temper and I felt that he had been known for hurting women in the past. I sensed that the men had attacked other women in a similar manner and they may have gone to jail for their attacks. The taller of the two had continued with his attacks against women for some time after attacking the two girls I was tuning in to.

I felt that the perpetrators had invited the girls to a party and told them that afterwards they would drop them off where they needed to go. The girls seemed to be very trusting and extremely innocent. I felt that the party was out of Brisbane and that they headed west for about an hour to get there. The area became more rural looking as they drove to the party, which was on a quite remote property. I felt that there were paddocks surrounding the place. It had a single-storey house, like an old Queenslander, with a verandah around it. I felt that a husband and wife lived at the house and the woman had a small child. The husband was quite a violent man and when he drank he became even worse. I felt that the woman who lived on the property had red hair and wasn't of a very big build. She knew what happened to the girls but was always too frightened to say anything, as she was concerned for her own safety.

The owner of the property was a workmate of the men who picked up the girls; they were manual labourers. None of these men had any respect at all for women. I could see that the girls started to become concerned as the night wore on. They began to ask the men who had picked them up if they could leave. The men said they would leave in the morning. The girls approached the woman who lived on the property and asked her for help. They tried to get her to take them to the local train station but the men told her to mind her own business.

The men seemed to be very aggressive and I could see that they started to come on to the young girls.

I then saw an old Holden that was a light-green or cream colour with a white roof. The tail lights were square and distinctive. I felt that it was a Holden EH model. The car had light-coloured vinyl seats and the girls were sitting in the back. I also saw a red ute. It was quite high off the ground, similar to what you would use on a rural property, like a Ford F100. I could see that the owner had a dog in the back.

Another vision was extremely disturbing. It was now night-time and the two girls were in the Holden EH. The two males were in the car, one driving and the other in the back of the vehicle, ensuring that the girls didn't get away. The girls were being driven on a country road that was very dark. There were no street lights; the only lights visible were distant ones on farming properties. The girls realised that they were going north instead of south, which is the direction to Goondiwindi, where the girls told the men they were heading. The girls were looking at each other with terrified looks on their faces.

I saw that the taller girl managed to jump out of the car while it was moving. The other girl was still stuck inside. I could see the car chasing the taller woman, trying to run her down. She ran into the bushes and the car followed her. She looked like a terrified rabbit stunned in the headlights. I felt that she gave up as there was nowhere to run. She was also very aware that her friend was still trapped inside.

The car stopped and the men got out holding the shorter girl. I could see that the girls tried a number of times to escape and I heard their terrified screaming. Unfortunately for the girls, nobody heard their cries. I saw that they were both scratched and bleeding and I felt that when the perpetrators finally caught them, they hog-tied and gagged them. I felt that one of the girls was dragged by the hair and then raped repeatedly. The second girl was subjected to the same treatment and I felt that their deaths were long and painful. The girls were attacked separately and one was made to watch and listen to her friend's attack.

I saw that both of the girls were hit about the head with a blunt metal object. It could have been an iron bar or a tyre lever. I picked up dreadful pain on the right side of my head. I could feel that the force was so strong that the victims' skulls were fractured.

I was given another flash. I felt that I had been brought forward a few years. I could see that wildlife had run through the murder site and I felt that the girls' remains had been scattered. I could see that the bones were bleached white as if they had been in the weather for some time. Clothing was scattered everywhere; it was faded and decaying due to exposure to the elements. I could see a denim bag and platform shoes with cork heels. The girls kept telling me that there was also jewellery scattered in the murder area.

There didn't seem to have been any effort to conceal the murder site. It was as if the girls had just been thrown away and discarded like their belongings. The feeling of lack of respect for life was extremely strong.

I felt that the perpetrators knew the area well and had frequented it in the past. It was as if they went there to drink with their mates around a campfire. I also felt that there was a river running close to where the girls' bodies had been found and I was hearing water running. I was told that the area was an old fishing hole, but I felt that the river may have now dried up. I was given the impression that the perpetrators had kept a trophy from the girls as a reminder of what they had done to them.

In the morning, we were on our way to film at a site an hour west of Brisbane, at Murphys Creek, near the rural town of Toowoomba. I was driven down a country road and when the vehicle stopped I was asked in which direction I wanted to go. I felt drawn to walk back up the road and then I was pulled to go into the bush. I could see that previously a road had led through the bush to the precise site I was drawn to.

Then the victims told me to head in a southerly direction. I got to a point in the bush where I was told to stop by the girls. I closed my eyes and the horrible events during the girls' final hours unfolded before me. I could hear them screaming desperately and trying to run away from the perpetrators, who chased them down like they were frightened wild animals. It was as though the men were hunting wild kangaroos or rabbits.

The girls then showed me where their bodies were found and where their belongings were discovered. I felt as if I needed to look for something and that jewellery may have been lost in the area. I told the crew that I needed a metal detector so I could search over the site. They later told me that the ring I had been given in the studio to tune in to was located with a metal detector on the site where I was standing.

I also located the riverbed that I had seen in my vision and, as I had thought, the river had long since dried up. There was an area with a burnt tree log, which looked like it had been the site of a campfire. There were broken bottles and rusty beer cans littering the area.

Later, I was told that the two women I had tuned in to for this cold case were two Sydney nurses, Lorraine Wilson, twenty, and Wendy Evans, eighteen. They had left Brisbane on 6 October 1974 to hitch-hike to Goondiwindi because Lorraine's car had broken down there and was being repaired. The girls were expected to return to work at St George Hospital, in Sydney, on 10 October, but they weren't seen alive after the night they left Brisbane. It wasn't until 1976, when the girls' remains were found in the bush at Murphys Creek, near the foothills of the Toowoomba Ranges, that it became clear they had met with foul play. By chance, two elderly bushwalkers came across the girls' skeletal remains. Their personal belongings and clothing were found scattered around in bush close to where their bodies were discovered. The girls had been raped, bound and gagged and bludgeoned to death with a heavy object. The car they were last seen alive in was a Holden EJ, the next model on from the EH that I had felt the men had driven.

Out of all of the cases I worked on for *Sensing Murder*, the victims from this case came through the clearest. Lorraine and Wendy deserve to have justice, as all of the victims do. At the time of filming, police indicated that they had suspects they were investigating.

My one wish through working on *Sensing Murder* was that the work of all of the psychics involved in the series would help bring closure to the families. At times, I felt frustrated or disappointed by the outcome of the work I did on the show because of its format and the way it was written. On the positive side, I feel extremely privileged to have been part of a groundbreaking Australian television program. I feel that the work of myself and the other psychics featured on the program was presented in a manner that showed the general public how the abilities of psychic individuals can be used to assist others.

On the world stage, psychic phenomena and medium-ship are widely accepted as tools that can help solve cold cases. Unfortunately, in Australia we are quite behind with the acceptance of the use of people like myself in solving such cases. My hope is that, in the future, our law-enforcement agencies will be permitted to work with psychics and mediums in an open and accepting manner, to help eradicate the large amount of cold cases that are filed away just waiting to be solved.

Chapter 17

Butterfly: The Story of Maria Scott

After *Sensing Murder* aired, I was approached by a detective in Wollongong named Jeff Little, who asked me if I could assist him with a murder case he was working on. Jeff needed help in filling in the missing gaps of what had happened to the victim for a report that he was preparing for the coroner. I agreed to assist, but told him that I didn't want to know anything about the case prior to meeting him.

On 16 May 2005, I went to Port Kembla Police Station to meet Jeff, who led me to an interview room at the back of the station. Immediately, I felt the presence of a female. She was of only a slight build, with mousy-brown hair just past her shoulders. She looked very black around the eyes and I felt that she had a problem with substance abuse.

Jeff introduced me to a female detective, Catherine Flood, and an officer from the police media unit named Todd Jeffree who was present to film the events that took place throughout the day. I told them that I felt the victim was already with me and described what I thought she looked like. All of them seemed quite shocked, because my description was correct, even though at this stage I hadn't been told anything about her and hadn't been shown a photograph.

Jeff went into the evidence room and returned with a small, brown paper bag containing items for me to tune in to. Prior to opening the bag, he warned me to put on gloves. As I had never done psychometry with gloves on before, I told him I didn't know if it would work. He insisted I wear gloves, as the items weren't all that nice to work with. I am so thankful that he insisted, as when the bag was opened a large amount of the victim's hair – which was indeed mousy-brown – fell out on the desk in front of me. Also in the bag were about ten silver bangles with little engraved patterns on them. All of them were deteriorated and rusted. The victim's skin was still attached to the metal bangles and some of it fell onto the table.

I tried to be calm and get down to the task at hand: receiving as much information as possible for the case. After I got over my initial discomfort at working with the items, the victim began to show me her life.

I felt very sad for this woman as she showed me how hard her life was. I felt that she was a prostitute, because she showed me she had a number of men around her. She told me that she had to keep turning tricks because of her problem. I felt that she suffered from addictions. She also showed me two children. I was then transported back to the past and she showed me how happy she was with her son.

I then felt immense pain in my chest and could see blood everywhere. I felt that she had been stabbed and I could see it was a frenzied attack. I also felt that she had been sexually assaulted.

I was shown a bloodied, serrated kitchen knife with a blade about twenty centimetres long and a wooden handle. The flashes began jumping all over the place: I felt that she knew the perpetrator and that he was a client of hers. I began to see a grassed area and gum trees on the edge of a clearing. She made a point of showing me a wooden picnic table with bench seats there. I could smell leaves rotting; it was a moist type of smell mixed with the smell of the ocean. I could also see a long driveway and hear the sound of gravel crunching under car tyres.

I then felt that she was cold and that she might not be fully clothed. I could see her face and it had water running over it. I felt that she was lying on her back and that she was wrapped in something. Jeff asked what I thought it was and I said a mattress protector or a doona without a cover, because the material looked white and it had sections with filling sewn into it.

The next flash took me inside a building. Firstly, I could see sky blue; then I felt that I was lying on my back. It looked like people had been squatting in the building, as there were mattresses all over the floor with sheets, blankets, pillows and lots of mess everywhere. The mattresses were dark blue, with a stars and moons pattern on them. I could then see the room covered in blood. The victim showed me what the perpetrator looked like. He was a heavy-set man about a hundred and eighty-two centimetres tall, with dark-brown eyes, brown hair and olive skin. When he became angry, he was very violent and frightening. His eyes almost went black when he went into a rage. I felt that he also had an issue with substances.

My mind flashed back to the little boy and whether he was okay. I kept seeing a symbol of a butterfly, which at that point didn't make much sense to me.

The victim also let me know that she was pregnant, by showing me her tummy suddenly growing with a baby bump. Again, a feeling of sadness passed over me. I felt that if only she had been more careful, she would still be alive today.

Jeff asked me whether I needed any more items to work with and I told him that I could try to see if any more information would come with another item. He left the room and returned a few minutes later with a much larger brown paper bag. He warned me that the smell could make me feel ill. Fortunately for me, I couldn't smell anything. Somehow, I think Running Horse must have been looking after me, as the others all went a pale shade of green and had to struggle to stay in the room.

The bag looked like something the butcher would put your meat in, because blood had seeped through it. I held on to it, still wearing the gloves. Jeff informed me that inside was one of the items that the victim had been wearing when she was found. I told him that psychically, without opening the bag, I could see that it was a white or light-coloured T-shirt with a logo of some text on the front. I felt that it had multiple cuts in the fabric from the stab wounds and that it was covered in blood. He agreed that I was describing the item and asked me how I could see into the bag without it being opened. I said I wasn't sure how it all worked and that the image just popped into my head.

After being interviewed and filmed for over an hour, I was taken to the murder site. I felt that the victim was very excited by this prospect. I felt her get into the car with us.

We headed down the coast and then started to drive up towards Moss Vale, on the escarpment south-west of Wollongong. I became a little confused and thought my messages must have been off, as I had sensed that I would smell salt air at the murder site, not mountain air. The officers put my mind at rest and said that when we got to the destination it would all make sense.

About an hour later, we arrived at a refuge for recovering drug addicts, owned by the Sydney City Mission, called Triple Care Farm, located at Robertson, south of Sydney. While driving through the grounds of the refuge, I spotted the gum trees and the clearing and the picnic table. The driveway was gravel and I could hear it crunching under the tyres, as in my visions.

When we got out of the car, I could smell gum leaves and moistness in the air. There was also a salt-air smell mixed in, coming up from the coastline below. I was being pulled to the bush at the edge of the clearing, to the right, but Jeff asked me to go down to the left. To this day, I regret not going to the right, as I feel that there were clues we missed that day. I saw a vision that the murder weapon was thrown from that area, at the edge of the escarpment. I could also see another victim being thrown off the edge as well. Jeff later informed me that it had not been possible to follow up this vision, as the area at the bottom of the cliff was completely inaccessible.

Jeff then took me to the murder site, about twenty-five metres into the bush, to see what I could pick up from that. While I walked down to the area, I felt like I was going to burst out crying. It was as if I had become the victim and was feeling her emotions. When I got there, the only thing I could see out of the ordinary was a pile of logs. What I didn't know was that the police had done an experiment with the carcass of a pig, which was wrapped in a doona and placed in the exact location where the victim's body was found, to try to understand why no one had detected any odour over the seven-month period for which she had been missing. The police had concluded that the doona and the thick pile of logs and other debris used to cover the carcass had been enough to conceal its smell. The carcass was actually still there when I was at the site, so the fact that I couldn't smell anything bad further demonstrates why no one was able to detect the body.

At the murder scene, the victim showed me that she was lying semi-naked; she had only a T-shirt on. She was lying on her back and was positioned with her head pointing downhill. The smell of rotting leaves now made sense, as did my vision of the water on her face. The water would have been running downhill and all over her.

Again, I saw the symbol of a butterfly. When we got closer to the site, I noticed a memorial plaque with the victim's name on it: her name was Maria Scott. Someone had left a number of butterflies around it.

Maria told me that her children had left the butterflies there for her. Her mum was now looking after her children, she told me, and at least they were safe. But she was so sad that she wasn't the one who was with her son now.

I had a strange feeling of being pulled up to the edge of the bush. I felt I had to look towards a building that was quite close to the murder site. I sensed that the victim had stood at the edge of the bush for a long time, waiting for someone to find her. She showed me that she would walk back and forth between the building and where her body was. I had a quick flash again of the light sky-blue colour I had seen in my earlier vision. Maria told me that the colour related to the building she was murdered in. On the property, there were a number of different buildings but the only one that was light blue was the one just near the murder site.

When we'd first arrived on the refuge grounds, the building hadn't made much of an impression on me. It wasn't until I was at the murder site that I felt there was some connection to it. The victim desperately wanted me to go inside it so she could show me what had happened to her.

The four of us moved up to the blue building. The feelings welling up in me were both of dread and excitement. I could feel Maria's anticipation that her story would finally be told.

When I first entered the building, the feeling I got was that it was completely different inside from the time that Maria was murdered. She showed me how the walls had been moved – they had been gyprocked – and that many things had been covered up. The refuge was in the process of renovating the building, which was used as accommodation.

She asked me to ask Jeff whether just she and I could walk around first so she could tell me what had happened. He agreed. I felt that, at the time of her murder, the perpetrator had lived in the building. She showed me that he had enlisted her services on many occasions. He was so well known to her that it almost felt as if she thought of him as a boyfriend.

She showed me how frightening he could be, but for some reason she kept coming back. I felt that, on the day of her murder, he had picked her up in the Wollongong/Port Kembla area and brought her up to the refuge at night. I felt that she wasn't really supposed to be there and that not many people would have known her whereabouts.

She showed me that a close girlfriend had warned her about hanging around this man. I felt that he had a violent history and may have been charged for or questioned about violence against other females in the past.

Maria led me into a room and asked me to open the cupboard door. When I did this, she said, 'This is identical to the one he wrapped me in.' It was a doona without a cover.

She then led me to another room and showed me a pile of single-bed mattresses. There were some with stars and moons on the sides of them and others with multicoloured patterns. I recognised the stars and moons pattern immediately, and I also felt that the stars had some other significance. I wouldn't know what that significance was for quite some time. All of the mattresses had mattress protectors made of the same material as the doona.

I called Jeff and the others and told them that these were the mattresses that I had seen in the visions earlier that morning. I then took them to the cupboard and pulled out the doona without a cover. Jeff said that as her body had been in the bush for seven months prior to being discovered, the material the victim was wrapped in had broken down so much that the police couldn't quite work out what item it was. He did say that the doona I picked out matched the material that was wrapped around the body.

Maria then took me into a room adjoining the one where the mattresses were stored. When I walked into it, I keeled over in agonising pain. I felt stabbing pains in my chest and my stomach. The feeling in my body was very strong and I felt that this poor woman had suffered greatly before her death. This room had very negative energy.

Suddenly, I was transported back in time. It was like I was a bystander watching the murder. I could see a couple of mattresses that had been placed haphazardly on the floor. The room was littered with belongings and rubbish. I saw an argument break out between the perpetrator and Maria. The fight became very violent and I could see him trying to overpower her. The perpetrator, who was much bigger than Maria, forced her down onto one of the mattresses on the floor. I could see that he had what looked like a kitchen knife and I could see him violently stabbing her with it. I also felt that he violently sexually assaulted her.

Jeff asked me where exactly I thought she had been murdered and I told him I was standing right on the spot. He acknowledged that I was correct.

The vision abruptly stopped and I was transported back into the present.

I told the detectives what I had witnessed and they asked me whether I could see anything else. I tuned back in and now the vision showed me that the perpetrator was in another adjoining room. In real time, the room was now a small bedroom but I was shown that in the past it had been a bathroom. I could see a sink and the perpetrator was standing there looking at me and washing his hands. I could see blood running down the drain. He just stood there looking at me. From his expression, I could see he was very pleased with what he had done.

He turned off the tap and abruptly came straight at me. It was like he walked straight through me. I felt quite ill from this experience, which made me very aware that he knew I was there.

I then saw him leave the room. He went out the front door and under the building. As the building was built on supports, there was almost enough room under it for a person to stand up straight. He began trying to hide some of the evidence. He appeared to be putting items of clothing and trinkets in pipes and up under the floor. He was tucking them in and putting rubbish over them to hide them.

I told Jeff what I was seeing and he said that when Maria's body had been found and a search conducted of the area, they had located some items under the floor.

Once we left the building, I walked around with one of

the police officers to see if any additional areas stood out psychically, while Jeff attended to some other business. The officer asked, in an offhanded way, where I thought the perpetrator was now. I said that I saw him going to Toowoomba and that I felt he had reoffended.

When Jeff returned, the officer asked me to repeat what I'd told him. When I did, Jeff just looked at me and then asked, 'How did you know that?' I told them that Maria told me.

As we were leaving, we drove past the place where Maria's remains had been found and I could see her standing there waiting. It was as though she was trapped in time. The sadness hit me so heavily in my heart. I only hoped that I provided enough information in order for her to find her peace and go into the light.

*

The hardest part of working on this type of case is returning to your family and trying to fit back into your normal life. What I had witnessed that day was not something I wanted to force on those I loved. It was distressing enough for me to see and feel such things, let alone tell my husband about it.

From doing my work, I have learnt over the years that I am able to make a positive difference. I feel that if my gift can help others in some small way, then I can learn to overcome the unpleasantness that comes with the job.

The following day, Jeff told me that I had uncovered many valid clues that would help him put together a report for the coroner. Over the next few weeks, more clues came through, which I also passed on to Jeff. But still, he said, there was one major thing about the case that I had missed. I couldn't think what that could be and it bothered me not to have picked it up. A couple of months later, I realised what I had missed, when Jeff told me that their chief suspect had killed himself before my help had been requested.

The suspect's name was Mark Brown. He lived and worked at Triple Care, Robertson, at the time Maria Scott was murdered. Three weeks after the murder, Mark Brown travelled to Toowoomba, Queensland. Three months later, he returned to the area and committed suicide inside a car at Carrington Falls, a few minutes' drive from the scene of Maria Scott's murder. After the coronial inquest, he was officially named as the perpetrator.

My mind went back to the day at the refuge and how the perpetrator came towards me and walked straight through me. I remembered how much this incident shocked me. So I had blocked out the obvious sign. If a person was living, then even psychically they wouldn't be able to walk through me in a vision. Only a spirit could do this.

I realised then that the murderer was in fact playing with me that day at the crime scene. Yes, he did know I was in the room – because he was there watching me. The perpetrator loved every minute of us being there; he had become *the star*.

Chapter 18

Alive and Well in the Spirit World

My job takes on many dimensions, from working on police investigations to making contact with lost loved ones on a daily basis. I often receive letters and emails from families who wish to make contact with those who have passed. The following stories are just some of the touching moments of contact I have been blessed enough to experience with some of these families.

In 2005, my Hotmail account went through a frustrating period of playing up. I just wasn't able to log in without the site dropping out on me and I was close to giving up on it. One particular night during this time, a nagging voice in my head said, 'Check your emails on Hotmail.' I thought there wasn't much point, as it probably wouldn't work anyway. Again, the voice in my head said, 'Check your Hotmail!' I thought, *What the heck? It can't hurt*, and to my surprise it opened. There before me in my inbox were over eighty emails.

I answered about sixty of them, by which time it was getting late and my eyes felt like they were going to drop out of my head. I decided I would finish off the rest the next day. As I went to log out, a little boy materialised beside me.

I thought I just must be overtired and continued logging out, but the little boy then started to plead with me. He pointed to the screen and said, 'Just one more. Please read just one more. This one here is from my daddy.'

He told me that Mummy was very sad because he had died and she wasn't able to see him any more. He wanted me to tell her that he was okay, and that he still played football and had his Jack Russell Terrier-cross puppy with him. He was standing there with a football under one arm and very proudly told me that the jersey he had on was his NRL team, the Wests Tigers, and that his best mate and favourite player was John Skandalis (Skando). John had visited him when he was in hospital, as part of his dying wishes. The little boy then told me that Wests were going to win the premiership that year. He showed me how he and the dog used to run around the house. He said that he would kick his ball and slide up and down the hallway in his socks.

He had been trying desperately hard to let Mum and Dad know how much he loved them and that he didn't want them to cry any more because he was all right.

When I read the email from his father, the whole story made sense.

Wednesday 9 February 2005, 9.28.25 pm

Hi Debbie. I have seen you on the TV show *Sensing Murder*. Debbie, our son passed away last year of a brain haemorrhage while having a bone-marrow transplant. We dearly miss our eight-year-old son Brendan Thompson. We are taking this loss very hard. I have seen you look at photos and receive messages back from the people. I was wondering if you can do that if we send a photo of our boy; we just want to know if he is okay. We have been to other people and they have told us different things that are not our boy. It's been very depressing. My wife is going through a very hard time, missing Brendan heaps and often thinks of going to be with him. I hope you can help us.

Warren and Susan Thompson

I emailed his parents right away to tell them everything that Brendan had shown and told me. Brendan then said he was just so excited that somebody could finally see him and that he was happy with what I had put in the email. I told him I needed to go to bed now. I felt his presence follow me upstairs, so I told him I couldn't do anything else until the morning and, with that, he disappeared.

In the morning, I made a phone call to his parents. His mum, Susan, began sobbing at the other end of the phone. Her husband, Warren, then spoke with me. I felt terrible that I had upset her so much and I apologised to him. Warren explained that contacting me was their last hope of reconnecting with Brendan. He told me how surprised they were that I had bothered to reply to them.

He said he was even more shocked by what I had put in my email. He kept saying, 'You have my boy with you. You have described our son.' I could hear the excitement in his voice and I felt so happy that I could give them contact with their darling little boy. We arranged to meet face to face at the first opportunity, which was two weeks later.

Warren and Susan were very excited when the day finally came for us to meet. They arrived at the door with a bag full of Brendan's favourite things and a photograph of their little boy. I tuned in to Brendan by holding his favourite stuffed toy tiger, named Timmy. I didn't really need to hold anything, though, as Brendan had arrived before his parents because he was also so excited.

Brendan showed me many signs that proved he was alive and well in the spirit world. He firstly showed me that he was being taken care of in spirit by Nanna Grace, Susan's nan. He also showed me how he tried to get his parents' attention: they had a lamp at home that could be turned on by touching it, so he would touch the lamp to make it flicker on and off. He also wanted me to tell his parents that his football boot was still on the roof of their house. Warren just started laughing and asked me how I knew that.

Brendan showed me the beautiful garden of remembrance in the backyard that his dad had made for him. He showed me that he was there with his dad whenever he was out there.

Brendan started to rub his mum's tummy and told me that she would be having another baby soon. Susan admitted that they were in fact trying to have another baby.

He wanted me to tell them how much he loved his

brother and sister, and that he wanted his sister to know that she could have his beloved tiger Timmy. He told me he knew that she slept with it and he was very happy she was taking such good care of it for him.

Brendan kept showing me a tow truck, and Warren said that he drove one and Brendan used to love to sit in it.

He began to show me a Parramatta football jersey and said he liked the team from Parramatta but the Wests Tigers would always be his team. Susan told me that when he was in hospital, some of the players from the Parramatta NRL team had come to visit him in hospital and they had given him a jersey, cap, scarf and football in Parramatta colours. He told his mum not to worry: she didn't have to keep going for Parramatta just to make him happy; he still liked the Tigers.

Susan began to laugh and said that made her happy, as she was only following Parramatta for Brendan, or BB, as the family called him.

He told me to tell his mum and dad that it was okay that they had to turn his life-support machine off. He told me that he was by their side when they did it and that he was never going to get any better, so it was best for everyone. Susan and Warren both started to cry. I felt so sad for them, but Brendan smiled and said that he was now an angel and that he was free to go wherever he wanted. He wasn't sick or in pain any more. He could play football whenever he wanted and he didn't have to go to hospital ever again. He wanted them to know he was so happy that he could still be with them.

*

A couple of months later, I was doing a reading for a female client when Brendan appeared beside her. When I conduct a reading, I never know if the main component of it will be a life forecast for the client or mediumship. Both of these components usually take place at the same time and I just go where spirit takes me. This woman had come to see me for advice about her career. Brendan interrupted and told me that this was the lady who granted his wish and then he showed me a star. I asked her if she worked for the Starlight Foundation, the wonderful charity that grants wishes to sick and dying children. She said she did but was wondering whether it was time to find a new job. Brendan said to tell the woman that she couldn't leave the Starlight Foundation, as she had many more people to help.

She looked quite startled and asked me how I knew Brendan. I explained to her how I had met him and then she told me that she was one of the people who helped grant his wish to go to Movie World on the Gold Coast in Queensland. As the reading concluded, Brendan asked me to thank his wish granter and he disappeared.

This woman had such beautiful, caring energy and I could feel how hard it was for her to even consider leaving her job at the Starlight Foundation. I am not sure what she did about her career path but, whatever it was, it would always include helping others.

I rang and told Susan and Warren that Brendan had made a guest appearance at work and they just laughed and said, 'That would be BB.'

About six months later, I did another reading for Warren and Susan, who brought along Brendan's little sister, Emily. As usual, Brendan came through loud and clear. He was so excited: I could see him jumping around the room. He cheered and told me that his beloved Tigers had won the 2005 Rugby League premiership. He told me that they won it for him and when I told his parents they agreed. This was the best present that he had ever received, even if he was now in spirit.

Once Brendan had settled down, he sat and held his sister's hand and then started to rub Susan's tummy. He told me that his new baby brother was on the way. Susan confirmed that she was pregnant.

When Susan had the baby, Warren rang to tell me they had a bouncing baby boy, called Tiger Nelson Thompson. Brendan was very pleased.

*

'Suicide' is a word that conjures up many thoughts and feelings. People don't like to discuss it and don't want to admit it has occurred in their family. But everybody is touched by it in some way, shape or form.

Many young people in particular disappear from this world through suicide. It is such a shame that more of us are not educated about the signs and how to help people who are suffering with a silent inner torture. People at risk of suicide need to be educated to understand the implications of their actions, and families need to learn the warning signs as well as how to deal with the loss of a family member.

On a weekly basis, I work with families who deal with the tragedy of suicide. Mitchell Davies' family is just one.

In March 2006, I was doing a reading for a lovely lady named Rachel when Mitchell abruptly made his presence known to me. Rachel had come for a reading to find out a number of things in her life but it was Mitchell who took the stage. He stood beside her and wouldn't go away until I told her that a young man was with her who had died tragically of suicide.

I told her that Mitchell was a good-looking guy about a hundred and eighty-two centimetres tall. He had the biggest blue eyes and dark-blond hair. His face lit up when he smiled and he had a beautiful, loving energy. He told me that he was a good friend of her husband's, Adrian, with whom he had worked. Rachel started to cry and pulled out a memorial booklet picturing the young man I was describing.

Mitchell had died nine months prior. He was very determined to tell Rachel that he was okay and that it wasn't anyone's fault that he had passed. He told me that he was angry about what he had done and that if he had known then what he did now, maybe things would have been different. He asked if Rachel could let his parents know that he had come through during the reading and tell them that he was sorry for what had happened.

Mitchell told me that he didn't need to fight the demons and voices in his head any more. He had been diagnosed with depression and he didn't like to take his medication all of the time as it made him feel slow and out of control, and when he took it he couldn't go out with his mates and have a drink.

He didn't want anyone to know that he had problems because he thought people would think he was weird. He had tried to not show it for so long, but the manic episodes were getting harder and harder to hide. Mitchell had a lot of friends on the outside but on the inside he was hurting badly. There were not many people that he let see the real Mitchell. Even though he had now passed, his energy was probably more vibrant than it had been when he was alive.

On the night of his death, Mitchell had been out with his mates. He'd had a bit to drink and had got into an altercation. He was told by his brother, Reece, that it was time he came home to calm down and that things would be all right in the morning. Unfortunately, for Mitchell the morning never came. He decided to hang himself in his bedroom.

Mitchell told me that he now struggled with his decision every day. He'd never really thought about what his actions would do to his family; he could only think about the pain he was feeling within himself. He had tried very hard from the spirit world to make amends for his actions and had done many things to try to get messages through to his family and friends.

I told Rachel that I felt we needed to help Mitchell go to the light. I felt that he was stuck due to what had happened. Mitchell had other ideas. He wasn't going anywhere until I got to meet his family. It is quite amazing the power a soul has, even when it has passed over.

After Rachel's reading, her husband, Adrian, rang to make a booking. But, the day before his appointment, he called to reschedule. Later that day, I received a phone call from a man named Phil. He said he had been given my number and wanted to make a booking with me asap, though he didn't say why. I booked him into Adrian's cancelled appointment.

Nothing happens by coincidence. It was very strange when I tuned in to Phil, as again I saw Mitchell. I described him to Phil and he became very emotional. Mitchell put his arm around him and I realised what the connection was: Phil was Mitchell's dad.

Mitchell told his dad he was fine but he was very worried about his brother, Reece, as he was struggling with his death. He wanted Reece to know he couldn't have done anything to stop it, as Mitchell had made up his mind. Mitchell spoke about his mum and sister and how the two had become very close since his death. He could see that the women in the family were coping a little bit better than the men. He said he hoped that Phil and Reece could try to communicate more, as he was worried about their relationship becoming distant because of what he'd done.

Phil told me that it was only since Mitchell's passing that he had begun to understand the problems that Mitchell was suffering with. He was so sad that he hadn't been aware of them before Mitchell's death. Mitchell told me to tell him that it wasn't anybody's fault and he didn't want his dad to feel guilty. He just wanted his dad to know how much he loved him and how worried he was that the family was falling apart because of his actions.

Mitchell used to be a surfer and he told me how close he was to his dad when his dad was in the surf. He knew that Phil had begun to surf again in their favourite spot. Phil asked me how I could know this, and when I told him it was because Mitchell had told me he just smiled.

By the end of the reading, Phil was like a different person. He seemed so much more relaxed. Of course, he was still sad about the loss of his son, but in some way he seemed more at peace within himself.

When it came time to meet Rachel's husband, Adrian, naturally my new friend Mitchell arrived right on cue. Mitchell wanted to allay his mate's fear that he could have prevented his early exit from this world. Mitchell was such a determined guy that when he had made up his mind, nothing would stop him.

Adrian told me that he was worried about Phil and hoped that he would come to see me. When I replied that Phil had already seen me, in his cancelled appointment, Adrian just sat there amazed, then said, 'That would be Mitchell.'

Two weeks later, I met Mitchell's mum, Barbara, and his sister, Rhiannon. When they arrived for their appointment, Mitchell was already at my office waiting patiently. The minute they sat down, he started giving me messages.

Mitchell sat between Barbara and Rhiannon. For someone passed, he was so alive. In all of the sessions I have had with Mitchell, I have never seen someone in spirit with such a big smile on his or her face. He started laughing and started to muck up his sister's hair like he used to do when he was alive. I relayed this message to Rhiannon and she started laughing. Rhiannon said that she had always danced and it used to take her a long time to get her hair just right for competitions, and just when she had it perfect Mitchell would come in and muck it up.

He told Rhiannon he knew that she wasn't doing her study and that she needed to hurry up and get her assignments for her year twelve assessments done. He told her that she was the smart one, not him, and that was why he'd left school early. Mitchell also wanted Rhiannon to practise driving more; he thought that she wasn't braking early enough. He wanted her to know that the voices in his head had finally gone.

He asked Barbara and Rhiannon to look after his brother, Reece, as he knew Reece had been very angry since he had passed. He was happy that Reece was wearing his watch, which had been his prize possession, but he had noticed that Reece had put a scratch on it.

He was happy to report that he had met his grand-mother, Barbara's mum, who passed away in March 2006. He said with a smile that sometimes she nagged him too much, though.

He brought forward a good mate of his named Hayden, whom he had played football with. Hayden had died nine years ago and now the two of them were together.

Mitchell started laughing and pointed to the tattoos that Barbara and Rhiannon had got in remembrance of him. He said it was funny how his mum hadn't wanted him to get any more while he was alive and now they both had one with his name on it. He put his arms around both of them and hugged them and just said to tell them 'thank you'.

He wanted his mum to know about the notes that he'd left in the drawers and said he hoped that she had found them. Barbara had a big smile on her face and said she'd found them tucked in different places in his bedroom.

He also wanted Barbara to know that the Robbie Williams CD that was found in his car was the second part of her Mother's Day present. He started laughing and said, 'You didn't think that I would listen to that stuff, did you?'

Mitchell said that next time he dies, he is going to have the wake first. He couldn't believe how many people were at his funeral and wake. He was happy that his mates had a celebration of his life instead of a commiseration of his death.

Mitchell also wanted the family to listen to a song called 'Behind Blue Eyes', as covered by Limp Bizkit, which is about a young man who hides his anger and sadness from the world. He said that this was his song and it described exactly how he felt. Aptly, Mitchell has the biggest blue eyes you have ever seen.

Mitchell said that he was happy that his mum and dad were starting to communicate better since my reading with Phil, and he wanted Barbara to know that he was doing all he could from the other side. As our reading drew to a close, Mitchell told his mum and sister how much he loved them.

After I do a reading, I usually feel quite drained physically and emotionally but after this reading I felt like I was now in some way connected to Mitchell's family.

Whenever I hear the song 'Behind Blue Eyes', I know that Mitchell wants to give me a message to pass on. I was driving back from Picton after working there on a ghost tour when the song came on the radio. I immediately felt Mitchell's presence and wondered what it was that he wanted to tell me.

When I got home and checked my emails, there was a message from Barbara to say that today was Mitchell's birthday and all of his mates went out on their surfboards at Mitchell's favourite spot, at Elouera, and joined hands to make a circle of friendship. They then all released blue balloons in remembrance of him. Mitchell told me he was blown away and couldn't believe what a great present he had received.

*

One Sunday morning a couple of months after my reading with Barbara and Rhiannon, my family and I decided that we would go for a drive down the coast for lunch. We were only five minutes into our journey when we came to a traffic jam on the highway between the Royal National Park and Engadine.

At first glance, we thought that a movie was being shot, as there was a cameraman and police everywhere, directing the traffic. But, on the other side of the road, in the middle of two lanes, was a blue tarp with something underneath it. There were three crumpled bicycles at the roadside and it was at that point that I knew there was a deceased person under the tarp.

Suddenly, I felt a very strong presence in the car. I felt total confusion and I started to cry uncontrollably. I felt like I couldn't breathe. My back was killing me and I felt great pain in my head.

My husband, Warwick, asked me what was the matter and I told him that the man killed on the bike was in the car with us. It reminded me of the scene in the movie *The Sixth Sense*.

Warwick looked at me and said, 'Can't we just have a peaceful drive with the kids, without you talking to dead people?' I knew he was absolutely right – this was family time. The trouble was that I couldn't help it if a spirit wanted to make contact.

After being stuck in the traffic for some time, we finally progressed on our family outing. The entire day, I could feel the man's presence with me. I mentioned to my husband that in some way I needed to help this man.

I ended up telling the deceased man that if he wanted my help then it was up to him to help his family find me. I just couldn't go through the phone book, ring them up and say, 'I have him with me.' They would think that I was a fruitcake.

That night on the news, there was a report about the accident. The victim, whom I'll call Jason, had been riding with two other cyclists, as the lead rider. One of the other cyclists went to go around him and the bikes clipped each other, causing Jason and his bike to be flung from the side of the road out into the main stream of traffic. He was hit by a car and then flung out into the second lane of traffic. He was killed instantly.

I write for a magazine and after watching the news I thought I should get to work and write my column. I had just turned on the computer when I felt there was a male presence behind me in my office. At first, I didn't recognise who it was, so I asked him to leave, as he was scaring me.

I turned back around and began to write; suddenly, I felt a breeze on my face. The doors and windows were shut, so I knew that something was going on. I turned again to face the presence behind me. This time, I realised that Mitchell Davies had come for a visit. I asked him what he wanted and all he said was, 'Check your emails. There is an important one from Mum,' and with that he disappeared.

Barbara had sent me an email to say that there had been 'another tragedy in our family, as my cousin [Jason] was killed in a bike accident at Engadine on Sunday morning'. In the days afterwards, the family had felt Mitchell's presence. Barbara and Rhiannon had driven out to Jason's home and, just before they arrived, they heard Mitchell's song on the radio. On their way home, they were driving past the room I give readings in, at Sutherland, when the song came on again. Barbara wrote:

> Rhiannon and I just looked at each other and laughed as we both said, 'Mitch, we know you're here.' We realise much more now how much he is around us. He keeps letting us know he is here in his special way.

When a guy whom I'll call Allan made a booking to see me in August 2006, I didn't really attach much significance to it; I just took down the booking and left it at that.

On the morning of Allan's booking, I first had an appointment in Wollongong. While driving down the coast, I had to pass the site where Jason was killed. Just as I was about to pass the area where I had first met Jason, I felt his presence beside me in the car. He started telling me that he would be talking to me later, but I didn't know what he was talking about.

I had my meeting, drove back to my office and started giving readings to my clients. Allan was my last appointment of the day. Prior to his arrival, I began to feel

Jason's presence even more strongly than I had before. The next thing I knew, Mitchell was standing with him, his arm around his shoulder. They both had very mischievous grins on their faces and looked like partners in crime.

The doorbell rang and I saw Allan standing there. Little did he know that Jason and Mitchell were now standing behind him laughing. I said hello and that it was good to see he had Jason and Mitchell with him as they had been hanging around me, getting impatient for him to arrive.

Allan looked quite puzzled; he asked how I knew that they were with him. When I outlined the story for him, I think he had second thoughts about whether he should be there or not.

Allan then told me that he was Jason's brother. He said he had thought long and hard about coming to see me, as his family was quite religious and he wasn't sure how their mother would cope with this sort of thing. I told him I didn't want to cause any problems – all I wanted to do was pass on messages from Jason, as he was beginning to become very impatient.

Jason asked me to describe him to Allan. Jason was the taller and more athletic of the two. He had hazel-brown eyes, whereas Allan had blue eyes. Jason wanted Allan to know that he was fitter – but he had to admit that Allan had more hair than him. He started to show me trophies and I told Allan that Jason wanted to show that he had won more sporting trophies than he had. Allan started to laugh and said that Jason would say something like that. Jason was a triathlete and was actually training for an event when he was killed.

Jason wanted Allan to tell their mum that he was okay and he also wanted his kids to know that he was trying to make contact with them.

As our session drew to a close, Jason repeated that he was the fitter one who had the most trophies, to which Allan said, 'Yeah, but I have the hair.' Seeing the two of them together gave me such a nice feeling. It seemed to me that Allan knew that even though his brother had died so tragically, in some way his spirit still exists.

Allan told me that he had wanted me not to know he was related to Jason when he arrived for his reading. He had wanted to test me out first, to see if I *really* had Jason with me.

He said his idea of hiding his identity got blown out of the water as soon as he arrived and I said that he had Jason and Mitchell with him. That was enough proof for him that I was actually speaking with Jason.

Barbara rang me the next month and said that since Jason and Mitchell had passed, the families were closer than ever before. I think Mitchell and Jason had a big hand in that. Each day, I feel so privileged to be able to give these glimpses to people who have lost someone.

*

On 9 April 2006, I remember seeing a report on the news that there had been a horrific car accident in Picton. Two young men had been travelling home after a party on a wet, slippery road when the driver lost control of the vehicle and hit a telegraph pole head on. They were killed instantly. The town of Picton was devastated to have lost two young men so prematurely. Matt Lye was twenty-two years of age and Jack Parker was only twenty.

Two weeks later, my brother, Michael, rang me and asked if I would mind seeing one of the ladies he worked with, Karen. All he said was that her son, Jack, and his mate, Matt, had died tragically in a car accident – at the time, I didn't connect it to the Picton accident.

Karen arrived a bit early for her reading because she was worried that she might have trouble finding my office. When I opened the door, I could see that she wasn't really sure whether she had made the right decision or not in coming to see me. She said that she was very nervous and had never done this sort of thing before. She didn't know if she believed in what I did, but as there was no other way to speak with Jack, she thought she would give it a go.

I told her not to worry, because Jack was already with me and had been waiting in my office all morning for her to arrive. I actually felt relieved to begin the reading. Jack has such a lively spirit; he kept pacing up and down in my office all morning and was very impatient about waiting for Karen to arrive.

Karen said she had been crying for weeks and hoped that she would be all right today. I said not to worry and that I got the feeling we would be having fun. She just looked at me strangely and I could tell she was wondering why I would say such a thing. Little did she know that Jack was telling me that Mum would have tears of joy, not sadness, by the time he had finished coming through to her.

Karen gave me a photo of Jack to tune in to, as well as his watch. All I could hear was laughter and him telling me how good-looking he was. The photo his mum had brought was one of his favourites. He was dressed in a tight-fitting black T-shirt and his biceps were bulging. He said that his hair was just how he liked it. And he had a very cheeky grin on his face in the photo.

He then made the statement: 'Live fast, die young and leave a good-looking corpse!' He asked me to remind his mum that he had been here for a good time, not a long time.

He was able to achieve many things during his short life and he hoped that his parents understood that. He wanted them to know that 'life is too short', you have to go for it and have no regrets. Karen later told me that this was something Jack constantly said.

I told Karen that I felt that Jack was an old soul even though he was the youngest of her three children. In Karen's words, 'Everyone knew this. Jack was our protector.' Jack's energy was so strong that I asked Karen if he was a bit hyperactive. Tuning in to him, I couldn't sit still. She replied that he was always in a hurry and couldn't stay still for long.

Karen told me that Jack had a saying he would use whenever he bought something new. To make certain that I was truly tuning in to her son, she asked me to tell her what the saying was. I quickly replied, ''Cause I can.' Karen sat there in disbelief and asked me to repeat what I had just said. I hadn't really thought about it myself; it had just popped out of my mouth.

Jack told me that his life had been progressing well just before the accident. He showed me that he was just about to purchase a second property and was planning to go away on a trip. I suddenly saw a map of New Zealand in my head and people skiing. Karen said that Jack had been planning a trip to Mount Cook to go skiing with some mates and confirmed that he was buying a second property.

Jack told me that he likened himself to the angel in the movie *Michael*, who was played by John Travolta: he wasn't perfect but he would get the job done. Karen later told me that she often sees Jack in her dreams with his chest out proudly and sporting magnificent wings.

He also started playing the song 'My Immortal' by Evanescence, because he wanted to pass a message to his mum to listen to it and pay attention to the words, especially those of the chorus. I tracked down a copy of the song myself later on, and the chorus, sung by a woman, poignantly describes how she has nurtured and cared for her loved one throughout the years and how, though he is now gone, his memory will never leave her and he will always have an essential part of herself inside him.

Jack was very worried about his brother, Trent. He wanted Trent to know that he was at the funeral listening to his speech. Jack worried that it seemed he was the golden boy of the two brothers, but he wanted Trent to know how special he really was and that Jack would always be there to help him.

Jack wanted his sister, Kirbie, to know that he was around her as well. He mentioned that he liked her boyfriend and thought he was a good bloke but he was worried that they had been arguing too much. Karen agreed they had and said she would try to help them.

Karen asked me if it was okay to give Jack's bicycle to his mate Dean for his twenty-first. Jack replied that it was a good idea, as he might be needing it sooner than he realised. Jack thought Dean might be about to lose his licence. In fact, when Karen gave the bike to Dean on his birthday, he had only three points left on his licence.

Jack then spoke about the accident that took his life. He described how an animal had run out in front of the car and that it wasn't anyone's fault. It was just an accident. He wanted me to tell Karen that neither of the boys felt any pain and that they were both together now.

Suddenly, Jack's mate Matt stepped forward. I could see that he was shorter than Jack and had a smaller build. He had brown hair and blue or green eyes – I wasn't sure which. Karen said that Matt wore blue contacts, so this explained why I couldn't quite pick up his eye colour.

It was very funny seeing these boys together. Matt stood there trying to fix his hair up and Jack would rub his hand over Matt's hair and mess it up – 'cause he could. I could see how close the two boys were. They both stirred each other up over who had the better physique and who was the better looking. Matt thought that he got all the girls, but then Jack started flexing his muscles. I described this to Karen and she burst out laughing. She said, 'You definitely are talking to the boys.'

Both of the boys started talking about a new baby arriving. Again, Karen started to laugh. She said that Matt's brother, Ben, and Ben's girlfriend, Rebecca, had just become proud parents of a beautiful baby girl. Karen said that at the time of the birth, Rebecca thought she had seen the boys at the hospital. When Karen asked me if that was possible, both of the boys looked at me and said yes, they had been there.

Matt was worried about Ben and Rebecca because they also were fighting too much. Karen said that Matt's mum had been discussing the same issue only the other day.

As the reading was drawing to a close, I told Karen that Jack was sitting beside her and giving her a cuddle. She told me to ask him to give her a kiss on her cheek. She quickly turned her head and went to kiss him on the lips, and Jack said, 'You weren't quick enough, Mum!' Karen burst out laughing and told me this was a party trick that the two of them used to play. She said she knew that Jack was really there.

Since that first meeting, I have spoken with Karen a number of times. A couple of months after the reading, I visited the crash site with both Jack's and Matt's families. It was a very emotional time for all of us. Since the boys' deaths, their friends had made a memorial out of the telegraph pole that they crashed into. On the pole, there are a number of photographs of the boys and messages from their loving friends. Their friends have placed a myriad of stuffed toys, flowers, poems and messages around the pole. The boys even have a chair each at the site, which are covered in messages from their mates.

Before I visited the crash site, I was always of the opinion that roadside memorials are not a positive thing for the departed. On going to the boys' memorial, though, all I could feel was their happiness and excitement. They felt like they were famous and were glad that everyone thought of them when they passed by on the road.

Karen told me that at times all of their mates would

get together and sit and have a few drinks at the site, in remembrance of the boys. Jack and Matt told me that they were very well aware they did this. Jack said it was okay, as long as they took his favourite drink with them, raspberry Vodka Cruiser.

Since my meetings with both of the boys' families, Jack and Matt have told me that they now feel more at peace. Karen came to see me the other day and she told me that the boys had come home, as the families went to pick up their ashes. It was quite a ceremony, as both of the boys owned very nice utes and both families used them to drive to the crematorium. Karen said it was like the boys were back when they drove the utes through town.

Jack told me that he had pride of place on the mantelpiece, as this is where his ashes are kept. He is happy that he is surrounded by his photos and that he can still see the TV from that position. Funny how when we pass we still have an interest in the earthly things we have left behind.

While I was writing this chapter, I had a strong message from Jack to ring Karen. When I rang Karen's number, it went to message bank, but I didn't bother to leave a message, as Jack said, 'Don't worry, Mum will ring you back. She's got something to tell you.'

Karen did ring me back, and she told me that both of the boys were having stars named after them. Jack just started singing: 'Twinkle, twinkle big star!' I told Karen and she started to laugh and then said, 'That's Jack!'

Karen sent me a letter some time later, which concluded:

Debbie, I thank you for all you have given me . . . In closing, I would like to comment that Jack wanted me to play Tracy Chapman's 'The Promise'. This came via a girlfriend of Jack's. He had told Natasha that if anything happened to him, he wanted me to play this song. In this song, it says that 'he would find a way back to me' and he certainly has through you.

Chapter 19

The Lost Lilies: The Claremont Murders

Back in early 1996, when I was pregnant with my third child, Shannon, I was still being bombarded by visions of the backpacker murders and was also having to cope with many other crime-scene visions, which came to me both in my waking moments as well as while I was asleep.

The newspapers were full of stories about a killer who struck in Claremont, an affluent western suburb of Perth, Western Australia. The first reported victim was an eighteen-year-old girl named Sarah Spiers, who, on 26 January, disappeared into thin air after leaving the Club Bayview nightspot in Claremont. It is alleged that, after Sarah left Club Bayview, she walked to the corner of Stirling Highway and Stirling Road to call a cab from a phone booth to return home, but when the cab arrived, she was nowhere to be seen. To this day, her disappearance remains a mystery.

On 9 June 1996, the next victim, a twenty-three-year-old girl named Jane Rimmer, disappeared not far from where Sarah went missing, only this time the location where she was last seen was the Continental Hotel (which is now called the Claremont Hotel). Jane's remains were found in bushland on the side of Woolcoot Road, Wellard, in a drainage ditch in August 1996.

On 14 March 1997, Ciara Glennon, a twenty-seven-year-old lawyer, also went missing from the same area and her body was found on a dirt track surrounded by bush scrub on 3 April on Pipidinny Road, Eglinton, Perth, about forty-four kilometres north of the CBD.

I remember at the time feeling great sadness that Australia had yet another serial killer on the loose. Watching the nightly news became even more difficult, as visions of the murdered girls began to flood into my head. I tried desperately to shut out these images, as the backpacker visions were already more than enough.

I did manage to shut them down, but I silently hoped that if I had successfully passed on enough information to help bring closure to the backpacker-murder victims, I would one day be able to assist on the Claremont cases.

Well, I have to say, be careful what you wish for, as you just might get it.

Fast track into the future; we are now in 2007. Over the past few years, the Claremont murders have been on my radar. While filming the program *Sensing Murder*, the producers raised the possibility of working on these murders, but they were informed that the police and also the bereaved families didn't have much respect for psychics.

In early 2007, I was approached by the producers of the program *Missing Persons Unit*. Once again, they said to me that they would love to work on this case for the series, but once again I was informed that the Western Australia Police weren't open to working with psychics. The producers decided not to proceed with the case and accordingly put it aside.

In October 2007, Scott Russell Hill from *Sensing Murder* approached me and asked me if I would like to work on a project named *Psychic Taskforce*. The concept was that the *Psychic Taskforce* team would join forces to gather clues for unsolved cold cases throughout Australia and present them live on stage to a theatre audience, who would be encouraged to contact us afterwards if our clues had triggered any relevant memories. This way, valuable leads could hopefully be passed on to the police. The idea intrigued me, as my psychic detective work had really come to the fore.

The other two members of the three-man team would be Scott Russell Hill and Anthony Grzelka, Scott being the team leader. Scott is a numerologist and psychic and he has the ability to see auras. Anthony is a very gifted medium who also communicates with spirits on a daily basis. Both Scott and Anthony use symbology and signs to gather messages, whereas my abilities are mediumship, channelling and psychometry.

Over many conference calls and emails, the planning began. It was to be another ten months of negotiation and planning before the *Psychic Taskforce* team was to meet in person.

Denise Blazek and Andrea Barry, the show's producers, along with Scott Russell Hill, were to be my main points of contact prior to me flying from Sydney to Perth to begin working with the team. Nova Radio in Perth was to be the promoter of the show, as Scott had his regular radio segment with DJs Nat and Nathan. During the year, Scott and Nat had made contact with Sarah Spiers through their radio show.

I had appeared on programs with Scott Russell Hill in the past, while filming *Sensing Murder*, although as all of the psychics worked separately during the filming we had only been introduced to each other very briefly.

In early June 2008, Denise rang me to tell me that Scott and the production team had made a decision that the first case was going to be the Claremont murders. She also told me that there was some other exciting news, which I would be hearing from Andrea later on.

I was very happy to hear that I would be given the opportunity to help provide new clues for this controversial case, although I was extremely mindful of the family members' dislike of psychics. The most important thing for me while working on this case was to work with respect for the families and the police.

At the time of the phone call, I was sick in bed with the flu, and the moment that Denise told me what the case was going to be, I began to get visions flooding into my head. I tend to find that when I am sick, I become more open to the spirit world and I don't always have control over when the spirits make contact.

After finishing our conversation, I tried to get back to sleep. However, the moment I shut my eyes, the visions of the murdered girls began to flood back into my head. All I could see was a sea of pretty female faces coming in and out of focus and then merging into one another.

Suddenly, one young woman came directly back into focus. She had shoulder-length, sandy-blonde hair and a pretty, round-shaped face. Her eyes were green and she only appeared to be eighteen to twenty years of age. I recognised the woman to be Sarah Spiers, who I knew was one of the Claremont victims. I received an image of Sarah walking down a darkened street, and then I could see a car following her. At first, I thought the car could have been an off-duty taxi, but I later felt that its driver could have followed her from the nightclub she had been visiting with friends. The vision was jumping about and I am not completely sure whether the car was privately owned or a cab. As I hadn't been to Perth at this stage, I wondered what colour the cabs were at the time of her disappearance. The car I was seeing was dark blue; the initial vision was of the driver sitting parked in a darkened car-park area and I couldn't see his features at this point.

I got the feeling that whoever was driving the vehicle had been waiting in a side street for Sarah. The feeling was that he was like a white pointer shark, waiting in the darkness to strike when his victim least expected. It was only when he struck with precision and purpose that his presence became apparent – which, for the victim, was all too late.

The vision then moved forward and I could see that Sarah was in the driver's vehicle. Frustratingly, I wasn't given any impression of how she had come to be there. The strange thing was that Sarah was travelling in the back, on the left-hand side. This is the position that you would normally sit in if you were being driven around in a cab. Sarah seemed to be dazed and confused by the situation.

I could see that the driver turned around to talk to her. She was asking him why she was in the car and he told her that he wanted to make sure she got home safely. He suddenly reached under the front seat and picked up a white cloth, like a handkerchief. He then turned, leant back towards Sarah and put the cloth over her face. The smell of being at the dentist's flooded my senses. I wondered if there was chloroform on the cloth. I then saw that Sarah had passed out on the seat.

As I was seeing this vision, I got a very clear view of the man. He was approximately twenty-two to thirty years of age. He had a Mediterranean look about him, with olive skin, dark-brown or black wavy hair down to his collar, dark-coloured eyes and a five o'clock shadow. He had a big smile on his face, showing his white teeth. He was wearing a button-up, short-sleeved, collared shirt, light blue in colour with a checked pattern. The most noticeable thing about him was how immaculate he looked, except for his hands. He had dirt beneath his nails and his hands were cracked. They looked like those of a tradesman, maybe even a mechanic, as they were considerably callused.

The next vision was of Sarah being driven south along Stirling Highway towards Fremantle. She began to wake up and I started to see through her eyes. Lights seemed to be flashing past in a blur. I could see that she felt extremely worried about the situation she was in and she tried to get out of the vehicle. The doors wouldn't open and I could see her fumbling at the door handle. I wondered whether or not there were child-safety locks activated in the car or whether the vehicle had central locking.

I felt that the perpetrator drove Sarah approximately twenty minutes south of Perth, passing Fremantle. The roadway became darker as they went along. Sarah asked the driver where he was taking her and he told her not to worry as he was taking her home. She told him that he was driving in the wrong direction and he was too far south. She pleaded with him to turn around and take her home but he ignored her plea.

He turned off a road close to an industrial area and pulled up in an abandoned car park that overlooked the water. Across the water, in the distance, I saw twinkling lights, which led me to believe that an island could be out there. The area looked as if it could get quite windy, as there was sand blown across the roadway. There were a number of sandy tracks around the place. One of them led down to the water, where fishermen launched their boats. There was a groyne to the north of the car park, made of dark-coloured rocks. Seagrass was growing along the shoreline.

I could see Sarah struggling to get out of the car and, when the perpetrator opened her door, she broke free and made a run for it. I saw her running towards the water through the sand dunes. She stumbled and fell, and the perpetrator caught up to her. He grabbed her by the hair and she turned and scratched the side of his face. This caught him by surprise, allowing her to once again break free.

Terribly, she wasn't fast enough and he grabbed her by the hair and placed a small piece of rope or cord around her neck. She fell down in the sand, gasping for air. He looked completely in control during the whole ordeal, and the precision with which he acted was frightening. The friendly smile he once had had now become more of a snarl.

He brought out a knife and began a frenzied attack, cutting her throat and then slashing at her fragile body. The knife was like a diving knife, with a black handle and a large, serrated blade. I was thankfully not given an image of him sexually assaulting her in the vision but I got the feeling that that is what he did. When he was finished with her, he covered her dead body in the sand amongst the dunes.

The vision abruptly ended and I woke up in a cold sweat, with my heart thundering in my chest. I knew that I wasn't just having a nightmare, as the memory was still so vivid in my mind.

Suddenly, the phone rang and it was Andrea. She was calling to tell me that a well-known national magazine wanted to do a feature about me concerning my spirit photography and police work. Boy, what a day! Everything seemed to be happening at once. I began to tell her about all of the experiences I was having with Sarah Spiers and the other Claremont victims. Andrea is also a crime reporter and she had a close interest in the case, so she offered to scan in some of her files for me to read through in case any of the information made sense.

Over the next couple of days, we had many conversations about the case and the images that came flooding through to me from the spirit world. These visions were building into a substantial bank of information. I felt that

I was receiving many new clues that might one day help to solve the case.

Andrea emailed me maps of the areas I described. They ranged from Claremont to the south of Perth down to the Rockingham area. This helped me to determine psychically which areas would be of most interest to investigate during my planned arrival in Perth.

Andrea picked out the key features from my visions that would indicate we were searching in the right place for Sarah Spiers' body, as follows:

- Fremantle is significant. It is not the actual location but there is some connection associated with the main road to Fremantle, around twenty minutes south of it.
- It is isolated. No one heard the victim scream.
- There are fishermen in the area.
- It has a beach car park.
- There is regeneration – dune stabilisation.
- The sand rises up higher in the location where she is buried.
- Grass has grown over the site.
- There is a beach daisy with leaves indicating that it is a succulent – it has purple-pink flowers (pig-face daisy).
- The sand has blown away due to windy weather to reveal items belonging to the victim – possibly a handbag or shoe.
- There is black asphalt – no kerb or gutter.
- There are birds – native ducks and guinea fowl.
- There is fresh water located close by, such as a pond or a swamp.
- The coastal area comes around in a bend.

- Fishermen go there to get worms.
- In summertime, there are boats.
- There is a low timber fence.
- There is seagrass on the walk to the beach.
- If you stand in the car park, you look down on the area.
- There are a few ripples in the water – it's not a 'classic' beach with big waves.
- Lights can be seen in the distance about one to two kilometres away – could be from a lighthouse or an island.
- There is a run-down caravan park that would be on the right-hand side of the road while travelling south past Fremantle.
- There is a connection to a pelican – a large, coloured, oval sign with what appears to be a statue of a pelican sitting on top of it.
- There is run-down-looking, single-storey accommodation nearby, which would be used by truck drivers or people travelling up and down the coast.
- The area is close to or part of an industrial area.

Andrea and Denise became so excited by the information that they decided to go on a road trip to see if they could locate any of the features I was seeing in my visions.

Nova Radio Perth was extremely supportive of what we were doing, so some of the people from Nova, including Nick, the producer of the morning show with Nathan and Nat, also joined the girls.

The idea was that the team would drive south and photograph anything that looked relevant. The photos would be sent to our mobile phones and we would discuss my feelings about them via my landline.

Considering I had never been to Perth before and the team were only working with my visions and Andrea's notes, they did exceptionally well. There were many things that were ticked off the list. When the team arrived at Kwinana Beach, they found vegetation similar to my vision and also located a road with sand blown across it. To my surprise, they also discovered a piece of faded material sticking up from beneath the sand. The excitement on my end of the phone was too hard to contain; I felt that we were on to something.

The team took video footage while at the location on a mobile phone and sent it through to my phone in Sydney. This way, I could instantly confirm that they were in the right area. When they arrived back in Perth, they emailed the photographs to me along with more video footage, which they had filmed on their video camera. This was extremely useful in helping me to tune in further to the locations. I have to say that technology is such a wonderful thing – to be sitting in Sydney and having people in Perth send me photographs so quickly was quite amazing.

I arrived in Perth late on 17 August 2008 and was there for five days for my first visit. Looking back now, I can't believe that so much was achieved in such a short period of time.

Denise, Scott and Kerstin (Scott's PA) picked me up from the airport. It was then off to Subiaco to meet the documentary film crew and to assemble the whole team of *Psychic Taskforce* for the first time in person, except for Anthony Grzelka, whom I met the following morning.

The next day, the first stop for me after being introduced to Anthony was to meet an extremely fascinating lady named Mary Rodwell, who was going to put me under hypnosis to see if I could gather any additional clues for the case.

Mary has many talents. She is a clinical hypnotherapist but, first and foremost, she is an expert in ufology and alien contact. She is an extremely spiritual woman and is attuned to the psychical phenomenon, so it was an absolute pleasure to be working with her.

Mary also has a very strong interest in spirit photography, so I took my computer with me to show her my photographs. However, it decided that it wasn't going to turn on for me, so that plan was thwarted. This was just one of the many malfunctions to my electronic equipment that I was to experience over my stay in Perth.

The documentary team met us at Mary's place as they wanted to film me going under hypnosis. I have been hypnotised many times in the past to work on police cases, and I go into hypnosis very easily. The crew wanted me to mock up the process for them for camera but, unfortunately, I went straight under and made contact with the victims immediately.

I could see Sarah Spiers right away and began to see images of what happened to her on the night of her disappearance. However, Sarah wasn't alone – another seven girls lined up behind her, patiently waiting to tell me their story.

My connection was abruptly interrupted when I heard Scott Wright from the film crew speaking in the distance, telling me that they had finished filming what they needed.

Poor Scott didn't realise that I was already in contact with the girls.

Suddenly, I was back in an armchair at Mary's place, feeling quite dazed about what I had just witnessed. Mary and I discussed what I had been seeing before we broke connection and I told her how there were a number of girls present.

We decided to begin the session again, so I relaxed and listened to Mary's soothing voice as it sent me back under hypnosis. The second time was much more difficult. Mary asked me to get Sarah to show me anything significant about the perpetrator. I began to see an image of a man in a workshop. He was wearing blue mechanics' overalls and was using a pulley with a rope and chain to lift an engine out of a vehicle. I could see that there were trucks parked in the car park of the workshop and there was an old, red diesel pump located just outside the entrance.

I could also see old tyres stacked up in a pile to the left of the door. Mary asked me to tell her if there were any significant signs to look for and I could see the letters TJM in a sort of logo for something. The logo was a red oval with a white outline and the letters TJM in white. I wasn't sure what the connection was but it came through as a clue.

I then could see the man's overalls up close and the name Joe was embroidered on them. Mary asked me what the man's surname was and I heard the name Garbonni or something similar. I didn't get the feeling that the surname was his; it was more a feeling that he might work for someone with a name that sounded like that.

Next, I could see a semi-trailer truck driving along a road. I didn't know whether he drove the trucks or the vision was to indicate that the man worked on trucks or for a trucking company.

Mary asked me what the man was doing now. I then saw that he had been married or in a relationship and had two children but I got the impression he had recently split up with his wife or partner. Mary asked me to tell her about the man's family and family life. I felt that he had a brother and a sister and that he had an ethnic background. I felt that he didn't have a good relationship with his parents and that his mother had put him down. His parents may have split up when he was younger and his siblings married before he did.

I felt that the man was a control freak and that his wife had left him due to this. I could see that he had violent outbursts and his wife and children were terrified of him. On the outside, he seemed to be very normal, but there was a cold darkness that only those close to him could see. It seemed that his family had suspicions that he had done bad things in the past but were too frightened to tell anybody.

I felt that he loved cars and that he had a connection to motor racing or motor sports. I could see that his vehicle was more important to him than his wife and children. He was also extremely neat and if his wife didn't have the house spotless he would fight with her over it.

Mary asked me what type of vehicle he drove and whether I could identify anything about it that stood out. I could see that he had access to a number of vehicles and then I saw a yellow vehicle door with a shield on it that looked similar to that of the RAC in Western Australia.

I felt that he kept trophies from all of his victims, perhaps locks of their hair. He also kept trinkets such as jewellery, key rings and other small personal items.

Sarah then communicated the following information to me while I was still under hypnosis:

- Head south of Fremantle on the highway and look for sand or salt piles on the right-hand side of the road in an industrial area.
- Look for a connection to a raceway.
- There is a strong chemical smell that is sickly sweet in the air.
- He drove over bridges to get to the location.
- The name Joe is very prominent.
- The name Carboni, Garbonne, Carbone or similar is important.
- Look for an old caravan or transient accommodation that could be used by long-haul truck drivers for cheap overnight accommodation.
- There are marshes to the right of the location that he took me to.
- The man smokes (Winfield cigarettes?).
- Look for an insignia on a vehicle door in the shape of a shield. The car door is yellow and the logo could be either dark blue or black, similar to the RAC logo.
- Question whether or not he is a mobile mechanic or attends to breakdowns.

As a point of interest, I thought that if he did have access to an RAC vehicle, the girls would trust him implicitly. He would be their knight in shining armour.

Unexpectedly, a new woman then made contact with me and she started to demand that I should help her instead of wasting my time with Sarah. This woman was older than the other girls I had seen earlier. She was very streetwise and she had straight, dark hair with highlights in it. Her skin was of a fairly dark complexion and her eyes were brown. She was extremely attractive, with a slender build. She was wearing eyeliner and ruby-red lipstick. The woman was wearing a white shirt, with a black skirt and black jacket and stiletto shoes. She was holding manila folders that were tied with ribbons, similar to what a lawyer might use.

I had absolutely no idea who this woman was (she looked nothing like Ciara, who was also a lawyer) and wondered what on earth she had to do with the Claremont murders. I desperately tried to break contact with her as I didn't feel that she was connected. However, she had other ideas.

She showed me that she drove a silver vehicle and that she was extremely upset about her children. I could also see a connection with netball and wondered if her children were netball players. She then began to show me how she had died and I felt a very sudden pain in the right-hand side of my head. This all became too much, so I tried to pull myself out of the hypnosis to take a breather.

Mary could see my discomfort so she agreed it was time to have a rest. Luckily, we were accompanied by a lovely lady named Julie, who was sitting patiently in the background taking notes of the whole session for my records.

I told Mary that I was becoming confused due to this new woman making contact. Mary told me not to worry, that it would all make sense in the future as everything happens for a reason. I was to later find out how prophetic those words were.

I tried one more time to go under hypnosis to gather any other information I could. All I could see, however, was the dark-haired woman, standing at the beginning of the queue. Sarah's energy had weakened and she stood back. I tried to make note of the ladies' faces so I could check who they were at a later stage.

Some of the women I recognised from the missing-persons reports I had seen on the internet while in Sydney. I could clearly see Julie Cutler, who went missing on 20 June 1988, Lisa Jane Brown, who went missing on 10 November 1998, Hayley Dodd, who went missing on 29 July 1999, and Sarah McMahon, who went missing on 8 November 2000. Also among the women were Jane Rimmer, who went missing on 9 June 1996, and Ciara Glennon, who disappeared on 14 March 1997. These last two have sadly since been found murdered. I wondered if this was a sign that all of these victims were linked to the same murderer or just that they wanted me to help them. (I have since worked with some of Hayley Dodd's items and now feel this is a separate case altogether.)

The session ended and it was time for me to leave. I had to meet the documentary team to film my studio interview. While I was in the car travelling back to meet them, my head was filled with many images, not to mention the new case I seemed to have picked up with the woman with the dark hair. I had no idea who she was but when I mentioned what she looked like everyone seemed to know who I was talking about. A lot of Perth cases don't make major headlines on Sydney news, and vice versa, and all Scott and Anthony would tell me is that I would find out about the case later.

I filmed my first interview as to my thoughts about Claremont and what I hoped to achieve working on the case with the team. Then it was off in the filming van with Scott, Anthony and the crew for a road trip to locations that each of us had come up with prior to meeting.

Scott and Anthony had visited a place at Yalgorup that they felt was important and I wished to drive to Kwinana and surrounding areas to look for the points I had seen in my visions.

First stop for us all was Claremont. It was great to actually be on the ground and in the location instead of only seeing visions in my head. A lot of the information I had received made more sense through the visit.

When I stood in front of the Claremont Hotel, I was immediately taken back to the night that Jane Rimmer disappeared. I could see a pretty blonde girl waiting at the front of the hotel. She didn't say anything to me; she just stood there with a look of great sadness.

Kerstin and I went inside the hotel and the feeling I picked up was that the perpetrator had been there numerous times and was very familiar with the area. He was like a wallflower that nobody noticed. He would mingle amongst the crowd and pick out his next victim. He would charm them and gain their confidence and then he would strike with lightning precision.

As I walked around, I was suddenly taken back in time and could see him leaning at the bar having a drink. He was alone and standing some distance from the other patrons;

328

the vantage point from this area would have given him a clear view of the room. The image finished and I was standing back in the empty bar.

After we left the Claremont Hotel, we walked along Bay View Terrace and turned right onto St Quentin Avenue. This is where Club Bayview is located and it was the last place that Sarah's girlfriends saw her alive.

I wanted to walk around to the back of the club to see if I could locate the car-park area in which I had seen the perpetrator's car in my visions. When I rounded the corner, I couldn't believe my eyes. Everything looked familiar and now began to make so much more sense. I began to tune in to the energy of Sarah Spiers once again.

I was transported back in time and began to receive a very strong feeling that Sarah walked out of the front entrance of Club Bayview and then went around to the back of the building, where Hungry Jack's is located. I feel that she went in this direction to see if there was a payphone at Hungry Jack's. When she didn't find one, she walked out of the restaurant and walked into the car park at the back of Club Bayview. Across from the car park is an entrance to a mall that leads through to Bay View Terrace. I feel that Sarah's intention was to head in this direction to get back onto Bay View Terrace to look for a phone.

Adjoining the Club Bayview car park is the Hungry Jack's drive-through area. I could see that the perpetrator had his car parked in this area. He had followed Sarah out of the nightclub, unbeknown to her, and he was waiting in his car, watching her. His car was a blue sedan, similar in shape to a Ford Falcon XE or XF. It was very shiny, perhaps from metallic paint, with tinted windows and mag wheels. I could hear the car idling and it sounded like it had a twin exhaust.

As Sarah came closer to his vehicle, he leant out of the window and offered her a lift. She stopped and spoke with him but refused his offer and then walked through the mall.

The perpetrator didn't like the refusal so he exited the car park and turned on to Bay View Terrace, driving slowly down the street in order to follow her. As Sarah was in an intoxicated state, her reactions were a little slow. I felt that she noticed the car coming up behind her and began to feel concerned. I saw her fumbling around in her bag for something and then dropping her keys on the ground. She hurriedly picked them up and continued walking down the street towards the Continental Hotel.

I felt that she headed in this direction towards the post office, where there were a number of public telephones located. (This theory is contrary to what police have announced. It is alleged that Sarah made her phone call from a phone booth located in the vicinity of Stirling Highway. It has, however, been confirmed to me by a number of officers that the exact location of the phone booth from which Sarah called a cab cannot be confirmed.)

In my vision, Sarah crossed Bay View Terrace and made her phone call at the post office. Meanwhile, the perpetrator drove up behind her and turned right into the car park adjoining the post office. I felt that it was in this location that the perpetrator struck and was able to get Sarah into the car.

Scott, Anthony and myself walked in the same direction

that Sarah did on that fateful night to see if we picked up any psychic impressions. When we arrived at the post office, the three of us had the same impression that the presence of Sarah vanished.

Our next destinations were Henderson, Kwinana and Yalgorup. As we headed south, I kept my eyes peeled for an oval sign with a pelican on top of it. I was also looking for run-down accommodation, such as a caravan or tourist park. There were many tourist parks on the drive down but no pelican signs to be found. There were a number of real pelicans flying overhead, though.

We stopped at the suburb of Henderson, which was near an old, abandoned power station. This area is right on the beach and from the car park you can see the water. There are two car-park areas and we parked at the furthest one first. I walked around the area and could see that there was a groyne with black rocks. I was getting the same sickly sweet smell that I had received during my visions. I was also able to locate the type of pink-purple daisy that I had seen only in my initial visions (it turned out that the only location where the daisy would be seen was at this location). There was also the seagrass vegetation that I had seen in my visions, and wild tea-tree bushes with grey-blue leaves were very prevalent in the area.

The crew told me that people did come fishing here and it wasn't a classic type of beach where families would come to swim; it was more of a place you would take your dog for a walk. People would also jetski in this area during the summer months.

The wind factor was certainly there on the day we were visiting and the crew informed me that when the

Fremantle Doctor (a cool, seasonal breeze native to this part of Australia) came up, the wind was extremely strong. There were roads in the area that had sand blown across them and there were plantings for dune regeneration all around. In the distance, there was an island called Garden Island, which is a naval base, and at night you would be able to see the lights from it in the distance.

The area had been recently upgraded and the public toilets and car parks were all new. Sarah went missing in 1996 and we were at the location in 2008. I felt that it was quite plausible that the demographics of the area had changed a lot over that time.

The location was quite secluded and had a strange, creepy atmosphere. I was later to discover that it was once the site of the Robb Jetty abattoirs. This explained the feeling of death that I was picking up on.

Scott wasn't picking up on anything from the area. However, Anthony also felt that something didn't feel right there. I still had the feeling that I needed to head further south, though, just in case I had missed something. So we drove down to Kwinana and, on the way, just past the abandoned power station, I saw the white piles I had seen earlier under hypnosis. There was a salt-processing plant on the right-hand side of the road. This confirmation helped me to feel that we were heading in the right direction. We also passed some very strange, shanty-type shacks or caravans on the right-hand side of the road. We drove around in this area and it had an extremely strange atmosphere. There were a number of signs with pelicans on the front of these holiday shacks but I wasn't convinced that this was the right location. If it was connected, though, it would have been a great place for the perpetrator to visit without being noticed.

Driving to Kwinana, we passed a lot of industry and I could still smell that disgusting industrial smell. We arrived at Kwinana Beach and I could feel that something bad had happened there. I could hear ducks and birds chirping, I could still see Garden Island in the distance but the main road was too close to the beach. Some of the puzzle wasn't quite fitting. I did, however, feel that evil lurked in this area at night and that violence had taken place there (which was correct, as I was to discover later on).

To my frustration, Scott and Anthony didn't feel a thing at this location, so we decided to push on to Yalgorup. When we got there, Scott and Anthony, who had previously visited the location, asked me what my thoughts were. It felt very ancient and connected in some way to Aboriginal energy. I definitely felt there were spirits and dead bodies in the area but it was the land and the ancient people that were generating the deepest reverberations.

There were significant connections with what we were looking for, though, as new pathways and roads were being constructed there at the time that Sarah went missing. Also, the location was right on a lake and I could hear and see birds flying past. It was extremely isolated and nobody would know you were there at night. Anthony found some bone fragments in an area that we all felt had a strange aura. While I didn't dismiss that there could be bodies in this location, though, I still wasn't convinced that this was where Sarah Spiers was to be found.

We then headed back north-west to a suburb called Wellard, where Jane Rimmer's body was found. We were using the book *The Devil's Garden: The Claremont Serial Killings* by Debi Marshall as a reference point.

When we arrived at our destination, we were held up by a freight train crossing for about ten minutes. While we were sitting there, I thought how interesting it was that we kept crossing train lines during our trip. This was the fifth time during the day that we had crossed them. Henderson had train lines that we had to cross and so did the Kwinana area. The other significant connection was that we were once again near big power lines. I wasn't sure what the relevance was but each location seemed to have similarities.

We drove up Woolcoot Road, Wellard, to locate where Jane Rimmer's body was discovered. A white cross had been placed at the site but we failed to find it. We drove the length of the road and stopped and went for a walk along it in case we could pick up anything. I felt that we needed to go back further down to where the big power lines were but the boys did not agree. We were running out of time so we abandoned the search. I felt quite annoyed that we didn't persist for a few minutes more. As we were driving away, I heard a voice in my head loudly tell me that we needed to go to the arum lilies, as that is where she was found.

Anthony and Scott didn't think it was important, but I did. When we arrived back at our accommodation, I did a search on the internet and discovered that Jane's body was found amongst arum lilies by a family who were picking them. I felt very strongly that it was Jane's voice I heard in the car telling me that we had missed the spot. I vowed that on my next trip to Perth I would visit both of the murder sites of the girls to see if I could pick up any extra information.

The boys decided that after dinner they wanted to have a séance to see if they could contact the girls. I wasn't particularly interested in doing this kind of thing as I didn't think that the clarity would be pure enough.

This was the first time I had ever participated in a séance and I found it extremely frustrating. I wondered what the use was as I could see, hear, feel and channel the victims so clearly. I certainly felt that there was energy building up in the room but the frustration of spelling out letters that didn't make any sense didn't impress me very much. The séance ended and I didn't really feel that we were any closer to finding the perpetrator or Sarah Spiers' body.

I went back to my room and the dark-haired woman in spirit followed me. My new iPhone was completely dead so I plugged it into its charger. The charger, however, wouldn't work, so I had to give up on it. I managed to turn on my computer but the internet connection would not work. I began to wonder what was going on with my electrical items. I questioned if the woman had something to do with it.

I decided to go to bed but I just couldn't get to sleep. The energy in the room was whooshing around all over the place. I decided to take some photographs while lying there. I soon discovered that I wasn't alone in the room; there weren't any living people but there were certainly a lot of spirit friends. I took one photograph of the TV and it looked like fireworks were coming out of the screen.

Now, I had seen the movie *Poltergeist* and I decided that I had seen enough activity for one night, so I tried to go to sleep. The dark-haired woman flooded my head with images and information. I made a promise to her that I would help her but not right now. I told her that if she needed my help, she needed to provide me with the tools to do it. I was later to find out that she would take me up on this.

The following morning, my first appointment was with the documentary crew to do an interview about what I had been experiencing during the hypnosis and the location searches. During the filming, I was given the surprising news that the team had made contact with a very respected, retired police forensic artist by the name of Terry Dunnett, who had worked for the Western Australia Police Force for thirty-two years. Terry had agreed that he would work with me to make a composite drawing of what I thought the perpetrator looked like at the time of the attacks. I couldn't believe how lucky I was. I certainly felt that the girls in spirit were doing everything possible to give us all the help they could in the short space of time we had to look for them.

I finished the interview and was driven off to meet Terry. On arrival at his place, I could feel his healthy scepticism about working with a psychic. He admitted to me, though, that he was open-minded and if the drawing helped to identify the man, then he felt it was worth it. He did warn me that in the past he had worked with another psychic and she was able to do a great description of a man who turned out to be her next-door neighbour, who had nothing to do with the case she was working on. With that in mind, I asked the spirit world to give me as much clarity as possible to bring the image in my head to life.

Well, it seemed that I was in luck, because the man's face came flooding back to me. Firstly, we looked at a database that Terry had constructed of different parts of faces that he had drawn and then separated. These images were based on images of real people. It was so interesting to see all of the noses, mouths, face shapes, eyes and hair flicking quickly past me on the screen. We reconstructed the man feature by feature, with Terry going directly to each part of the face that I needed to choose from. In about an hour, Terry had managed to produce an image of a man that looked very close to the perpetrator. It was extremely unsettling to have this man staring back at me from the screen. I felt that he could now be seen by all the world; he wasn't just an image in my mind.

The interesting thing when we finished was that Terry told me he remembered having drawn this man before. I truly hoped that this might be the break we were looking for and that the Claremont killer could be put where he belonged, once and for all.

When we had finished, Terry said that he would make some final adjustments to the image and email it to me as soon as it was ready. I couldn't wait for the rest of the team to see our 'man'.

After finishing the identikit with Terry, it was back to meet with Scott and Anthony. To my surprise, two detectives from the Western Australia Police Force were waiting with the boys to meet me.

I knew that earlier the boys were having a meeting with these officers but didn't realise that I was to be involved. Scott asked me to tell the officers about the woman I had seen the day earlier under the hypnosis. I asked him which girl he meant and he replied that it was the woman with the dark hair. It was only then that what Mary had told me came to light – everything did happen for a reason. The officers were talking to me about the woman who broke through the hypnosis session to make her presence known.

We discussed what I had seen and I could feel her presence very strongly in the room. I asked were there any personal items of the woman that I could hold to tune in to. I was given a diary that belonged to her and immediately began receiving messages from her.

I strongly felt that she had been murdered. Once again, I saw a silver sedan and felt it belonged to the victim. She had a lovely energy and I could feel her distress about leaving her children.

The woman once again showed me the law files and this confirmed to me that she was a solicitor or barrister. She also flashed the symbol of scales in my mind, signifying justice. I asked the officers if it was possible to go to the site where she was found. We were extremely privileged that the officers agreed, as the case was current and unsolved. (In fact, the investigation is still ongoing at the time of going to print, so I'm afraid I have had to omit some of the details, including the name of the victim and the names of the officers I assisted.)

Anthony and I joined the officers, as Scott had to do his interview with the film crew. We were driven to a street not far from where we were staying. I was holding the woman's diary as we drove in the car.

Anthony was drawn to a particular part of the street. I felt compelled to get out of the car and have a walk around to tune into the energy. I could hear the woman telling me to turn right and head down past the tree and look at the lamppost. She then told me to look at the ground and there would be a sign connected to murder.

I spoke with one of the officers and he agreed that indeed it was the exact spot where her car had been found. I then could see some very strong images of people connected to the case and relayed that information to the officer.

As I have worked on lots of police cases in the past, I understand that it is protocol for officers not to be able to relay details to confirm or deny psychic information. It was, however, confirmed to me that what I was saying made sense to the case. For me, that was all I needed to know, because I then knew for certain that I was on the right track.

When we got back to the car, we were driven to a bush area a few kilometres away. There were a few roads we needed to drive along before we knew that we were close to where the woman was found.

Anthony received a message that we needed to look for some bollards. I wasn't sure until I got out of the vehicle which exact location I would be drawn to. Anthony and one of the officers walked up a sandy track in the bush. I was behind them but didn't feel drawn in that direction. Suddenly, I felt myself being pulled by the woman and I began to go off into the bush on the right-hand side of the track.

I felt the urgency to keep on walking, so I ventured in about two hundred metres off the main track until I came across a hot-pink pot full of tulips sitting in a large, circular indent in the earth. As soon as I arrived at this spot, I heard the woman loudly say to me, 'It's about time you got here!' I was suddenly overcome with emotion and began to cry. I started to see visions of the woman's two children and the sadness she felt about not being with them as they grew up.

While heartbreaking, this experience was extremely fulfilling and it confirmed for me that I could locate a site where a crime had taken place. I passed more information on to the officer concerning the case and then it was time to head back to where we were staying.

I decided to call it a night, but my new-found friend with the dark hair had other ideas. The previous night was bad enough but that was only the beginning. The light bulb in the kitchen in my hotel room blew and the energy in the room was electric. I took more photographs, just to prove to myself that I wasn't imagining things. I was a little surprised to see the room full of orbs. I tried to go to sleep but the night seemed to drag on. The images in my mind just wouldn't stop.

I was extremely tired in the morning when it was time to meet up with the team. We had a radio interview first thing at Nova with Nathan and Nat. It went very well, in spite of my tiredness, the three of us doing readings on air for the listeners. I was also given the pleasure that morning of meeting the rest of the Nova team in person, all of whom had been gracious enough to go on the first road trip to Kwinana to help track down where my visions were directing me to. In the afternoon, we went back to Subiaco to film our interviews about our findings for the case. The rest of the day went by at a much slower pace than the rest of the week.

After dinner, Denise, Scott, Kerstin and I decided that we would visit Claremont during the night to get a better feel for what it was like when the girls went missing.

We parked at the back of Club Bayview and walked around to get our bearings. Quite coincidentally, a blue Ford was parked in the same location where I had seen the perpetrator park his car on the fateful night of Sarah's disappearance. We all made a remark that it might be some kind of a sign.

We walked the path that we thought the perpetrator may have driven while following Sarah, and the images felt very plausible. We passed the Claremont Hotel and crossed to the post office. If Sarah was abducted from the car park at that location, the view wouldn't have been completely clear from the hotel across the road. The phone boxes were located towards the car-park side of the building and he could have easily fled from the car park down a lane adjoining the site.

The location matched the images I had been receiving; the only problem was that this was not the line of enquiry the police had been following.

We went back to the car and drove down the fairly deserted lane. It passed by the back of shops and meandered down to Stirling Highway. It was a perfect getaway route; he could quite easily have driven down the lane without being noticed.

The following day, I returned to Sydney. I felt extremely tired but very excited that maybe, just maybe, the Claremont case could be solved. If not, it certainly wouldn't be through any lack of commitment.

On 28 August 2008, on the Crime Investigation channel on pay TV, a program aired about the Claremont murders. It showed exclusive CCTV footage of a man who was seen talking with Jane Rimmer prior to her disappearance. I could not believe my eyes: the man was the height of the perpetrator in my visions, he had dark wavy hair (I couldn't tell whether it was black or brown, as the footage was black and white) and he was neatly dressed, with a coloured shirt and tight-fitting jeans.

While watching the footage, I felt that the man had met Jane prior to this meeting and it was the reason she had left her friends behind when they'd decided to head home after their night out. My feeling was that the man had waited until Jane was alone to make his move. In the footage, she looks so pleased and excited to see him.

Unfortunately, no front-on view of the man's face is shown in the footage, which jumps back and forth from different vantage points, but his general appearance was enough to convince me I had a match, and that was where the identikit image I had reconstructed of his face could step in. I felt excited that I was on to something.

I returned to Perth on 23 September and stayed until 30 September 2008. Denise picked me up from the airport and I stayed at her place for most of the week. During my first night there, I received visions about a silver four-wheel-drive Hilux Ute. I couldn't see the driver but I could see the vehicle passing me by. I then saw a view of the ute from behind; it was driving along a bush track that led off from an asphalt road in a country area. I didn't think much about it, except I wondered what the significance was. I was to find out the following day.

Andrea, Denise and I planned to visit the sites where both of the girls' bodies were found and revisit the Henderson and Kwinana areas for further clues. We travelled to Pipidinny Road, Eglinton, first. It was an hour and a half's drive to the location and when we arrived at the site the road was deserted. We parked the car near where I felt the site could be and started walking to see what we could see.

I knew that I was looking for a large grass tree on the eastern side of the road. It must have looked a sight, three women in the middle of nowhere walking along the road. It is only when I think back that I realise what a risk the three of us were taking.

A man drove past us in a silver four-wheel-drive ute and gave us a strange look. A couple of minutes later, he came back and asked us what we were looking for. He then casually asked if we were looking for the site where Ciara Glennon was found. When we said we were, he told us to get back in the car and he would lead us there.

He drove about two hundred metres up the road and then turned off onto a sandy track with thick bush almost covering the access. I suddenly remembered the vision I had during the night. Andrea jokingly said, 'I hope that he isn't the murderer.' I began to panic and told Denise, who was driving, not to follow the car in. I kept telling her to back up and get onto the road. Both Denise and Andrea at this stage had no idea about what I had seen the night before.

They both told me not to panic, as there were three of us and one of him. Fat lot of good, I thought, if he had a weapon. We ended up following the car into the track and it led into a loop. The man stopped the car and walked back to us and told us he would lead us down to where a cross had been placed as a memorial to Ciara.

Andrea asked him what he was doing out in this area in the first place and he replied that he was looking for snakes and goannas. She then asked him what his name was, and he told her 'Ken' and said he was a local. He got back in his car and drove off just as quickly as he had appeared.

I told the girls about my vision the night before and they then understood my strange behaviour. We all agreed that it was a very strange coincidence that he just happened to come along at the time when we needed him. I do feel that the perpetrator has a silver four-wheel-drive ute, but I don't feel that the man who assisted was connected to the case in any way. I felt that Ciara and Jane were doing all they could to help us solve their case.

I then walked down to the area where the cross was placed. I quietly stood at the spot and put my hand on the white metal cross signifying the final resting place of Ciara. The feeling was overwhelming: my hand became extremely hot and I could see the perpetrator's vehicle on the track. I felt that he dragged Ciara to the location by her hair and that his handiwork ended her life at this spot. I didn't see much of a struggle at this location and wondered if she had been drugged once again, like I had seen him do to Sarah.

I asked Ciara how he had managed to get her in the car in the first place and she told me that she was walking home and he had followed her out of the hotel. He had driven up behind her and offered her a lift and she had declined. She then showed me that she continued to walk away from the car. I saw him driving up onto the footpath and nudging her from behind with the vehicle, which knocked her over. It wasn't fatal, but I saw that he was able to pick her up and put her into the vehicle without much resistance. I wondered if there were any signs on her remains of damage to her lower limbs.

Ciara was an extremely streetwise young woman; all she could say to me was that she had travelled throughout Europe and the United Kingdom and yet she had met foul play in her own backyard.

She told me that he had made advances to her at the bar when she was with her work colleagues and that she had declined them. She had thought nothing more of it until he approached her in his car. It was only when she saw him in the vehicle that she began to panic. At this time in her life, Ciara didn't have a care in the world. She was excited about her sister's upcoming wedding and that event was all she was focusing on.

I felt that Ciara had put up a bit of a fight and that she had insulted him by telling him that he wasn't her style. This had sent him into a rage. I felt that he'd managed to get her into the back seat of the car and knock her out with the chloroform.

Ciara then showed me that there was some form of restraining device in the back of the vehicle. When she came to, she was restrained, with her hands and feet tied up. One notable thing that she showed me was that he had seat covers on the front seat and something covering the back seat and the floor at the back. I am not sure whether they were plastic or vinyl coverings but there was certainly a difference between the front and the back seats.

Suddenly, I was back standing at the cross where Ciara was found. The images suddenly stopped but Ciara was still communicating with me. I got the feeling that the perpetrator kept a trophy of her and she told me about a brooch he had taken that was extremely special to her family. It was what represented her family and their closeness. I also felt that he took some of her hair, as I saw him rubbing it on his face. This image was extremely disturbing. She showed me that he may have taken her undergarments and I saw him quickly putting something in his pocket.

I began to feel quite queasy in the stomach that such a person was still running around in public. It really makes you think and question how one individual can inflict such atrocities on another human being. You also wonder what happened in that person's life to make him turn into such a monster. I believe that we all begin this life as innocent little beings. What is it that flicks the switch that turns someone into a murderer?

Andrea and Denise asked me what I was experiencing, and Andrea took notes as I spoke. Once I had finished the contact with Ciara, we drove down to Wellard to visit Jane Rimmer's site.

It was interesting that when we passed Henderson and turned off to Wellard we crossed train tracks again. I am pleased to say that Andrea, Denise and I did locate the site this time. Her cross was located near a drainage ditch on the left-hand side of the road.

Andrea's partner did some research for us and provided us with a rough map to guide us. It confirmed all of my feelings on my previous visit to the site. There was a big overhead electricity transformer just opposite it and the area was completely covered with arum lilies on both sides of the road. Some people think of arum lilies as death lilies, and in Jane's case they were. I actually see them as beautiful, elegant symbols of life as well as death.

As a memorial to the three girls, I decided it would be respectful if we picked the lilies exactly where Jane's body was found and had them on stage when we did the *Psychic Taskforce* show at the Burswood Casino on the upcoming weekend.

While at the location, I could see the disrespect for human life that the perpetrator had. I could see that he quickly stopped the vehicle and just discarded Jane Rimmer's body into the drainage ditch without so much as a second's glance. He then drove off as though nothing had happened.

This location is not as isolated as where Ciara's remains were found. There is a house about three hundred metres up the road on the opposite side. Adjoining the site where Jane was found is a paddock with horses and a house about five hundred metres back from the road. It just goes to show how brazen he was.

After we picked the lilies, we drove down to the Kwinana and Rockingham areas to see if I could pick up any more information. On the way, we passed the Kwinana Motorplex. This was something I hadn't noticed on my first trip down to this area. Next, we passed three RAC vehicles within a minute of each other. All three of us noticed them and we laughed and wondered whether it was a sign that we were on the right track.

We drove to the industrial area in front of the grain silos that Andrea and Denise had visited in June with the team from Nova. I still felt that there was something wrong with the area but couldn't put my finger on it. We drove along some other roads that were across from the beach and had a walk around. This area was extremely creepy and I felt that there was definitely negative energy here.

We then drove to Rockingham and out past the naval base. We did see a few pelican signs but none of them fitted what I was looking for. It was getting close to 4.30 pm, so we decided to head back to Henderson.

On our way there, we saw a sign of a pelican advertising a new housing estate. It hadn't been present the last time I had been in Perth, and I felt that it was pertinent to the case. We stopped to take a photograph of it and, from the position it was in, you could look down onto the salt works and the old Henderson power station, which was our next destination.

We parked the car at the car park next to the amenities block and proceeded to walk amongst the dunes to see what I could pick up. We had just got to the top of the dune area when a burnt-orange metallic Monaro with black tinted windows and personalised plates pulled up. The windows were so dark that we couldn't see the occupants of the car; all we could see was an arm with a white, short-sleeved T-shirt up against the passenger's window.

The vehicle parked parallel to the back of ours and the occupants just watched as we walked away. I said to both of the girls that something felt extremely wrong and told them to get back into the car. I had already had enough adrenalin for one day and now the sun was beginning to set, so the sooner we got back into the car the better.

The passenger in the front of the Monaro then opened his door and began to get out. We couldn't see his face, just his foot and arm as he began to exit the car. When we quickly got back into our car, the man abruptly jumped back inside his and shut the door. It felt like we were in a Mexican stand-off; it was quite a few moments until they drove off and stopped hemming our car into the parking space. We all vowed to come back to the location the following day, during the daylight hours.

While driving home, Denise admitted that she had seen the same vehicle earlier that day while we were driving in Kwinana and she had recognised the number plate, as it was personalised. I don't know what they wanted, but I was extremely glad that none of us ever found out.

As we headed back to Perth, signs seemed to be popping up in front of us. At a roadside memorial, there were two crosses, one bearing the name of 'Sarah' and the other 'Jane'. These were not connected to the case, but we all felt that it was a sign from the girls that they were pleased with what we were trying to do to help them. When we stopped at lights, a four-wheel-drive vehicle stopped close by bearing a personalised plate that said 'Jane'. I silently hoped that this meant Jane was happy that we had picked the lilies in remembrance of the three girls.

The following day, we drove back to Henderson and this time we were extremely cautious about who was in the car park. We walked down the beach towards the abandoned power station and discovered that there was an area nearby that had fresh water and was filled with reeds and native ducks. The ducks seemed to be having a wonderful time diving and swimming in the lagoon.

The area seemed to fit in with a lot of my visions: there was a wooden fence, black rocks made into a groyne and Garden Island was opposite. The succulent pink-purple daisy was present in the area and the seagrass was prevalent everywhere. Seagrass is quite creepy when it is bleached by the sun; it looks like bone fragments sticking up from the sand. I looked very closely in some areas, just in case Sarah's remains could be found. In my vision, I could see that the wind had blown enough sand away to expose some material and bleached white bones.

The tea trees were also growing rampantly in the location, which also confirmed my thoughts. As I walked amongst the dunes, I found a piece of material sticking up from the sand. It was bleached white by the sun and weather. However, when I picked it up it was a black T-shirt with a print on the front, and I didn't feel it had anything to do with Sarah.

We walked around the area for quite some time until I satisfied my feelings that it could quite possibly be the location we were looking for. My only concern was that I hadn't noticed the power station in my visions. Perhaps, because it was disused at the time of Sarah's disappearance, it would just have been a blackness in the dark, rather than something that was lit up, making its presence known.

Another pertinent thing that I noticed was the humming sound of the electricity substation built right next door to the old power station. I wondered whether there was a connection to electricity in some way, as at both Jane's and Ciara's murder sites there were power lines close by.

After we drove back to town, it was time to meet Scott and Anthony, as they arrived on the Friday night before the *Psychic Taskforce* show. I asked them whether or not they could return with me to the locations the following morning, as I felt it was extremely relevant. Unfortunately, though, they didn't have the time. I was disappointed by this but I also reminded myself that we all work differently. My next thing to focus on was doing the *Psychic Taskforce* show at the Burswood Casino in Perth. The Saturday-night show was in the Burswood Ballroom and the Sunday-night one was in the Burswood Theatre.

It was quite overwhelming to be in something on such a grand scale as this, although I felt that if it helped to find Sarah and unearth new clues to assist the police then it had to be worth it.

Terry had graciously given me permission to show the composite of the man I believed to be the perpetrator on the stage, and I felt that this could help to jog something in the public's mind in case there was anyone out there who recognised him, especially since the CCTV footage had also just been released.

During the first half of the show, Scott, Anthony and I did readings for the audience, while the second half was focused on bringing up new facts on the Claremont case.

The Sunday event was the more fruitful of the two. In the second half of the show, I read out to the audience the clues I felt most vital to the case, including my psychic profile of the suspect, and we again revealed the composite. The audience gasped when the image was displayed on the screen. One woman in the crowd stood up; her voice was quivering with emotion and she couldn't stop herself from shaking. She admitted that the psychic profile fitted that of a man she knew. She said the composite only confirmed her suspicions of him and she stood there in disbelief at seeing his image staring back at her, larger than life. She had always felt his connection to the murders but didn't have enough evidence to come forward to the police. I felt that the knowledge this woman possessed could be a major turning point in finally solving the Claremont murders.

A number of other audience members came forward on the Sunday with information about the composite, and this information has now been passed on to the police for investigation. I found it interesting that one young woman came forward when the footage was shown of the team standing at Kwinana Beach, where I felt that something bad had happened. I remember telling the boys that I felt there was a significance to the area, yet they didn't agree. The young woman was sexually assaulted right where I had been standing. This was confirmation that my psychic gifts were truly on the trail. It was a sad realisation, however, that someone had suffered at the hands of another.

After the shows, I met up with some of the audience members and have since had many conversations with them in preparing a report for the police. I understand that some members of the Western Australia Police Force do not accept the work of psychics but I hope they will consider listening to the members of the public, as they are the ones with the factual information.

It was also passed on to me later that a member of the Macro unit – the police team in charge of the Claremont investigation – wanted me to know that the way I had asked for the arum lilies to be arranged on stage exactly matched the logo of the Macro unit's badge. She was astounded as to how I would even know this, and I was also shocked, because I didn't know that they had a badge like that. All I can say is that the girls had told me exactly what to do.

After returning home to Sydney, I was hit by the reality of the Claremont case. I realised that I had once again got myself a little too close for comfort. I couldn't stop thinking about what I had experienced over the past week and felt pleased that Denise, Andrea and myself had made it home unscathed, albeit for a few close calls at Henderson and Eglinton. I truly felt that the information received while working on the *Psychic Taskforce* project was very viable.

The bigger task at hand now was to get the Macro unit to listen to my information. I had numerous conversations with the police spokesperson for the Macro unit, Jim Stanbury, and his constant line was that 'The police don't work with psychics'.

I totally understood that statement – it is imprinted inside my brain – but I knew that it was not completely true. I told him that I had assisted numerous officers in New South Wales for the past fifteen years, but that didn't impress him very much. I asked him could he at least listen to the witnesses who had come forward and speak with them about their experiences. He agreed that he would, so I rang them all and passed on his details.

The witnesses attempted on many occasions to speak with Mr Stanbury and a number of them let me know that he wasn't at all interested in their information if it related to their recognition of the composite. I felt extremely frustrated that he was taking this line of reasoning. The case is cold, it is at a dead end, so why wouldn't they at least look at this information? I do understand, though, that psychics in the past had caused a lot of grief to the families of these girls.

Thursday 2 October 2008 was a night I won't forget. I was abruptly woken from a sound sleep by another Claremont vision. This time, the vision was in the present and the perpetrator was now older.

I was suddenly watching a scenario taking place at a restaurant with full-length glass windows overlooking the water. I felt that it was at Fremantle. Lots of tables were being cleared and then reset for the following day. It was the end of the evening and people were starting to leave. The perpetrator had been chatting to a very attractive-looking woman who was in her late thirties to early forties and was dressed in evening wear. Her top was a pink-peach colour and was shiny like satin, and she had a string of pearls that looped three times around her neck. Her eyes were blue-green and she had thick, blonde, straight hair just past her shoulders. The woman bid her colleagues farewell and then turned to the perpetrator to tell him that she was calling a cab.

The perpetrator offered to give her a lift home, saying that it's not safe to get a cab as the Claremont serial killer (who has been suspected of being a taxi-driver) had never been caught and he couldn't forgive himself if anything happened to her. The woman thanked him profusely and accepted the offer.

Next, he was driving south on Stirling Road and I felt

354

that he was heading south past Fremantle. They crossed over a bridge and turned off to the left, doing a kind of a loop. They passed a number of playing fields on the left-hand side of the road. The woman began to worry as he started to drive towards an area that was less lit up. She questioned him as to why he was heading to this location. He ignored her questions and just kept on driving.

I heard her say loudly that he was going in the wrong direction and why were they driving to the sailing-club car park. I now think that it could be the East Fremantle car park, as I have googled the location and it looks similar to the vision. He then abruptly stopped the car and she asked him what on earth he thought he was doing.

He then turned to her and said, 'And you were worried about the Claremont serial killer. Well, now you have met him!' He then started to strangle her with her strand of pearls and everything went black. In the distance, I heard him say that he just needed a little trophy and he told her that he wanted some of her hair.

I woke up with my heart pounding and his voice lingering in my head. I immediately took note of what he looked like, as this time I was seeing things through the victim's eyes and the image was very clear.

His eyes were blue-grey in colour, his hair was now greying and he had put on some weight. His face was a little paunchy and more lined than before. I then went back in my mind to see what other things identified the route he took to where he finally strangled her.

The entrance to the yacht club went down a hill and there was a sign at the front of the building. The car park was on the left-hand side and when the car was parked I could see that there were houses elevated above me. There was a sandstone retaining wall on the right of the car park that was on the property of the sailing club, and above this area were houses. To the left of the car park were the water and boats.

What I didn't see was whatever it was he did with the woman when he was finished with her. I really hope that it was only a dream – my only problem is that when I have dreams like this, they are usually true. Let's hope that this time it was just a bad dream. I find it very frustrating to see such alarming visions and not be able to circumvent them. I am told constantly how lucky I am to be able to do what I do, but let me tell you it comes at a price. The saving graces are that I am able to help police with clues and provide families with messages from their loved ones, which in many cases gives them closure. In this case, I was also very glad that I was able to work with Terry Dunnett again to produce a new composite image of how the killer looks now, based on my latest vision.

My strongest wish is to help stop the Claremont serial killer from doing it again. I understand that psychics don't solve cases – police do. It would be nice, though, if my work could become an accepted tool, to assist the police in theirs. When you think about it, they use sniffer dogs and forensics: what is the difference with using a psychic? Fingers crossed that the future will see a change.

Chapter 20

You Are
Never Alone

While watching the first episode of *Ghost Whisperer*, starring Jennifer Love Hewitt, I received one of the very few visits I have ever had from my nanna, Jean Gee, who passed in 1985, when I was twenty-one years old.

Before I left for my working holiday in Queensland, Nanna had informed me that it would be the last time that I would see her alive. This statement worried me but I thought that she was being silly. At that time in my life, my psychic abilities were not tuned in to the level they are now, so I was quite oblivious to what she was trying to tell me. I deeply regret that I didn't pay more attention to her words, because I would have made a more concerted effort to phone her and write to her while I was away.

You would think that I, being a medium and psychic, could easily talk to my own dead relatives, but unfortunately this is not the case. I am much better at contacting the deceased family members of other people.

But as the opening scenes of *Ghost Whisperer* played out in front of me, I felt a change of energy in the air and a coolness surrounded me. Then my nanna appeared beside me.

Nanna started to communicate with me as clearly as when she was alive. She told me that she was always aware that I had a gift and that she also was psychic. The program I was watching faded into the background and it was as though I was watching my own childhood on the television screen. My nanna took me back to the time when my poppa had died. She told me that she knew then that I had the gift. When she was alive, we had never discussed such a thing, so it was quite a surprise to be talking about it with her now.

Nanna reminded me that when I was about nine years old she bought me a game called ESP. I loved to play this game, even though I wasn't very good at it. My mum had a habit of putting things at the top of the cupboard, out of the way, if she thought that we shouldn't play with them, and my ESP game was quickly relegated to the top of the cupboard. Realising that Mum didn't approve of her encouraging these talents in me, Nanna decided not to talk to me about my psychic gift, in case it caused friction between the two of them.

Nanna spoke with me now for about an hour. She told me that for her it had been very hard to live with this gift (or curse) as at times family members thought that she was going mad.

She then took me back to a time when I was aged ten and she came to stay at our house for a week. I saw that Mum and Nanna had an argument when Nanna informed my mother that she should throw out all of her aerosol cans because she could see that using them was going to cause a big hole in the atmosphere and damage the environment in the future. My mother of course thought that Nanna was going crazy and told her that she didn't know what she was talking about. Mum told Nanna that she wouldn't throw out any of the cleaning products because she had just bought them. Years later, my mum relayed this same story to me and said she now understood what Nanna had been talking about. Mum realised that Nanna was talking about the ozone layer and the damage that CFCs in aerosol cans caused.

Nanna also reminded me about a book she bought me around the same time that had information about all of the pollution going into the atmosphere. It was only the other day, when I was looking for a book for one of my children's assignments, that I found that very book. It was quite ahead of its time, as it was published in the early 1970s. Isn't it amazing? In hindsight, if this amazing lady had been listened to, maybe the damage to the planet may not have been as bad as it is today.

Nanna then took me forward to a couple of days before my wedding and showed herself sitting on my bed waiting for me with my poppa. When Nanna was alive, she always told me that her one wish was to live long enough to see me walk down the aisle at my wedding. On the television screen, a scene from my wedding began playing before me. There, in the front pew on the right-hand side of the church, were Nanna and Poppa, dressed in their Sunday best and smiling happily at me. I had always felt in my heart that they were present at my wedding but to see it actually playing out before me was the most wonderful gift I could receive from them.

The screen suddenly changed and my children's faces were looking back at me. Nanna was trying to show me that she knew all about her great-grandchildren. She then showed me that there was another little girl that she was taking care of in the spirit world and I knew that she was referring to the miscarriage I'd had. Again, the television screen changed and a dream I'd had in the past played before me.

In the dream, I was at my nanna's house and she was cooking in the kitchen, just like she did when she was alive. I could see a little girl who was about four years of age. She had blonde wavy hair down to her shoulders and big hazel eyes. The little girl looked just like me when I was a child and she also looked very similar to my oldest son, Ryan, when he was a baby.

It was my little girl Brooke, and she was playing at Nanna's kitchen table with a doll in a toy cot, happily putting a blanket on the doll and feeding her a bottle. I was sitting in the next room when suddenly Brooke turned around and saw me watching her. She got up and, with the biggest smile on her face, came running straight towards me. She put out her arms as if she was going to give me a cuddle.

Unfortunately for both of us, when she got close enough to hug me she realised that there was a glass partition separating the two of us. I could see her disappointment when she realised that I was not able to touch and cuddle her. She burst into tears and so did I at this point.

Next, Brooke placed her hand on the glass wall between us and I put my hand up on the other side opposite hers. We knew that neither of us could cross through the barrier. I felt an overwhelming sadness that we couldn't be together.

Nanna then came from the kitchen, walked towards Brooke, took her hand and gave her a cuddle. She looked at me and smiled, indicating that Brooke would be safe with her and that she would look after her for me. They both turned away and walked back into Nanna's kitchen, where Brooke began to help Nanna with the cooking.

Nanna showed me that the dream I'd had was really a message from her informing me that my daughter Brooke was indeed with her and having a lovely time in the spirit world. I remembered the times that I would spend in Nanna's kitchen making cookies and baking cakes, so it was lovely to see Brooke now doing this with Nanna.

The television screen abruptly went back to the episode of *Ghost Whisperer*. I had tears streaming down my face. I felt mixed emotions of sadness and joy. At least I now knew that the darling daughter I had lost was in safe hands, with someone I loved dearly who would always take care of her.

*

Since coming to terms with my gift, I have experienced many emotions about it. At times, I have asked the question 'Why me?' I have wondered why I had to be given such a challenging life. But when I sat back and thought about my experiences, I came to realise how blessed I am and how special I feel to be able to do what I do. I have seen evidence that confirms that what I do is real. I have had many clients tell me that after they had a reading, their life was changed in some way, whether through making contact with a lost loved one or by clarifying their life's purpose.

My life has changed hugely over the years and I never would have imagined the path that it would take. I have experienced many triumphs and at times met with disappointment. I feel so blessed that I have been given the opportunity to help others and to bring closure to those who have lost loved ones.

It has been a major journey to try to perfect my connection with my spirit guides and my ability to interpret their messages. I am still working on these skills constantly. I have come to the realisation that every day I learn something new from the beautiful unseen beings that share this world with us all.

However, the responsibility of being given this gift is huge and at times it can be a burden. There are many sceptics out there who wish to ridicule and attack people like me.

People have asked me if I am a Ghostbuster. I feel that this is a horrible way to describe what I do. I am a medium and I do spirit photography. It is a privilege if a spirit wishes to communicate with me or their loved ones or show up in a photograph, and I always thank them for their cooperation. The most important thing for me is to use my gift to assist as many people as possible, whether they are alive or in spirit. I feel that I was given this gift for a reason, so I plan to use it in a positive way.

I am sometimes criticised for assisting lost souls. My answer is: imagine if you or a family member died due to tragic circumstances and became trapped in the form of a ghost or spirit, unable to leave the scene of death, not being given the chance to go to the light? I believe that everyone, dead or alive, deserves to find peace and I feel it is a privilege to be of any assistance, no matter how big or small.

I myself began life as a sceptic, although I have always had an open mind. I don't expect to change everyone's mind about what I do – my aim is to challenge people's perceptions and let them make their own decisions.

Remember, the world is a wondrous place and there are many things that we still don't understand. Our brain is a mysterious part of our make-up and remains relatively unexplored. Be open-minded in your journey and be willing to accept the unexplained. You might just be surprised by what life has to offer.

And always remember, you are never alone!

The Power to Be

You ask the question of what it is to be,
It is the power within that guides your soul,
You feel the warmth from within,
It is a light that shines for all to see,
It is the feeling you have when a child is born,
A smile that touches your heart,
The warmth you feel when you help another,
It is what helps you to inspire others,
When the sunrise welcomes you with awe,
When the moonlight ignites you deep within,
It is something that can't be measured,
Or what others try to understand,
When you connect to the source, the possibilities are endless,
It is only the pressure from the day to day
That makes you lose the feeling of what it is to be,
So remember to take pleasure from every moment,
And feel the power from within,
Then you will truly remember what it is to be.

Debbie Malone

Acknowledgements

To Rowena Gilbert, thank you for being such a dear friend and for being so ahead of your time. Your website, www.castleofspirits.com, was one of the first paranormal/spirit websites in Australia. The site has been a platform for educating and informing the public about all things paranormal. I seemed to have been suffering writer's block while writing one of the chapters of this book and during this time I received the extremely sad news that you had passed. The positive thing about this is that I have been able to communicate with you since your passing, and I am so glad that you now have all the answers that you sought.

To my dear friend Wendy and her husband, Michael Hancock, thank you for being such a great support. You have been there every step of the way.

To Kay Sutton, the most wonderfully inspirational woman I have ever met, you have been there for me when at times I doubted my path. I thank you for your encouragement and guidance throughout my journey.

To Reverend Patricia McRae of the Church of Spiritualism of Australia, you are my living angel and I thank you for your help and guidance with my psychic journey.

To the wonderfully dedicated police officers I have met throughout the years, thank you for being receptive to what I had to offer. Some of you cannot be named, but you know who you are. I would like to personally acknowledge the following officers, for whom I have the utmost respect: Gae Crea, Steve Rose, Jeff Little, Catherine Flood and Terry Dunnett, as your openness and understanding have given me reason to never give up.

To Jackson Luke Baker, thank you for accompanying me on many trips to pursue my quest in spirit photography. You have been an inspiration to work with.

To the Maye, Davies, Thompson, Parker and Lye families, thank you for allowing me into your lives. It has been a privilege to meet you and your beautiful children, and to share their inspirational stories.

To the many other families I have met throughout my journey, I am sincerely grateful for the privilege of being allowed to be the go-between for you and your lost loved ones.

To Melanie Ambrose and Denise Blazek, two amazing ladies whom I have been blessed to meet, both of you have been an amazing addition to my life, and your help and insight have been inspirational.

To my guides and the messengers who have allowed me to be a conduit to the spirit world, your connection never ceases to amaze me.

Finally, to the readers, thank you all for being part of my journey. I hope you feel your own connection to spirit and realise that you are never alone.

Other products by Debbie...

Clues From Beyond:
True crime stories from a real–
life psychic detective

ISBN: 978-1-925924-62-6

In *Clues from Beyond*, psychic medium Debbie Malone seeks the truth about some famous real-life Australian crimes. In it, she shares more personal experiences with the spirit world, conveys messages from the departed and describes the ripple effect they create in extending proof that life and love still go on across the veil.

The book seeks the truth about some famous Australian criminal cases such as the Rozelle fire and the death of six-year-old Keisha Abrahams, and connects the disappearance of Dorothy Davis with the convicted murderer of New South Wales woman Kay Whelan. She investigates unsolved murders, including the killing of Shane Barker in Tasmania and the 1974 Murphy's Creek murders, and explores the mysterious disappearance of teenagers Kay Docherty and Toni Cavanagh from the Wollongong area in July 1979, and Bob Chappell from his yacht moored in Hobart harbour on Australia Day in 2009.

Available at all good bookstores or online at
www.geldingstreetpress.com